ON LOCATION
The Film Fan's Guide to Britain and Ireland

Brian Pendreigh

ON LOCATION
The Film Fan's Guide to Britain and Ireland

MAINSTREAM
PUBLISHING

EDINBURGH AND LONDON

For Jenny, with love and thanks

First published in Great Britain in 1995 by
MAINSTREAM PUBLISHING COMPANY (EDINBURGH) LTD
7 Albany Street
Edinburgh EH1 3UG

ISBN 1 85158 729 2

A catalogue record for this book is available from the British Library

Picture Acknowledgements

Every attempt has been made to contact the various copyright holders
of the pictorial material reproduced in this book. We apologise if, by
being unable to trace photographic sources, we have unknowingly failed
to acknowledge copyright material

Typeset in Bembo by Litho Link Ltd, Welshpool, Powys, Wales

Printed and bound in Great Britain by Butler & Tanner Ltd, Frome

CONTENTS

CHAPTER 3

Locations Far From the Madding Crowd: The West Country

CHAPTER 4

Brando, Bond and Public School Revolution: Central England

CHAPTER 8
Educating Rita in Geography: Dublin

CHAPTER 9
Ryan's Daughter, Daniel's Foot and Tom's Dingle: Ireland, except Dublin

CHAPTER 10
Robin Hood Goes on Tour: Everywhere except Sherwood Forest

ACKNOWLEDGEMENTS

The author wishes to thank the following, without whom this book would have been impossible:

Jenny Pendreigh, Ewen McDonald and Jim Brunton; Mary Alleguen, Richard Attenborough, Daniel Baber, Bath Film Office, Simon Bosanquet, Jeff Bowen, Amanda Sparks and British Film Commission, British Film Institute, British Gas, Peter Broughan, John Box, Seamus Byrne, David Brown, Buena Vista, Channel Four, Malcolm and Penny Christopher, Columbia TriStar Films, Shane Connaughton, Patrick Cooke, Corbett and Keene, Eric Coulter, Mark Cousins, Bill Cunningham, Nick Daubeny, DDA, Kevin de la Noye, Micheal de Mordha, Larry DeWaay, Eastern Screen, George Carlaw and Edinburgh and Lothian Screen Industries Office, Sid Kiman and Edinburgh Film Guild, Charlie Cartwright and Edinburgh Filmhouse, Neville Elder, Peter Elford, Enigma Productions, Jeanne Ferber, Film Institute of Ireland, Ray Freeborn, Lewis Gilbert, Assheton Gorton, Harvey Edgington and Greenwich Film Office, Andrew Grieve, Gwynedd Film Office, Keith Hatcher, Paddy Higson, Jenny Howarth, Charles Hubbard, Wilym Hughes, Allan James, Phil Kohler, Bill Lang, Lynn Saunders and Liverpool Film Office, Joe Marks, McDonald and Rutter, Andrew Macdonald, John McDonnell, Hamish MacInnes, Gillies MacKinnon, Merchant Ivory Productions, John Mollo, Kevin Moriarty, Mark Mostyn, Ronald Neame, Russell Needham, Northern Screen Commission, Martin O'Malley, Grania O'Shannon, John Pym, Karel Reisz, Simon Relph, Scala Productions, Lee Leckie and Scottish Screen Locations, Screen Wales, Anne Skinner, Iain Smith, South West Scotland Screen Commission, Roy Stevens, Siobhan Synnot, Caroline Thompson, United International Pictures, John Hefin and Wales Film Council, Alan Wands, Chris Wheeldon, Michael Winner, Working Title Films, Franco Zeffirelli, Fred Zinnemann, many other film companies who are individually acknowledged in the book and hundreds of property owners, curators and custodians, librarians, hoteliers, publicans, ministers, journalists, press officers, councillors, council officials, tourist information officers, estate agents, sub-post masters and mistresses and local residents.

FOREWORD

Thick mist covered the countryside and deadened the sound of my footsteps and my shortening breath as I followed the track up the hill. I had been told that the scenery is spectacular but I could see only a few yards ahead as I pursued my solitary path, the dampness running down my face. Then, suddenly, I reached the top of the hill, and, in the middle of nowhere, the rough track became a cobblestone street.

On my right and left were the foundations of stone houses long gone. It was like stumbling upon the evidence of an ancient civilisation. But the civilisation that had briefly flourished at this historic location was not that ancient. A quarter of a century ago film director David Lean had built an entire village here for his epic Irish drama *Ryan's Daughter* and when he was finished he knocked it down again. Now there is nothing but the cobblestones, the mist and the sheep, where once there was the sound of technicians shouting instructions to each other as they set up cameras and equipment for stars like Robert Mitchum, Sarah Miles, Trevor Howard and John Mills, who won an Oscar as the village idiot. About a mile away an empty stone schoolhouse still stands steadfast against the Atlantic storms on its lonely spot above the cliffs of Ireland's Dingle peninsula – further testimony to the solidity of Lean's vision.

Two days later, on Saturday, I stood on the platform of the old country station in County Galway where John Wayne pulled Maureen O'Hara from the train in *The Quiet Man*. On Sunday I found the field by the Erriff River that caused so much grief for Richard Harris in the film called *The Field*. And on Monday, across the water in south-west Scotland, I followed in Edward Woodward's footsteps among the weathered gravestones with their skulls and crossbones, in the grounds of Anwoth Old Kirk; a location unchanged and easily recognisable from the cult film *The Wicker Man*, which Christopher Lee rates as his best.

Not all films are made in the studio. These days most films use real places, either as themselves or as somewhere completely different, be it a Merseyside athletics ground as the Paris Olympic Stadium in *Chariots of Fire* or Milton Keynes as Metropolis in *Superman IV*. Everyone must at some time have wondered where a film was actually made, but although there are many literary guides to Britain and Ireland, there has never been a guide to film locations aimed at the general public. No central records exist of where films

NOTE

Many films used locations in more than one region. They have been placed under the region which provided the principal locations or the most locations.

There are references in some entries to other films, which may not have entries of their own.

Individual places and films are fully indexed at the back of the book.

were filmed. But by speaking to directors and producers, to location managers – the film professionals who organise the use of locations – and to local people, it has been possible to produce a book that contains not merely the raw facts about where films were made, but also the stories behind why those locations were chosen, as well as first-hand accounts of adventures and mishaps that happened between that first call of 'Action!' and the opening credits appearing on screen before an expectant first-night audience.

CHAPTER ONE
American Werewolves and Other Odd Sights
LONDON

ALFIE (1966)

A new breed of amoral, hedonistic hero, Alfie embarks on a sexual odyssey through London, from the back streets of Kings Cross to the tourist landmarks on the Thames. Many other English films of the period were set in northern towns and pursued a gritty, realist, almost documentary, feel. But director Lewis Gilbert rooted his working-class anti-hero firmly in the capital, making extensive use of well-known and lesser-known London locations. And, although the film was ultimately more poignant than most, Gilbert rejected the realist approach in favour of Michael Caine's jokey running commentary direct to the camera.

While working as a street photographer, Alfie is seen opposite Big Ben and the Houses of Parliament, and he has Ruby (Shelley Winters) pose in front of Tower Bridge. Gilbert recalls that the actors used the beefeaters' rooms in the Tower of London to get changed and put on their make-up: 'One thing that I always remember, that always struck us as funny, was when Michael was getting made up and a beefeater came in, dressed up in all his gear. He looked at Michael and said, "Wearing make-up, you do look a bloody fool." And he was dressed in this damned beefeater's outfit!'

The film begins with Alfie and Siddie (Millicent Martin) making love in his car behind Kings Cross Station, in front of the gasometers which have featured in numerous films over the years. Siddie is the first in a whole series of women Alfie sees only as objects for his pleasure. For a while he lives with Annie (Jane Asher) at his flat in Chepstow Road, near Ladbroke Grove, but she runs out on him after a row. 'The police weren't too happy when we filmed at night because of the lights being on,' says Gilbert, 'and they kept on saying that motorists were finding it difficult. In those days we had quite big lights to light streets. Nowadays it's much easier.'

Most of the interiors were shot at Twickenham Studios and the film-makers did not go far afield when it came to shoot the scenes at the convalescent home where Alfie meets Harry (Alfie Bass) and his wife, Lily (Vivien Merchant). They were shot at the local town hall. 'At the back of it there are very nice gardens and things,' says Gilbert. The flats inhabited by Ruby and Gilda (Julia Foster) were both in the Notting Hill Gate area, though Ruby's was an expensive modern flat, borrowed from a famous actor and dancer, and Gilda's looked as if it might well be situated in a gritty northern town like Nottingham or Salford. Gilda has Alfie's baby but, rejected by Alfie, she marries someone else. She discusses the possibility of marriage with her neighbour, during her lunch break, in the grounds of St Mary's Church, on a little promontory overlooking the Thames in Battersea. And it is there that Alfie later watches his son and Gilda at the christening

Michael Caine and Shelley Winters at London's Tower Bridge in Alfie *(Paramount). Picture supplied by BFI Stills, Posters and Designs*

of her second child, only now beginning to realise what he has lost.

The film was a major box-office hit and won five Oscar nominations, including best picture and best actor. Although he lost the Oscar to Paul Scofield in *A Man for All Seasons*, Caine enhanced his reputation enormously in a role that had been turned down by Laurence Harvey, Terence Stamp and Anthony Newley.

AN AMERICAN WEREWOLF IN LONDON (1981)

Although *An American Werewolf in London* is a comedy, it has a wonderfully chilling and atmospheric opening sequence in which two American backpackers are attacked by a mysterious creature on a dark, lonely moor and then stumble into a sinister pub called The Slaughtered Lamb, which falls suspiciously silent as they enter. The northerners they find there are close-knit and tight-lipped and a pentangle is scratched on the wall. However, it might not have been such an atmospheric opening if audiences had known that the young heroes were not on the Yorkshire moors but deep in London's Stockbroker Belt. The Slaughtered Lamb was The Black Swan, in Effingham, near Leatherhead – a traditional old pub which has appeared in several films and television programmes including *Inspector Morse* and *Just Good Friends*. It is situated in a secluded area and so served *An American Werewolf*'s requirements.

Location manager Ray Freeborn recalls that most of the footage of 'moors' was shot at Windsor Great Park, where corgis are spotted more often than werewolves. The mountainous Brecon Beacons area of Wales was used for wider shots, given that the sight of Windsor Castle on a lonely Yorkshire moor would have been incongruous to say the least.

There was extensive location filming in London itself. David Kessler (David Naughton) turns into a werewolf and kills three tramps near Tower Bridge and another man is killed on an escalator at the Aldwych tube station. Aldwych was readily available for the film because it was only used during rush hours: it has subsequently closed. David wakes up next morning, back in human form, in a cage at London Zoo. When he realises he is responsible for the overnight carnage, he accosts a policeman in Trafalgar Square, beneath the famous statue of Nelson, and asks to be arrested. David eventually turns into a werewolf again and causes mayhem in Piccadilly Circus at the climax of the film, which was written and directed by John Landis.

Probably Hollywood's top comedy director of the eighties, Landis also made *Trading Places* and the cult hit *The Blues Brothers*. Freeborn recalls: 'John Landis phoned me up from the States and said he was coming over and he was making a film called *American Werewolf*. I asked, "Where are you going to make it?" He said, "Piccadilly Circus." I said, "Well, unfortunately, Piccadilly Circus has been closed (to film-makers) for some 15 or 17 years because a previous crew had been in there and caused havoc. Where was your second choice?" He said, "The second choice is, I don't come."' Landis got his way and still talks enthusiastically about the Piccadilly Circus scenes.

Piccadilly Circus is one of the busiest roundabouts in Europe. Every day thousands of vehicles circle the famous statue of Eros – not that it was intended to be Eros. When it was erected in the nineteenth century, the intention was that it should represent the Angel of Christian Charity. But Eros seems more appropriate to an area famous for its prostitutes. It was going to be quite a proposition to close Piccadilly Circus down. Freeborn says that he discovered there was a new chief inspector in charge and showed him a model demonstrating everything they proposed to do. He then invited the policeman to come and see them rehearse the stunts and eventually managed to persuade him to let them have Piccadilly Circus for two nights. 'We had camera crews all over the place, on various levels of various shops and stores . . . We finished up with a 19-vehicle crash in Piccadilly Circus.'

An American Werewolf in London was not one of Landis's most successful films at the box-office, though many regard it as one of his best. It did get into *The Guinness Book of Movie Facts and Feats*, however, on the basis that it took longer to put on David Naughton's werewolf make-up than it took for make-up on any other British film – a total of ten hours.

BLOWUP (1966)

This classic portrait of Swinging Sixties London revolves around David Hemmings's strange adventures in a public park and what he does or does not see there.

Hemmings plays a fashion photographer who takes some snaps in the park only to be pursued by a mysterious woman (Vanessa Redgrave) who demands that he hand them over. He develops them and believes the blowups show a corpse and a man with a gun. Hemmings returns to the park and finds a body, but in the morning it is gone. The film ends with mime artistes playing tennis without a ball – even though we hear the sound of a ball on the soundtrack – just to underline writer-director Michelangelo Antonioni's theme of reality and illusion.

The park was Maryon Park in London, off the Woolwich Road, on the south bank of the Thames. The park is still there, very much as it was when Hemmings found stardom in it. Even the tennis courts survive, though nearby buildings, which also featured in the film, have been subject to redevelopment.

Antonioni also shot in west London, with the photographic studio situated in Holland Park. He worked without a script and never mixed with cast or crew. One of Hemmings's co-stars, Sarah Miles, wrote in her autobiography *Serves Me Right*: '*Blowup*, for me, was a cluster of clichés bundled up in a fashionable emperor's new clothes.' She walked out in the middle of filming.

But *Blowup* struck a chord with the public. While other films were questioning established standards and practices, *Blowup* questioned the nature of reality itself. Its subversive attitude, its mysticism, its confident and superficial stylishness and its daring, though brief, full-frontal nudity all served to make it a big cult hit.

CHAPLIN (1992)

It was Charlie Chaplin who inspired Richard Attenborough to become an actor when Attenborough's father took him to see *The Gold Rush* at the age of 11. More than half a century later, Attenborough was to channel his passion for Chaplin into a feature-film account of his life, with Robert Downey Jr in the title role and some of the locations Chaplin frequented making an appearance in the film before the action switches to America.

Chaplin *(Carolco/Le Studio Canal Plus/ RCS/Lambeth) Cheney Road, at the back of Kings Cross Station, served as London's East End at the beginning of the twentieth century in Chaplin. The film-makers erected houses on both sides of the street (picture courtesy of producer-director Richard Attenborough)*

Chaplin *(Carolco/Le Studio Canal Plus/ RCS/Lambeth). Picture courtesy of Richard Attenborough*

Chaplin is first seen as a small child in a velvet suit and Eton collar on the stage of Wilton's – the world's oldest surviving music hall – in London's Whitechapel area. It was doubling for a music hall in Aldershot. Wilton's closed in 1880 and served as a Methodist mission and rag warehouse before Greater London Council stepped in to save it. It can be found in Grace's Alley, off Ensign Street – though it would be easy to walk right past, for the front is boarded up and the paint flaking away. There is no sign to identify this silent ghost of a building, incongruously adjoining a smart new block of flats.

The casual passer-by might be forgiven for thinking it was merely something the demolition men forgot, but in recent years it has been used for the BBC's *Bleak House* dramatisation, the Tom Cruise film *Interview with the Vampire* and the 'Relax' video by Frankie Goes to Hollywood.

Charlie would go to Hollywood in due course too, but his showbiz career begins more modestly when he takes over his mother's routine after she dries up. He turns out to be a natural showman. Chaplin's mother, Hannah, is played by his own daughter, Geraldine. She descends into madness and, in 1903, young Chaplin commits her to London's Cane Hill Asylum, represented here by St Pancras Chambers, the great redbrick building over St Pancras Station. It was one of the grand railway hotels, but had been largely unused for decades at the time of filming.

Attenborough recreated the East End of Chaplin's time in Cheney Road, tucked away behind Kings Cross Station. It is one of the last cobbled streets in London and has several gasometers in the background. The film-makers added extra 'houses' to the scene. The adolescent Chaplin is seen pushing his wheelbarrow of scrap-iron past a host of cockney characters who were to reappear in his films – the oversize policeman; the old man crippled with rheumatism who inspired Chaplin's distinctive walk; the glazier who would be the central figure in *The Kid*; and the blind girl selling matches who becomes a blind flower-seller in *City Lights*.

Chaplin's brother, Sydney, signed up as one of Fred Karno's comedians before Chaplin did. It was Sydney who persuaded Karno (John Thaw, television's *Inspector Morse*) to give Chaplin an audition. In the film this takes place beside the Thames at Cliveden Reach on the former Astor estate, now owned by the National Trust. In 1931 Chaplin had indeed visited Cliveden, not to audition for Karno, but to dine with David Lloyd George.

The teenage Chaplin is seen performing a routine as a drunk at the Hackney Empire, where Chaplin did perform in the early years of the century. It was one of the first all-electric theatres in Britain. After serving as a television studio and bingo hall, it has been restored to its original use.

Chaplin falls for a dancer called Hetty Kelly (Moira Kelly) and proposes to her at Covent Garden over jellied eels. But the fashionable Covent Garden of the 1990s was considered an impossible setting, so the film-makers recreated the old Covent Garden under the giant arch of Smithfield, London's traditional meat market, dressing it up with fruit and vegetables, horses and carts, barrows and baskets. Kelly turned Chaplin down. He went off to America and she died a few years later, but Chaplin never got over her. Throughout his life he was attracted to young women who reminded him of Hetty Kelly.

THE CRYING GAME (1992)

A surprise hit on both sides of the Atlantic, Neil Jordan's IRA thriller – with a very definite twist in the tale – was filmed in both Ireland and England. The hairdresser's, where Dil (Jaye Davidson) worked, and the exterior of the Metro bar where she gets to know Fergus (Stephen Rea) were vacant properties 'dressed' by the film-makers, but the interior of the bar was real enough. It is the London Apprentice at 333 Old Street in north London. And the bar where Fergus and Jude (Miranda Richardson) plot the assassination of a judge was the Lowndes Arms in Chesham Street, Belgravia – one of the most exclusive districts of London, only half a mile from Buckingham Palace.

The first half of the film was set in Ireland where the IRA kidnap Jody, a British soldier (Forest Whitaker) who had been visiting a carnival. The carnival was the carnival at the little seaside resort of Bettystown, on the coast near Drogheda, though the filming was not done there. In fact, the film-makers took the carnival apart and reconstructed it a few miles down the coast at Laytown. Irish location manager Martin O'Malley says, 'It was more suitable: it had that railway bridge and the river.'

Fergus strikes up a rapport with Jody only to be faced with the task of taking him into the woods and shooting him when the British authorities fail to meet the IRA demands. The hideout scenes were shot at Shepperton Studios in Middlesex and those in the woods, where Jody makes his ill-fated break for freedom, were shot at Burnham Beeches – the 600-acre Buckinghamshire woodland, which is convenient for both Shepperton and Pinewood and has been used in many films, including *Robin Hood: Prince of Thieves.* After

Jaye Davidson in The Crying Game *(Palace)*

Jody's death, Fergus decides to track down his partner, Dil.

The film was originally and more imaginatively called *The Soldier's Wife*, before a last-minute change of mind resulted in it following the fashion of cashing in on the titles of classic songs.

Many of the English scenes were shot in north London. A vacant property at 3 Fournier Street was turned into a hairdresser's and another, 28-30 Coronet Street, was used for the exteriors of the Metro bar. The interiors and exteriors of Dil's flat were shot just round the corner in Hoxton Square, though the building site, where Fergus finds work, was not exactly convenient. It was right on the other side of London, at Dartmouth Terrace, Blackheath.

The film did amazing business at the box-office, taking more than $60 million in North America, and was nominated for six Oscars, including best picture. Neil Jordan won the award for best original screenplay. In this case the term 'original screenplay' was extremely apt. No other film had ever constructed two such enormous obstacles to true love as those faced by Fergus and Dil.

84 CHARING CROSS ROAD (1987)

This was the ultimate film for pen-pals and bookworms, based on the memoirs of the American writer, Helene Hanff, and her long-term, long-distance relationship with an antiquarian bookseller, Frank Doel, at Marks and Company, 84 Charing Cross Road, in the centre of London.

The forthright Hanff (Anne Bancroft) and reserved Doel (Anthony Hopkins) correspond for 20 years before she finally manages to visit London. But by then the bookshop is up for sale and Doel has died.

By the time the film was made, the shop had changed significantly. It was occupied by Covent Garden Records during the eighties and the first half of the nineties, at which point it was subject to further redevelopment. So, although 84 Charing Cross Road gives the film its title, it was reconstructed at Shepperton Studios, near London. Producer Geoffrey Helman told *Films and Filming* magazine: 'We built the shop on a stage looking out through doors to a large open space which we were able to develop into our own Charing Cross Road, complete with cars and buses which change as time passes from the late forties to the seventies.'

The film-makers did go on location for scenes of Doel's neighbourhood, though not to Muswell Hill in north London, where he lived. They wanted somewhere nearer Shepperton and opted for Richmond, one of London's western suburbs, using a vacant flat as Doel's home and shooting in local streets and at the railway station. There was also extensive filming in New York.

FULL METAL JACKET (1987)

Stanley Kubrick, cinema's ultimate perfectionist and one of its greatest illusionists, managed to recreate the Vietnam war in the capital of the United Kingdom. He turned the sprawling, derelict Beckton Gas Works on the north banks of the Thames, out beyond Docklands, into a deadly combat zone, blowing up buildings and tearing the place apart

Full Metal Jacket
*(Natant/Warner) filmed
at Beckton Gas Works
in the East End of
London (picture courtesy
of British Gas)*

while Matthew Modine and his fellow U. S. Marines try to survive the nightmare of war.

The film, which takes its title from soldiers' body armour, follows Modine (Private Joker) and his squad through Da Nang into the urban battlefield of Hue, represented by Beckton. The crumbling buildings were considered a suitable match for the buildings of Vietnam's colonial past; the palm trees were added by the film-makers.

Beckton was no ordinary gas-works, having won its place in the *Guinness Book of Records* as Britain's biggest and covering 300 acres. As well as the gas plant, the site included offices and workers' houses, but it had been closed for many years before Kubrick's arrival. The demand for the production of gas using the old, traditional methods – which involved carbonisation of coal – had declined following the arrival of natural gas from the North Sea. In the early nineties, British Gas had plans for an ambitious waterfront and leisure complex on the site, but Beckton's redevelopment has not been considered a priority and various other film and television productions have filmed there.

The site is very definitely closed to the public. A British Gas Properties spokeswoman said some of the buildings that were blown up by Kubrick were now half-up, half-down and considered unsafe.

A HARD DAY'S NIGHT (1964)

This is the film in which the Beatles get on a train in London, travel 2,500 miles and arrive at their destination, where they are to play a concert. And it turns out to be London!

The film was rushed through production and into cinemas to cash in on the Beatles' phenomenal popularity, before it waned. They began filming on 2 March 1964 and the film premièred four months later on 6 July – an incredibly short period for a full-length feature. Yet throughout the eight weeks of shooting, the Beatles fitted in other engagements including recordings, interviews and their first appearance on *Top of the Pops*.

The first week of filming was spent on a train travelling back and forth between London and the West Country. Mark Lewisohn notes in his excellent book, *The Complete*

Beatles Chronicle, that the Beatles joined the closed-shop actors' union, Equity, on the platform of Paddington Station in London only minutes before filming began. They were proposed by Wilfrid Brambell and Norman Rossington. There was no filming at Paddington itself – the film's opening scenes of the Beatles being chased through a station by fans were shot later at Marylebone, with additional footage from outside, in Melcombe Place and Boston Place. The train ran between Paddington and Minehead, Taunton and Newton Abbot, with the Beatles boarding and disembarking at suburban stations *en route* to avoid most of the fans.

The sequence in which the Beatles run alongside the train asking a snooty first-class passenger if they can get their ball back was shot at Crowcombe Station, on the line which subsequently became the privately-run West Somerset Railway. One of the young actresses playing schoolgirls on the train was Pattie Boyd, who became Mrs George Harrison.

The Beatles play themselves in the film, which has a quasi-documentary style as it follows them on their journey. Rossington plays Norm, their manager, and Brambell plays Paul McCartney's grandfather. He turns out to be a womaniser and gambler, though it is continually pointed out that he is very clean – obviously a reference to his role as a rag-and-bone-man in the popular television sitcom, *Steptoe and Son*.

When they arrive in London (again) Paul's grandad sneaks out gambling at Le Circle Club, passing himself off as Lord McCartney, while John, Paul, George and Ringo go to a disco. The Beatles would not have needed to look far to find his lordship. Both sequences were shot in Les Ambassadeurs club in Hamilton Place, off Park Lane.

The venue for their televised concert was the Scala Theatre in Charlotte Street, though a shot of the Beatles coming down the theatre's external fire-escape staircase was done at the Hammersmith Odeon, now Labatt's Apollo. The Scala was demolished years ago.

Paul's grandad stirs up trouble between Ringo and the others and Ringo goes AWOL just before the concert, walking along the Thames towpath on the south bank just west of Kew Bridge and visiting the Turk's Head pub in Winchester Road, close to the film's base at Twickenham Studios.

Chase scenes were shot in Notting Hill Gate with actors as policemen, supported by real policemen, holding back hundreds of screaming fans. Other locations included Gatwick Airport and Thornbury Playing Fields in Isleworth, Middlesex.

Given the rushed nature of the film, it could have been dreadful, but, like the Beatles themselves, it is greater than the sum of its parts and widely regarded as the best pop film ever. The Beatles, particularly John Lennon, seemed ideally matched to the dry humour of Alun Owen's script; and the mix of realism and surrealism in Richard Lester's approach as director works extremely well. The Beatles appear sharp, witty, cool and full of creative energy, which bursts loose in classic songs such as 'Can't Buy Me Love' and 'A Hard Day's Night'.

HELP! (1965)

Made at the height of Beatlemania in 1965, the Fab Four's second film, *Help!*, opens with a scene of them arriving in a quiet residential street of terraced brick houses. As they step from their limousine and approach the front doors of four adjoining houses, one middle-aged woman (played by Gretchen Franklin who was to become a regular on the *EastEnders* soap opera in the eighties) turns to her friend and observes how fame has not changed them at all. Her friend, played by Dandy Nichols who was shortly to achieve nationwide fame herself as Mrs Alf Garnett, observes: 'Just so natural and still the same as they was before they was.' And just at that point the Beatles disappear through their respective front doors and into one long communal dwelling.

It is a scene that wonderfully captures the cheeky charm and surreal humour of the four young stars from Liverpool, though the film was not written by them, but by Marc Behm and Charles Wood. It was directed by Richard Lester, who had directed the first Beatles film, *A Hard Day's Night*, and it included the songs 'Ticket to Ride' and 'You've Got to Hide Your Love Away'. Some writers have suggested that the latter may have been a reference to Beatles manager Brian Epstein's homosexuality.

Whimsical, silly and lightweight, *Help!* was underrated at the time, especially as it followed *A Hard Day's Night*, which was shot in black and white and whose story of a 'typical' day in the life of the Beatles was much closer to the social realist fashion. *Help!* centres on the increasingly desperate attempts of the members of an eastern cult, led by Leo McKern and Eleanor Bron, to bump off Ringo because he is wearing their sacrificial ring.

It was filmed largely in Austria and the Bahamas – which was apparently chosen entirely for tax reasons rather than artistic considerations. Interiors were shot at Twickenham Studios, but, because of who the Beatles was after they was, extensive records have been preserved of locations in London and elsewhere in the south of England. It is Ailsa Avenue, not far from the film studios, that is immortalised on film at the beginning of *Help!*, with Ringo approaching the door of No 5, John of No 7, Paul of 9 and George of 11, before they all emerge on to one of the Twickenham Studios sets. Mrs Beatrice Pennington, who lived at No 7 Ailsa Avenue, was quoted in the press as saying: 'It is very quiet around here but this certainly broke the monotony . . . I loved the whole thing. I had them all in to tea and they gave me an autographed picture to put in the sitting-room. It was no trouble. We even got the front door and windows painted into the bargain.' Young female fans set up a series of lookouts to spot the Beatles as they approached.

Ailsa Avenue was the first of the English locations, with shooting taking place on 14 April 1965, after the overseas scenes had been completed. And with the switch to English locations came a change in title to *Help!*. The film was previously to have been called *Eight Arms to Hold You*. There was further location work in April at Strand-on-the-Green in Chiswick where the Beatles encounter McKern's followers disguised as bagpipers. The Beatles are seen coming down Post Office Alley on to the River Thames towpath and, after encountering the villains, they enter the City Barge pub. The interior was again shot at Twickenham Studios.

Ringo cannot get the sacrificial ring off his finger, so they go to Asprey's, the jewellers in London's New Bond Street, for advice; while the Rajahama Indian restaurant was in fact the Dolphin Restaurant in Blandford Street, London. The scene where Ringo posts a letter and one of the villains is hiding in the postbox was shot in South Western Road in St Margaret's, Twickenham, and a similar scene involving the sort of weighing scales on which you stand was shot in Winchester Road, Twickenham.

Ringo's situation becomes increasingly fraught and the Beatles are forced to record under the protection of the Army on Salisbury Plain, before being installed by their Scotland Yard minder, Patrick Cargill, in what is captioned as 'a well-known palace'. The exterior is clearly Buckingham Palace, but interior scenes were shot at the vast nineteenth-century Cliveden House near Maidenhead in Buckinghamshire.

Cliveden is now owned by the National Trust, though the house itself operates as a luxury hotel. Built in the middle of the last century for the Duke of Sutherland, it passed to the American millionaire William Waldorf Astor in 1893. It was a key political and social centre between the wars – Lady Astor was a noted hostess and became the first female Member of Parliament in 1919. It was at Cliveden in 1961 that the Secretary of State for War, John Profumo, met showgirl Christine Keeler and began a relationship that was ultimately to bring down the government.

The Beatles are seen lounging around among the gold and gilt finery of the French dining-room, playing cards and discussing the possibility of cutting off Ringo's finger. Cliveden's extensive grounds can be seen through the windows. The film's mock 'inter-mission' sequence was shot in woods on the estate. During filming, Lord Astor was recuperating in bed after illness, but the local press recorded the fact that Lady Astor watched an outdoor scene from her bedroom window. An end-of-filming relay race was run in the gardens – a four-way contest between the electricians, the carpenters, the camera crew and the Beatles, and much to everyone's surprise the Beatles won.

The film was rushed out in July, just two months after filming finished, and went on to become the highest-grossing film of the year in Britain.

HOWARDS END (1992)

Although the centrepiece of Merchant Ivory's film is a private house, fans can follow in Anthony Hopkins's and Emma Thompson's award-winning footsteps by eating at Simpson's-in-the-Strand, shopping at Fortnum and Mason's in London's Piccadilly and visiting numerous other public locations that represent England at its most elegant and charming.

E. M. Forster's novel revolves around the house of the title, which is a symbol both of heritage and of privilege for the Wilcox family. They are outraged when Ruth Wilcox (Vanessa Redgrave) leaves it to her friend Miss Margaret Schlegel (Emma Thompson). For Howards End, Merchant Ivory used Peppard Cottage, overlooking Peppard Common, near Henley-on-Thames, Oxfordshire. The name suggests a fairly small house, but the seventeenth-century, ivy and wisteria-covered building has four public rooms, six bedrooms and a self-contained flat. Forster was a friend of Lady Ottoline Morrell, who owned the house in the early part of this century, prompting speculation that it was the model for Howards End in his novel, which was published in 1910. At the time of filming it was owned by Hatton Garden silver dealer Roger Shapland and his wife, Caroline, who said: 'I am sure some people would loathe the disruption, but we loved every minute of it. '

In the film Evie Wilcox destroys her mother's last note – Evie was played by Vanessa Redgrave's niece, Jemma Redgrave. But Evie's actions do not guarantee the family's

Samuel West and Helena Bonham Carter in Howards End *(Merchant Ivory/ Nippon Herald/ Channel Four)*

happiness or the future of the house, which is to be the scene of a tragedy affecting all the characters. Peppard Cottage was in the news a few years after Merchant Ivory's visit when the Shaplands faced a terrible family tragedy of their own. Captain Harry Shapland, son of the owners, was shot down by 'friendly fire' over Iraq while serving with the United Nations. Peppard Cottage has subsequently been resold.

Hilton railway station near Howards End, where oafish young Charles Wilcox (James Wilby) complains about the inefficiency of the staff and declares that he would sack them all, was Bewdley Station, Worcestershire, on the Severn Valley Railway between Bridgnorth and Kidderminster. It is run by a preservation society and was also used in the 1978 version of *The 39 Steps*. In *Howards End* the train is seen crossing the Victoria Bridge, which replaced the Forth Bridge as the scene of Richard Hannay's daring escape in the most recent of the three films of John Buchan's thriller.

For the local village, Merchant Ivory used Dorchester-on-Thames and its attractive half-timbered white houses in Oxfordshire. The Schlegel home was another private residence, among the white townhouses of London's Victoria Square, not far from Buckingham Palace. The Schlegels' bright and spacious environment is contrasted with that of Leonard Bast (Samuel West), whose flat was located in Park Street, Southwark, London – venue for the Borough Market, a very old wholesale fruit and vegetable market held early every morning except Sundays.

For the Wilcoxes' London flat, which was supposedly situated within sight of the Schlegel house, Merchant Ivory used the St James Court Hotel in Buckingham Gate, formerly the home of Lord Dacre. Director James Ivory shot exteriors in the courtyard. The buildings around it are Victorian and Edwardian, with an attractive appearance that combines red brickwork and white pillars. The courtyard boasts the longest terracotta frieze in the world, depicting scenes from Shakespeare.

An unlikely relationship develops between Margaret Schlegel and her late friend's stuffy husband, Henry Wilcox (Anthony Hopkins), while Margaret's sister Helen (Helena Bonham Carter) is increasingly drawn to Mr Bast, prompting the Wilcoxes to fear for her sanity. Helen first met Leonard Bast after she took his umbrella by mistake when leaving a lecture on music and meaning. He follows her to her home in Victoria Square to retrieve it – which must have been a very uncomfortable walk in the heavy rain, as the lecture took place more than 50 miles away in Oxford Town Hall. The town hall is open to the public and houses the Museum of Oxford.

The film used so many locations that it would be possible to write an entire book on them, though quite a few are private homes or buildings closed to the public. One of the more interesting ones was the Baltic Exchange, St Mary Axe, which appears as a bank where Mr Bast seeks work. Not long after filming it was bombed by the IRA.

Among the London locations which are readily accessible are Admiralty Arch, Chiswick Mall and St Pancras Station – the great Gothic railway palace where Ruth Wilcox and Margaret Schlegel buy tickets for Hilton only to bump into the rest of the Wilcox family returning to London, forcing them to postpone their plans. Ruth and Margaret go Christmas shopping at Fortnum and Mason's: grocers and provision merchants by royal appointment. William Fortnum and Hugh Mason began trading on the same Piccadilly site way back in 1707. The royal link was established at the outset by Fortnum, who was a footman to Queen Anne, and, as such, entitled to receive the partly-used candles of the Royal Household, which he then sold second-hand.

On their way to Fortnum and Mason's, Ruth and Margaret are seen passing Admiralty Arch, designed as a triumphal arch for Queen Victoria, though her triumph ended before its erection in 1910 – the year Forster's novel appeared. After Ruth's death Margaret and Helen meet Henry Wilcox by chance after a party in Chiswick Mall; a street full of expensive properties on the Thames.

Subsequently, Margaret and Henry have lunch with Evie and her fiancé, Percy, in Simpson's-in-the-Strand; a London institution that even merited a mention in *The Bridge on the River Kwai*, when the prisoners look forward to going home. It began as a chess club early in the nineteenth century and it remains a proudly old-fashioned establishment, serving plain English cuisine. *Howards End* shot in the west room and the whole sequence serves as the sort of advert for the restaurant that a million-pound advertising campaign could not buy. Hopkins's character comments that the restaurant is 'thoroughly old-English' and offers some advice on the menu when Margaret (Thompson) declares her intention to order fish pie. 'Fish pie! Fancy coming for fish pie to Simpson's . . . Roast beef and Yorkshire pudding and cider to drink. That's the type of thing to go for.'

Director James Ivory and producer Ismail Merchant found their film winning audiences on both sides of the Atlantic. It was nominated for nine Oscars, including best picture, and won three – best actress, Emma Thompson; best adapted screenplay, Ruth

Prawer Jhabvala and best art direction. Thompson repeated her Oscar success in the British Academy Awards, when the film was preferred to *Unforgiven* for best picture.

Orson Welles and Oliver Reed in I'll Never Forget What's 'is Name *(Scimitar)*

I'LL NEVER FORGET WHAT'S 'IS NAME (1967)

Although Michael Winner is hardly the critics' favourite these days, this was rated an instant classic of Swinging Sixties London. *Leonard Maltin's Movie and Video Guide* describes it as 'excellent comedy-drama'.

Oliver Reed quits an executive position in advertising for a job on a small literary magazine, but Orson Welles's mogul determines to buy back his soul. 'Splashes of sex and violence in trendy settings,' says *Halliwell's Film Guide.* And none were trendier than the original Biba shop in Kensington Church Street, which took style to the working classes. Director Michael Winner recalls that Carol White's character bought her clothes there and they looked so good that 'one of the posh newspapers' said that it was ridiculous dressing a secretary in designer outfits. 'At the time a suit was about £4,' says Winner.

He goes on to recall: 'Orson Welles visited Oliver Reed in his house-boat on Chelsea Reach. We also used the National Film Theatre, as it then was, for an advertising film festival.'

THE JOKERS (1967)

Locations ranged from the Tower of London and Eton College to Michael Winner's flat in South Kensington and the restaurant that became Tramp's nightclub, in this Swinging Sixties comedy about two brothers (Oliver Reed and Michael Crawford) who decide to steal the Crown Jewels.

Director Michael Winner filmed in the Tower of London itself, but there was building work going on in the main courtyard, so he used the courtyard at Eton College in

Michael Crawford,
Michael Winner, Lotte
Tarp and Oliver Reed
outside Buckingham
Palace during the
making of The Jokers
(Adastra/Gildor/
Scimitar)

Berkshire as a stand-in. Always careful with a film's budget, Winner used his own flat as the brothers' apartment, where they hide the Crown Jewels. He also shot in the Society Restaurant in Jermyn Street, which subsequently became the famous Tramp's nightclub, haunt of the rich and famous.

'We shot in the real Stock Exchange,' recalls Winner, 'and all the stockbrokers saw us and started throwing paper darts at us. Then they took the trousers off one of our assistant directors when he went down on the floor to "direct" them . . .

'We had to put the Crown Jewels in the Scales of Justice on top of the Old Bailey and we were surprised when a phone call resulted in us getting permission to use the real Scales of Justice. They used one of their high-wire cleaners to double as Michael Crawford putting them in.'

THE KRAYS (1990)

Notorious gangsters Ronnie and Reggie Kray move up-market in Peter Medak's film, from London's East End to Greenwich.

The East End had been extensively redeveloped since the Krays' hey-day, with many of the old houses demolished and new skyscrapers erected. The film-makers found what they were looking for on the other side of the Thames, using Greenwich to represent the Kray twins' home patch and shooting extensively in Caradoc Street – a traditional, working-class area, with brick, terraced, two-storey houses which open on to the street, without front gardens.

Location manager Bob Jordan told *Screen International*, Britain's main film industry magazine: 'There was a gap between the houses. We filled it in to go through three different decades – we built a false front for the 1930s, put a load of rubble in the road to look as if it had been bombed for the forties, and for the sixties we put up corrugated iron.'

The Krays were played by Gary and Martin Kemp from the rock group Spandau Ballet, though their screen appearances have been fewer than those of Caradoc Street, which figured in the 1985 film *Plenty*, with Meryl Streep and Charles Dance, and has been used frequently for television and commercials.

THE LADYKILLERS (1955)

Two of London's great Victorian railway stations and a little old lady's small lopsided cottage formed the setting for this wickedly dark Ealing comedy, starring Alec Guinness as the boss of a gang of thieves and directed by Sandy Mackendrick – the most subversive of Ealing's directors.

Katie Johnson plays Mrs Wilberforce, the scatter-brained owner of the little lopsided cottage. She rents out her spare room to Professor Marcus (Guinness with sinister, ill-fitting dentures) and his string quintet, the others being Peter Sellers, Herbert Lom, Cecil Parker and Danny Green. In reality they are violent criminals, using her house as the base for an elaborate robbery. When she discovers the true nature of their business, they have to decide which one of them will ensure her silence. Suffice to say, only one of the principal characters survives to spend the loot.

The hold-up took place just at the back of Kings Cross Station in Cheney Road, in front of the gasometers, whose screen career was to prove longer than that of most film stars. They went on to appear in *Alfie, Shirley Valentine* and *Chaplin*.

Mrs Wilberforce's house appears to be situated at the end of a cul-de-sac immediately in front of a railway track, just as it disappears into a tunnel. When she opens her front door she is faced with the ornate Gothic clock tower of Kings Cross Station's neighbour, St Pancras. The house was built by the film-makers at the end of Frederica Street, which has now been redeveloped, off Caledonian Road; the tunnel was Copenhagen Tunnel; and the view of St Pancras was merely one of the tricks of the film-makers' trade. Although Mrs Wilberforce was not far from St Pancras, she certainly would not have seen it from her front door.

There was tremendous debate lasting for most of 1990 in the correspondence columns of *Steam World* railway magazine on the exact locations. Writing in the magazine in 1992, Philip J. Kelley, a former photographer in British Rail's public relations office, said: 'During 1955 we were asked to find a suitable site for *The Ladykillers* . . . Copenhagen Tunnel was suggested. A situation over a tunnel was called for in the script. We used the goods lines in order not to obstruct the main line. Filming was to take place on Sundays and we had to provide two empty wagon trains facing in opposite directions . . . The wagons had to be empty for the "bodies" to drop into them!'

Kelley detailed how the cottage was built over the tunnel and how he advised on the construction of a replica tunnel mouth at Ealing Studios for close-ups.

This was one of the last and one of the best of the Ealing comedies, managing to create a homely, Little-English village in the shadow of Kings Cross and having a gang of homicidal villains thwarted by an eccentric Little-English lady. Katie Johnson, a long-time character actress, became a star in her late seventies and won a British Academy Award as best actress. Ealing Studios were sold to the BBC and Mackendrick, who had previously directed *Whisky Galore!*, moved to Hollywood, and made the classic *Sweet Smell of Success*.

1984 (1984)

For the film of George Orwell's bleak novel that introduced the concepts of Big Brother and the Thought Police, director Michael Radford needed to find a large square that he could take over for a week. It was to serve as Victory Square, assembly point for speeches and rallies in Airstrip One, where the hero, Winston Smith (John Hurt), works as a civil servant at the Ministry of Truth.

The film-makers found just what they were looking for, in London, which is where Orwell had in mind when he created Airstrip One. Location manager Richard Craven recalls: 'To find Victory Square was a problem. How could we dress an entire square over a period of a week, remove all traffic and pedestrians, and shoot for five days with thousands of extras?'

They found the answer in Alexandra Palace, in the Muswell Hill area of north London. The historic 'people's palace', built over one hundred years ago as a grand exhibition and concert venue, had been gutted by fire in 1980 and was no more than a roofless shell at the time. 'When the inside walls were dressed they looked like the interior walls of a square,' says Craven.

The Alexandra Palace, or Ally Pally as it is popularly known, was originally built in 1873 as a 'pleasure palace of the people' and named after the Princess of Wales. It was destroyed by fire a fortnight after opening. The present building was opened in 1875 and lasted rather longer before being damaged by fire. It was from Alexandra Palace that the BBC first broadcast television in 1936. It has now been restored as a multi-purpose entertainments centre. Located at the top of Alexandra Park, it affords one of the best views over London.

1984, which also shot on location in Wiltshire, was Richard Burton's last film and he gave one of his most memorable performances as O'Brien, a complex character whom Smith believes to be a prominent subversive, but who turns out to be an undercover agent of the ruthless totalitarian state envisaged by Orwell. Burton delivered a subtly shaded performance, all the more remarkable considering filming was well under way before he was cast.

The choice of the year for the title of the novel was not determined by any particularly scientific method of prophecy by the author. He had intended to call it 1948 – the year in which it was written – but was persuaded to transpose the last two digits.

NUNS ON THE RUN (1990)

Robbie Coltrane and Eric Idle dressed up as nuns and found they had a hit on their hands in both Britain and America. They play two crooks, Charlie and Brian, who fear their boss, Casey, is about to terminate his association with them – in the most permanent way possible. They carry out one last job, robbing the Triads, but instead of handing over the money to Casey they intend to flee the country.

Director Jonathan Lynn filmed in Gerrard Street in London's Chinatown, just round the corner from Leicester Square and some of Britain's big showcase cinemas.

Things go wrong for Brian and Charlie and they end up wanted by Casey, the Triads and the police. They plunge through a door in a wall and hide out in a building, which turns out to be a convent, where the nuns include Janet Suzman and Doris Hare, from *On the Buses*, the popular television sitcom of the early seventies. The film-makers used St Michael's and All Angels Church in Priory Avenue, west London, for exterior shots of the convent. Interiors were filmed at the United States International University in Bushey, Hertfordshire.

Brian's girlfriend, Faith (Camille Coduri), goes to see them in the convent, but is grabbed by the Triads. They free her, but she walks into a lamp-post and is taken to hospital with concussion. Charlie and Brian first go to her flat for a scene with a collapsing drainpipe. It was shot at the rear of the Culross Building, in Cheney Road, right beside Kings Cross Station. They subsequently discover her true whereabouts – for which a combination of Putney Hospital for exteriors and the German Hospital in Ritson Road for interiors was needed.

Other locations included Wimbledon Town Hall as a bank and Chelsea Football Club's ground at Stamford Bridge which doubled as Wembley Stadium carpark.

'Achingly predictable jokes,' said *Empire* magazine, 'lacking any sense of surprise or spontaneity'. But you cannot argue with the box-office.

PATRIOT GAMES (1992)

The Royal Naval College at Greenwich not only served as Buckingham Palace, where renegade IRA terrorists attack the limousine of the Queen's cousin; but also as an actual naval college, where American intelligence analyst Jack Ryan has been giving a lecture. This was the second Jack Ryan film, with Harrison Ford taking over the central role from Alec Baldwin, who had been Ryan in *The Hunt for Red October*.

Skilful cutting enabled the makers of *Patriot Games* to show the limousine of Lord Holmes (James Fox) coming through the ornate gates of the naval college, while Ryan is leaving the college itself – though the viewer is expected to regard them as two completely different places, otherwise it would have seemed Ryan had been giving his lecture in Buckingham Palace.

Ryan intervenes in the IRA attack and kills a young terrorist. Later the film has an IRA operative emerge from a bookshop – which serves as an IRA contact point – and try to elude his police pursuers in what would seem to be an adjacent underground station. The bookshop was in Burlington Arcade, off Piccadilly. Built in the early nineteenth century, it is largely occupied by expensive jewellery and clothes shops. Top-hatted beadles enforce traditional rules that prohibit whistling, singing and hurrying.

Piccadilly Circus station is about a quarter of a mile away, but the film-makers used Aldwych, which is over a mile away. At the time, Aldwych Station was open only during rush hours and therefore easier for film-makers to use. It closed down in 1994, though it is still available for film purposes.

The escape of terrorist Sean Miller (Sean Bean) from police custody was filmed at Canary Wharf. He resurfaces in America, where most of the film is set, determined to kill Ryan.

REDS (1981)

England provided locations that doubled for both America and Russia in Warren Beatty's epic about the Russian Revolution and the radical American journalist John Reed, played by Beatty himself. Location filming was done in the United States, Finland and Spain as well as England. But the fact that the production was based at Twickenham Studios meant that the film-makers could keep costs down by using as many locations in England as possible and minimising expensive trips to locations elsewhere. 'It's cheaper to keep the crew at home, an English crew, rather than having them away on location,' says location manager Simon Bosanquet.

So Bolshevik revolutionaries went into action just a stone's throw from Buckingham Palace, storming Lancaster House, the former stately home now used by the Government for official functions. 'I seem to remember that Government ministers were being shown around that day and were absolutely outraged that this should happen,' says Bosanquet, 'and they banned filming in it for about ten years after that; although it suited our purposes very well. And we had Kerensky's son playing his father in a scene in the big state ballroom on the first floor, which was interesting.'

Lancaster House was built in the early nineteenth century for the Duke of York and was subsequently home to the London Museum before the Government took it over.

Lancaster House, which is open to the public at weekends, was used to represent the interiors of the Winter Palace in St Petersburg. Exteriors were shot in Finland. 'There were lots of interiors that were shot all over the place, rooms and offices that we found in London and Manchester,' says Bosanquet.

The Zion Institute building in Manchester was used as a Chicago hall during Reed's campaign against American involvement in the First World War. It was built as a church just before the war and subsequently served as the home of Northern Ballet and as rehearsal rooms for the Halle Orchestra and Choir. The film-makers also used the Central Methodist Hall in Storey's Gate, London, and the great hall and rotunda of nearby One Great George Street – headquarters of the Institution of Civil Engineers since Edwardian times and now a major conference venue. 'The big exteriors weren't done here, because none of the film takes place in England,' reveals Bosanquet. 'We shot rural exteriors where you wouldn't know where you were.'

They built a house at Frensham Ponds in Surrey, with its Great Pond extending over more than 100 acres. It served as the house on the shore at Provincetown, Massachusetts, when Reed's lover, Louise Bryant (Diane Keaton), has an affair with playwright Eugene O'Neill (Jack Nicholson).

Reds was nominated for 12 Oscars and won three, including best director, though it lost out on the best picture award to *Chariots of Fire*.

THE SERVANT (1963)

Joseph Losey's film about the shifting balance of power between a young playboy (James Fox) and his scheming servant (Dirk Bogarde) appeared at the end of a year of government scandals, including the Profumo affair, when it was revealed that the Secretary of State for War shared a girlfriend with a Soviet diplomat. The public was increasingly questioning the established order and the Tory government would be voted out the following year.

Fox's character sets himself up in a Georgian townhouse and hires Bogarde to run it; before long he is doing this only too well. The film was shot in a house off the King's Road, in Royal Avenue, Chelsea, opposite that of Robin Maugham, who wrote the novel on which Harold Pinter based his screenplay.

James Fox was from a well-off background himself and his mother was outraged when she saw the film. Sarah Miles's parents accused her of disgracing the family name with a piece of 'sexually perverted tosh'. Miles plays Bogarde's lover, brought into the house to seduce Fox and strengthen Bogarde's hold on him. Miles was actually James Fox's partner at the time.

Although *The Servant* did not figure in the Oscars, Bogarde and Fox both won British Academy Awards.

SHIRLEY VALENTINE (1989)

Although Willy Russell's plays are set firmly in Merseyside, the film of *Shirley Valentine*, like *Educating Rita* before it, was made elsewhere. *Educating Rita* shot in Dublin, whereas most of the British filming for *Shirley Valentine* was done in London – though on this

occasion there were at least a few scenes shot in Liverpool.

Shirley Valentine's house was in Twickenham, not far from the film's base at Twickenham Studios. 'Those kind of streets are the same all over England, with the pebble-dash stuff on the outside,' says director Lewis Gilbert. 'Willy writes about characters and people he knows. He writes about Liverpool, but his characters could live anywhere in the world.'

Pauline Collins won a British Academy Award and an Oscar nomination for a superb performance as a dowdy housewife whose personality is being crushed by routine and a husband, Joe (Bernard Hill), who used to be fun but now expects his tea on the table at six – and it *has* to be steak on Thursdays. He is none too pleased when Shirley gives him egg and chips, having fed the steak to her vegan neighbour's dog.

Shirley Valentine was originally a one-woman play and the film retains the technique of its central character talking to the audience – the best use of straight-to-camera commentary since *Alfie*, which was also directed by Lewis Gilbert. By the time Shirley starts talking to the camera she has already convinced us she converses with the kitchen wall. Instead of being an awkward story-telling device, talking to the camera is a perfect illustration of the drudgery of her life.

Shirley leaves her husband and almost grown-up family for a holiday with a female friend in Greece. Under the Mediterranean sun and the influence of a different culture, she is transformed into a sexy, mature woman with a new zest for life. *Shirley Valentine* was

Wendy Craig, Dirk Bogarde and James Fox in The Servant *(Springbok)*

*Bernard Hill and
Pauline Collins in
Shirley Valentine
(Paramount)*

actually shot back-to-front, with filming beginning on the Greek island of Mykonos in September 1988, where Shirley has a holiday romance with a waiter (Tom Conti), before cast and crew returned to London to shoot the preparations for the holiday.

'We shot on Marylebone Station where she was getting her pictures taken for her passport in the photo booth,' recalls Gilbert. 'We shot in Littlewoods in Oxford Street when she went to buy all her stuff for the journey and she bought – well, she didn't *buy* them – the black panties, and the neighbour saw her. ' It was the Oxford Circus store, not the Marble Arch one. The scene in which Shirley is splashed by a limousine containing a posh, former schoolfriend (Joanna Lumley), who subsequently turns out to be a high-class hooker, was filmed at the Marlborough Hotel in Bloomsbury, an up-market hotel with an impressive restored Edwardian entrance, though the hotel interiors were constructed in the studio.

'We did take some shots in Liverpool, just to get the flavour, round the docks and things,' says Gilbert. By the time Gilbert and Collins reached the last day of filming, at Liverpool's Pier Head, it was late November. Gilbert wanted it to look as cold, wet and miserable as possible, enough to make anyone pack up and head for Greece. 'I was told it was always cold and wet in Liverpool,' he said at the time. It was certainly cold, but rain had to be supplied by artificial means.

CHAPTER TWO

Four Weddings and a Lot of Stately Homes
SOUTH-EAST ENGLAND

ANNE OF THE THOUSAND DAYS (1969)

Richard Burton and Genevieve Bujold played Henry VIII and Anne Boleyn on the very location where the couple had courted more than 400 years earlier. Hever Castle, near Sevenoaks in Kent, was the Boleyn family home. It was subsequently owned by the American multi-millionaire, William Waldorf Astor, who built an entire Tudor village behind the castle.

Today, Hever looks a little like a Tudor theme park. One of the most distinctive estates in England, the solid, square, medieval castle sits behind not one, but two neat square moats. Within the courtyard are half-timbered Tudor buildings. The land between the moats contains a maze and formal garden as well as the Tudor village, which was built for guests and staff, but is now let out for conferences. In addition, the estate includes a 35-acre lake, used in *The Princess Bride*. The castle also featured in *Lady Jane* – another film about a queen who had her head chopped off – and in Michael Winner's *Bullseye*. The castle actually began as a farmhouse in the thirteenth century and was transformed into a crenellated manor house in the fifteenth.

After the execution of Anne and her brother, George, Henry gave Hever to his fourth wife, Anne of Cleves. It subsequently fell into a long decline before Astor bought it in 1903. He spent a fortune on restoration and sympathetic extension and on various art treasures, including ancient Roman sculptures. The house and gardens are open to the public from spring to autumn.

For Henry VIII's Greenwich Palace, which stood on the site of the Royal Naval College, the film-makers used another grand location, Penshurst Place, near Tunbridge Wells in Kent. The manor, which was built in 1340, has been greatly extended in Gothic style over the years. Penshurst was the home of the Elizabethan poet, Sir Philip Sidney, and has been in the same family ever since. It is open to the public and has featured in various films and television productions, including *Young Sherlock Holmes* and *Love on a Branch Line*.

BATMAN (1989)

Not many people know this, but Batman shared an English stately home with Queen Victoria. *Batman* was one of those films that most people would assume was made in America and to all intents and purposes it is an American film, made by an American studio, Warner Brothers, with American stars – Michael Keaton as the dark knight, Jack Nicholson as the Joker and Kim Basinger as Vicki Vale. But it was filmed in England, albeit almost entirely in the studios at Pinewood, where most of the sound stages were taken over by the film and the nightmarish futuristic city of Gotham was created.

Anton Furst, the production designer, based his vision on the worst aspects of New York, but with the buildings taller and streets narrower. The secret identity of Gotham's masked crime-fighter is Bruce Wayne, a wealthy playboy. Wayne's home had to provide a contrast to this ultra-modern urban hell so Warners were looking for Old-World style and opulence, with perhaps something of the same dark quality that characterises Batman on screen. They opted for a combination of two stately homes just outside London, both in Hertfordshire, off the A1. Knebworth House was used as the exterior of Wayne Manor and Hatfield House was used for interiors.

Knebworth has been the home of the Lyttons since the fifteenth century, but is best known, apart from rock concerts, for the magnificence of its nineteenth-century Gothic exterior. The castellated frontage gives the building the air of a fortress and conceals the Tudor home within.

Hatfield House, one of the largest and most splendid Jacobean mansions in England, was built in the early seventeenth century for the Earl of Salisbury in red brick with stone dressing. In its Victorian heyday, it was possibly the most celebrated weekend retreat in the country and guests included Queen Victoria herself, Disraeli, Gladstone and the Shah of Persia. Both houses are open to the public.

Batman went on to become one of the highest grossing films of all time. The sequels *Batman Returns* and *Batman Forever* were filmed in America.

BLACK BEAUTY (1994)

The bustle of nineteenth-century streetlife was recreated in the courtyard of one of England's great stately homes, Blenheim Palace, near Oxford. It was here that Winston Churchill was born and that Black Beauty worked as a cab-horse for Jerry Baker (David Thewlis), with the palace appearing in the background as an opera house. 'It was great,' says writer-director Caroline Thompson. 'It worked well for us because it was completely controllable — we didn't have to worry about traffic.'

Queen Anne conferred the estate on one of Churchill's ancestors, the First Duke of Marlborough, for his victory over the French and Bavarians at Blenheim in Germany in 1704. Parliament voted him the astronomical sum of £500,000 to build Blenheim Palace, an enormous edifice spread over three acres, set within a 2,500-acre park. The palace was designed by Sir John Vanbrugh and the avenues and trees were laid out by Capability Brown, supposedly in accord with a map of the Battle of Blenheim. Both the palace and the gardens are open to the public from spring to autumn.

The house of the kindly Squire Gordon (Peter Davison) was Hall Barn, a seventeenth-century house in Buckinghamshire, while the home of Lord and Lady Wexmire (Peter Cook and Eleanor Bron) was Ditchley, an eighteenth-century house not far from Blenheim Palace. Churchill was a regular visitor there. For about 350 years, Ditchley was the home of the Lee family that included the famous Confederate General Robert E. Lee. It is now used as a conference centre, but can be viewed by arrangement.

'It was fun shooting at Ditchley because no one ever had, but that also made it a little dodgy because the guy who owns it was very nervous. Film crews are notoriously destructive even though we don't intend to be . . . ' admits Thompson.

The grand room in which Black Beauty has to pose for Lady Wexmire to paint him, surrounded by marble busts, and where he relieves himself on the carpet was shot at Stratfield Saye House in Hampshire. It is another house which was presented to a victorious general after defeating the French – on this occasion to the Duke of Wellington in 1817. He altered the existing seventeenth-century building, intending to create a Waterloo Palace to rival Blenheim, but he never fulfilled that ambition. Stratfield Saye is open to the public and includes a special exhibition on the famous duke. 'The only part of the house that we used was the interior where Eleanor Bron's doing the painting – we did lots and lots of exteriors there,' says Thompson.

Thame Park, a private estate in Oxfordshire, was also used extensively for exteriors. (For full details on the strange history of Thame Park, see the entry on *The Madness of King George*.) The drunken ride of Reuben Smith (Alun Armstrong) was shot in Black Park, beside Pinewood Studios; and the railway that appears in the film, when the Gordon family set off to live abroad, was the Bluebell Railway at Sheffield Park in Sussex, where steam trains run daily in summer and on Sundays throughout the year.

Black Beauty was the directorial début of Caroline Thompson, who had written *Edward Scissorhands* and Tim Burton's *Nightmare Before Christmas*; and it was Peter Cook's last film.

BLACK NARCISSUS (1947)

Powell and Pressburger's melodrama with Deborah Kerr and Jean Simmons, which dealt with illicit passions in a community of Anglican nuns in the Himalayas, won Oscars for its stunning colour cinematography and its art direction. Michael Powell and Emeric Pressburger were jointly credited for writing, directing and producing their films, but Powell was primarily responsible for directing and Pressburger for writing.

Powell was a man who would go to great extremes to get exactly what he wanted at a time when location shooting was much less common than it is now. It was fully expected he would want to go to India for *Black Narcissus*, but he had a surprise in store for colleagues when they met to plan the film.

Rumer Godden, author of the original novel, had said her setting was a combination of a number of places, and the art department had a large portfolio of photographs ready for the meeting. Powell was asked if he had a specific location in mind. 'Yes,' he said. 'Horsham.'

He recalls in the first volume of his autobiography, *A Life in Movies*, that cameraman Chris Challis was the first to recover his composure. 'Do you mean Horsham in Surrey, Micky?' he asked. 'In Sussex,' corrected Powell. 'There's a famous house and gardens there called Leonardslee . . .

'I reminded them how British merchant princes and pro-consuls, when they retired and came back to Britain to live, would bring whole trees and bushes wrapped in matting to remind them of India. Himalayan plants and trees do well in the British climate. Rhododendrons and azaleas grow like weeds and Leonardslee had a deep and steep little glen planted with cedars and deodars. You would swear you were in the Himalayas.'

Powell had decided that the style and colour of any Indian location footage would never match the style and colour of footage shot at Pinewood Studios in

Buckinghamshire. He wanted complete control over the look and atmosphere of the film and decided to build the main set on the lot at Pinewood, with a painted Himalayan backdrop, complemented with location footage from Leonardslee. The end-result was an exotic, erotic, slightly unreal setting that matched the tone of the film.

Leonardslee is privately owned, but the gardens are open to the public in summer. Located in a natural valley with six lakes, they are noted for camellias and magnolias in April and rhododendrons and azaleas in May. There is a rock garden, bonsai exhibition, Alpine house, wallabies and deer.

A CANTERBURY TALE (1944)

Half a century after Powell and Pressburger borrowed her house to use as the residence of Eric Portman's eccentric squire, Elizabeth Montgomery was still living at Wickhambreaux Court, with vivid memories of the commotion the production caused in the Kent village. 'I could have shot the lot of them!' she says, and she is not talking about filming them.

Only the exterior of the Tudor manor house appears in the film; the interiors were reproduced in Denham Studios near London. But the film-makers needed access to photograph the inside to help with the construction of studio sets and leading lady Sheila Sim (subsequently Lady Attenborough) requisitioned one room as her dressing-room.

'They walked in and out of here as if they belonged to the place,' says Mrs Montgomery. 'It would have cured you of being film-struck. They had a caravan parked out on the green with all the recording stuff in it and Sheila Sim drove her cart through the green. It took them six weeks here. It was quite a thing . . . They even cut branches off the trees to get the shadows right.'

Mrs Montgomery was not the only one who did not appreciate Michael Powell and Emeric Pressburger's film. Even by their own standards, it is a strange film.

An American serviceman (John Sweet) gets off at a small village station by mistake, instead of Canterbury, and meets a landgirl (Sim) and a British soldier (Dennis Price). As they leave the station, a shadowy figure leaps out and pours glue on the landgirl's hair. Suspicion quickly falls on the local squire (Portman), whose lecture on the Pilgrim's Way is well attended, supposedly and perhaps rather oddly, because young women are frightened to be outdoors. The four main characters subsequently complete the journey to Canterbury and the squire admits he is the mysterious 'glueman', motivated by a wish to deter girls from going out with American servicemen and to boost attendance at his history talks.

It was only in the seventies that the film was critically re-evaluated. There is a great deal to admire in the film, which opens with a sequence involving a medieval falconer's bird taking to the air and transforming into a Spitfire – a sequence which predates Stanley Kubrick's legendary bone-to-spacecraft jump cut in *2001* by more than twenty years. But the critics have still never quite managed to explain what *A Canterbury Tale* is all about and how it supposedly embodies the qualities for which England was fighting at the time of its production.

It was clearly a deeply personal film for Powell. He was born in Kent and went to King's School in Canterbury. In his autobiography *A Life in Movies* he recalls his mother

Jean Simmons and Sabu in Black Narcissus *(The Archers)*

John Sweet, Sheila Sim,
Dennis Price and
Eric Portman in
A Canterbury Tale
(The Archers)

reading him *The Canterbury Tales* as a child and cycling along the old Pilgrim's Way with his mother and brother in 1918. He wrote of loyalty to Canterbury – 'to the High Street and cattle markets that are no more, to the Christchurch Gate opposite Kit Marlowe's statue in the Butter Market, to Cave's café, to the cathedral standing amid the hushed green lawns of the precincts, to the vast silence of the nave, where a chair dragged across the echoing flagstones made one think of Becket's body dragged by armoured men, pierced and slashed with swords, to die before the altar in the side chapel. All this I have tried to get into the last 25 minutes of *A Canterbury Tale*. '

He also wrote of the narrow medieval lanes – Butchery Lane and Mercery Lane – between overhanging black-and-white houses. 'You can see them in my film when the marching soldiers turn left to their route to the cathedral. ' Although there was extensive shooting in Canterbury, some of the cathedral scenes had to be done elsewhere. Canterbury's organ and its stained-glass windows had been removed for safe-keeping. The scene in which Dennis Price's character, Peter Gibbs, a cinema organist in civilian life, plays the cathedral organ, was recorded at St Albans and the nave of the cathedral was reproduced at Denham Studios.

Canterbury was formerly the Roman town of Durovernum and, as Cantwarabyrig (borough of the men of Kent), it became the capital of Ethelbert, king of Kent, in the sixth century. After the murder and canonisation of Thomas Becket, Archbishop of Canterbury, in the twelfth century, it developed as a centre of international pilgrimage. Earlier this century, however, not long before Powell and Pressburger's film, it was a target for Hitler's bombs. The cathedral is the mother church of Anglican Christianity and a great, grey stone, ecclesiastical skyscraper. It dates from Norman times, though much of it is later and Gothic in style. The main entrance was built to commemorate Henry V's victory at Agincourt in 1415. Henry IV is buried here and there was a shrine to Becket, who was murdered by Henry II's supporters in one of the regular conflicts between church and state, until it was destroyed at a time of escalating conflict when Henry VIII was king. He founded King's School, within the cathedral precincts.

The traditional pilgrims' route followed the High Street and Mercery Lane, which was once packed with traders selling Becket souvenirs and medallions – the medieval equivalent of the people who sell programmes and T-shirts at pop concerts today. Although the Pilgrim's Way approaches Canterbury from the west, Wickhambreaux and many of the other locations that Powell and Pressburger used were east of the city.

The two men are jointly credited with writing, directing and producing the film, but Pressburger did most of the writing and Powell did most of the directing. Powell wrote in his memoirs that Pressburger was denied permission to visit Kent because it was wartime, the county was a restricted area and he had been born in Hungary.

The village, where Bob Johnson (Sweet) gets off the train by mistake and meets the other characters, was called Chillingbourne. Elizabeth Montgomery recalls visitors, who had managed to follow the film-makers' trail to the village of Wickhambreaux, asking directions to Chillingbourne without realising that it was a fictional village made up of shots from various places. Powell mentioned a few in his book, including the village of Shottenden, where Bob Johnson, who has been brought up in the lumber business in

Oregon, chats with an old English wheelwright. Mrs Montgomery reels off more – the railway station at Selling, the Red Lion at Wingham, the town hall at Fordwich, where the squire delivers his lecture – all of which are still there. Although tiny, Fordwich is officially a town rather than a village, with a town hall complete with ducking-stool. It was the port for Canterbury when ships came right up the River Stour. Wickhambreaux Court, like Chillingbourne, is no longer a single entity, having been sub-divided into several private residences.

Mrs Montgomery says that long before her time, Powell had visited the house as a boy. There may have been changes, but change comes cautiously in these parts and there is much that Powell and Pressburger's pilgrims would recognise in Canterbury and the surrounding villages today.

THE DRAUGHTSMAN'S CONTRACT (1982)

The location is absolutely central to Peter Greenaway's charming atmospheric and at times bamboozling costume-drama; a film that has been described as a seventeenth-century thriller about class, sex and landscape. Mrs Herbert (Janet Suzman) hires a draughtsman (Anthony Higgins) to produce 12 drawings of her husband's home, Compton Anstey, while he is away. Both she and her daughter, Sarah (Anne Louise Lambert), also use the draughtsman as a possible means of providing an heir who will one day inherit Compton Anstey.

It is a film of rare elegance, though it cost only about £300,000 to make. Peter Broughan, one of the producers, claims the credit for finding the location and recalls how they exploited the valuable historic contents of the house. 'The teaset Janet Suzman uses is worth more than the entire budget of the film,' he says.

The Draughtsman's Contract was made almost entirely on location in a single stately home. 'We got it for next to nothing – about £500 a week,' says Broughan. But neither the house nor its grounds were open to the public and the owners insisted the location remain a secret. However, the house has since changed hands and it can now be revealed that it is Groombridge Place, a moated mansion, near Tunbridge Wells on the Kent-Sussex border. It was built for the Royalist, Philip Packer, in the seventeenth century after the Restoration, with gardens designed by the diarist, John Evelyn. The moat, in which Mr Herbert eventually turns up dead in the film, surrounded an earlier castle on the same site. Neither the house nor, unusually, the neat, formal, walled gardens have changed much since they were built. The gardens reflect an increased interest in horticulture among English gentlemen during the reign of King Charles II and are evocative in Greenaway's film of a bygone age of privilege, leisure and order.

Greenaway was not the first individual in the popular arts to be inspired by Groombridge Place. Arthur Conan Doyle used it as the inspiration for Birlstone Manor in *The Valley of Fear* 70 years earlier. The previous owners also owned the village of Groombridge and the surrounding farmland, but the estate was broken up after their deaths and many of the contents were auctioned off by Sotheby's in 1991. Groombridge Place's new owner, businessman Andrew de Candole, provoked controversy with plans for a new visitor carpark, but at least the gardens are now open to the public.

A FISH CALLED WANDA (1988)

John Cleese's rise to stardom began while he was a student at Cambridge University and a member of the famous Footlights Revue. But it was 'the other place', Oxford, that was to play a key role in his greatest success, *A Fish Called Wanda* – an enormous hit on both sides of the Atlantic.

Python teamed up with Ealing for this comedy classic. John Cleese wrote, produced and starred in it, while 77-year-old Charles Crichton, who made *The Lavender Hill Mob*, directed. They had been collaborating for several years on the story about a gang of jewel thieves – two English, two American – who carry out a major robbery and then fall out with each other.

Cleese played Archie Leach, the barrister representing the crook who ends up in custody and who also happens to be the only one who knows where the jewels are hidden. Crichton shot exteriors at the Old Bailey, London's Central Criminal Court, but the English court system does not facilitate feature films, so the interiors were shot in the former courtroom which is part of Oxford Town Hall. An impressive wood-panelled chamber, it still has the staircase leading directly from the dock to the cells. It is occasionally used for meetings, but is maintained in its former judicial state. And although the film's press release says gang leader George (Tom Georgeson) is 'a prized guest in one of Her Majesty's better known prisons', it was in fact Oxford Prison. Hardly Barlinnie or Wormwood Scrubs, the prison is an ornate stone fortress, easily overlooked among the city's other architectural gems. Crichton and Cleese also filmed at Twickenham Studios and in and around London.

George instructs Ken (Michael Palin) to bump off the little old lady (Patricia Hayes) who is the only witness in the case. But Ken, an animal-lover and owner of the fish called Wanda, accidentally kills her dogs, one by one, as she leaves her home in Onslow Gardens, a solid old street of whitewashed terraced houses, near South Kensington underground station. The London Underground is definitely an underground train system and not a subversive political movement, no matter what gang member Otto (Kevin Kline) might think.

In the dog-killing sequences, you can see the number 69 on the pillar by the little old lady's door. The dogs are subsequently buried in a real pets' cemetery, called Silvermere Haven, set in woodlands just off the A3 near Cobham in Surrey. Pet owners pay hundreds of pounds for a good funeral and some come every week to tend the graves. 'Gone for long walkies,' says one epitaph. Even some rats were loved sufficiently to merit a decent send-off.

The money from the big job in the film would have bought gold coffins for an entire menagerie. The robbery itself was filmed in the Hatton Garden area, an international centre for the jewel trade. Archie Leach's chambers were in Lincoln's Inn Fields – the address in Holborn that shows you have made it to the legal premier league. His up-market house was a private home in Esher, Surrey, and the flat he borrows for his romantic liaisons with gang member Wanda (Jamie Lee Curtis) was a warehouse converted into a flat on the Thames. Location manager Bill Lang recalls: 'That was a lovely flat in a warehouse. I suppose it was really in the Docklands. It's on the South Bank, opposite

Tower Bridge, opposite Tower Hotel. It was one very early conversion on a top floor and we had to lift everything in by crane.'

There is double-cross, triple-cross, the murder of various dogs and fishes and some meditation from Otto – using a Buddhist technique that the monks used to focus their anger before battle – before the film concludes at Heathrow Airport, with a question mark still hanging over who exactly will be on the flight to South America.

A Fish Called Wanda grossed $60 million on its initial North American release. Not only was it the fourth-highest grossing film in the UK in 1988, but it was in the 1989 Top 20, too, at No 12. It was a critical hit as well as a commercial one. Despite the sex, violence, extensive cruelty to animals and John Cleese in the nude, *A Fish Called Wanda* is essentially a very sharp and very funny study of English manners and mannerisms. Probably uniquely, its three leading actors all won Academy Awards. The incredibly versatile Kevin Kline, a regular Shakespearean actor, won the Oscar for best supporting actor for his psychopath Otto, a man who claims to be a CIA public relations officer keeping the neighbours informed that they are debriefing a KGB defector nearby. John Cleese won the British Academy Award for best actor and Michael Palin won the British Academy Award for best supporting actor.

One final footnote on names: Cleese's character was called Archie Leach, which was Cary Grant's real name; Tom Georgeson's character, George Thomason, was a play on his own name; and the man who disturbs Archie and Wanda in the waterside flat was called Iain Johnstone, which is the name of the former film critic for the *Sunday Times*, who has subsequently collaborated with Cleese on the script for the sequel to *A Fish Called Wanda*. In addition, George gives Ken a scrap of paper saying the old lady lives at 69 Basil Street – obviously a reference to Cleese's character in Fawlty Towers.

FOUR WEDDINGS AND A FUNERAL (1994)

With crowds flocking to see it again and again, many viewers must have wondered exactly where the four weddings and one funeral took place. One Australian screening was interrupted by a shriek of recognition when St Michael's Parish Church in Betchworth, Surrey, appeared on screen, with the proud declaration, 'that's the church where I got married.' Bookings have soared for the honeymoon suite at Amersham's Crown Hotel, where Carrie (Andie MacDowell) and Charles (Hugh Grant) make love on a four-poster bed. But when *Four Weddings and a Funeral* began filming, no one had any idea that it would become the biggest hit of the year in Britain and one of the most successful British movies ever, grossing $200 million worldwide in its first six months.

It was shot on a tight budget of about $4. 5 million (£3 million), including the usual cash from Channel 4. The budget would not stretch to a trip to Scotland. So, for one of the weddings, instead of Perthshire the film-makers used Albury in Surrey, 'where we found a bit of bracken, and which looks remarkably like Scotland', according to Richard Curtis, who wrote and co-produced the film. The wedding ceremony of Carrie and Hamish (Corin Redgrave) takes place in a stately home in Hampshire, with members of the London Caledonian Society recruited to provide the 'local' colour on the dance floor. Every day a piper piped them to the catering caravans for lunch.

The film opens with Charles and his flat-mate, Scarlett (Charlotte Coleman), late for a wedding in what is described in Curtis's script as 'an idyllic, sun-soaked, small country church in Somerset'. It was filmed at St Michael's, a traditional stone village church, in Betchworth, near Dorking. It was certainly sun-soaked – it was so hot one elderly extra fainted. It was a long way to the reception, however, which was held at a marquee in the grounds of Goldingtons, a privately-owned Georgian manor house, near Sarratt, in Hertfordshire.

By the time the film team shot at Goldingtons, the weather had changed for the worse. It was freezing cold and the dialogue in the marquee had to be re-recorded because of the sound of thunder and the rain on the canvas. The only person not in danger of hypothermia was Simon Callow, who plays Gareth. He had been 'padded out' underneath his clothes to make his character seem larger-than-life. Producer Duncan Kenworthy said: 'We asked an awful lot of the weather and when you have a small budget one of the risks you take is that you are completely at the mercy of the elements. You have to go with what you are given on the day, but, fortunately, we got what we wanted almost on cue.'

The owner of Goldingtons, who preferred to remain anonymous, later told *The Times*: 'The film company were no trouble at all. We were a bit nervous about our lawn. We were worried about the chickens and the ewe which were put in the couple's car, but nothing went wrong. We watched from the top floor just to check.'

Later that night Charles and Carrie meet again in a country inn called The Boatman, the exteriors of which were shot at the King's Arms in Amersham, Buckinghamshire, and the interiors down the road in the Crown Hotel, High Street, Amersham, a coaching inn dating from the sixteenth century. Stephen Quigley, general manager, reveals: 'In the film, the hotel has green fields around it. Our hotel doesn't actually have green fields around it.' So, Charles gets out of the Land Rover at the King's Arms and steps through the door into the Crown Hotel and ultimately up to Carrie's bedroom.

Director Mike Newell recalled: 'Everything was running late. We were still up to our eyes in cables, arc lights and with cameras shooting from every angle at 6 p. m. The hotel staff were tearing their hair out. They were expecting a honeymoon couple to arrive at 8.30 p. m. and they probably had a picture of the happy couple walking into their beautiful bridal suite and finding Andie MacDowell and Hugh Grant in their bed. In the end they threw us out and furiously got to work on making the suite habitable. We had to finish the scene by building a replica set.'

But the panic was certainly worth it in the long run for the hotel, which has inquiries every day about the room and has taken bookings from as far away as Japan. Stephen Quigley adds: 'There is no question they are fans of the film. The question is, are they getting the suite that was used in the film and the answer is yes. If that's the bed they book, that's the bed they'll get. It started when we had a young couple come from the North of England, travelling down 300 miles, to see it. They got engaged here. She had seen the film about five times and he brought her here without telling her where they were going. That story made the press. On the back of that, the *Travel Programme* did a feature on us and I did a few radio interviews.'

The second wedding, presided over by Rowan Atkinson's nervous priest and

Hugh Grant and Andie MacDowell in Four Weddings and a Funeral *(Working Title/Channel Four)*

supposedly in a grand Roman Catholic church in London, was shot in the chapel of the Royal Naval College at Greenwich. The college was built in the seventeenth century as a new palace for King Charles II and the chapel was rebuilt by James 'Athenian' Stuart in the late eighteenth century. The reception was held at Luton Hoo, an eighteenth-century Robert Adam stately home at Luton, Bedfordshire. Because it is so close to London and the film studios, it has become one of the most frequently used locations in Britain. It produces its own CV, listing more than 30 feature films and television programmes, including *Oliver, Never Say Never Again, Harry Enfield* and *Inspector Morse*, and pointing out the variety of uses to which different parts of the house have been put on screen. While the sitting-room has doubled as Queen Victoria's bedroom, the white-tiled kitchen area has represented hospital corridors. Luton Hoo is run by a charity and is open to the public.

By this time Carrie is engaged to Hamish, but is accompanied by Charles when she goes shopping for a wedding dress at Albrissi, Sloane Square, London, followed by coffee in The Dome in Wellington Street, London WC2. London also provided the characters' homes, with Fiona and Tom residing at Holland Park, Matthew and Gareth in Cranley Mews and Charles and Scarlett in Highbury Place. Producer Duncan Kenworthy says: 'The day we shot the rain scene in Highbury Fields with Andie and Hugh was the coldest day in 40 years and at one point the temperature dropped eight degrees in 30 minutes. The rain was unbelievable, but no real rain could be as heavy as the hundreds of gallons of movie rain we drenched those poor actors with.'

Carrie and Hamish's 'Scottish' wedding takes place just outside London at Albury Park, near Guildford, in Surrey. Albury is a Tudor mansion remodelled by A. W. N. Pugin in the mid-nineteenth century and subsequently sub-divided. There is limited public opening in summer. The reception was down the road at Rotherfield Park, a Victorian Gothic house in extensive grounds, at East Tisted, near Alton, Hampshire. It is privately owned but open to the public on specified days.

The series of weddings is punctuated by the sudden death of Gareth and his funeral at St Clement's Church in West Thurrock on the Thames. It dates from the twelfth century and has clearly seen many sad funerals over the years. The churchyard was the final resting place for an officer and 16 teenage trainees from H. M. Training Ship *Cornwall* earlier this century. St Clement was the patron saint of sailors. The church is now surrounded by industrial development and ceased to function as a church in 1977. It was subsequently restored as a community facility by Procter and Gamble, which occupies a neighbouring site, and the churchyard is maintained as a wildlife sanctuary for flowers, insects, birds and small mammals. The churchyard is always open and access to the church can be arranged through Procter and Gamble.

Southwark Cathedral in London was the original location for the final wedding, but arrangements fell through shortly before the scenes were due to be shot and the film-makers switched to the Priory Church of St Bartholomew the Great, tucked away on a patch of land, off a street called Little Britain, not far from London's Smithfield meat market. The surrounding area includes high-rise flats, professional offices and pubs which service the meat market and nearby Fleet Street. The church had fallen into terrible disrepair in the last century and the cloister was being used as a stables before rebuilding and restoration began. The outside of the church is dominated by its brick clock tower, but on entering the building the visitor seems to move back several centuries through time into a great, high-ceilinged hall of stone arches and pillars. Parts of St Bart's date from as early as the twelfth century. It survived the Great Fire of London in 1666 and is the oldest church in the city of London by 500 years. As well as *Four Weddings and a Funeral*, it featured in *Robin Hood: Prince of Thieves*. Because of the high ceiling, lighting was a problem for *Four Weddings and a Funeral* and it took five days to rig up before filming. Church of England rules have been tightened to stop couples getting married in churches other than their own, but there has been an increase in the number of visitors to St Bart's.

There is never any guarantee of living happily ever after, but the success of *Four Weddings and a Funeral* certainly made life sweeter for the film-makers in the short to medium term. *Four Weddings and a Funeral* was the first British film to reach No. 1 at the American box-office since *A Fish Called Wanda* six years earlier and Hugh Grant, who had been working away largely unnoticed in British films for years, was transformed into a major box-office star and an unlikely transatlantic sex symbol.

GENEVIEVE (1953)

Much of this classic comedy about the London–Brighton vintage-car rally, and the two rival owners who challenge each other to a race on the return leg, was shot nowhere near the London–Brighton road. And it was not just the locations that differed in reality from those in the film. The story was meant to be taking place in summer, but it was shot in mid-winter, making filming an uncomfortable experience for the four principals – Kenneth More, Dinah Sheridan, John Gregson and Kay Kendall – particularly as director Henry Cornelius insisted on take after take before he was satisfied.

Most of the filming was done on the convenient country roads around Pinewood Studios in Buckinghamshire, reportedly causing traffic congestion at times. For close-ups, the veteran Spyker and Darracq cars were mounted on trailers which could also accommodate lighting and camera crews. Gregson could not drive prior to filming and so his driving in a valuable machine was kept to a minimum.

Cornelius did have to venture into London for the big city locations, which included the Strand, Hyde Park and Westminster Bridge. The Spyker is supposed to get stuck in the tramlines on the bridge, but the film-makers discovered they had been lifted, which is why the background suddenly becomes Lewisham.

GREAT EXPECTATIONS (1946)

Half a century ago David Lean was already showing some of the traits that were to make him one of cinema's great perfectionists. Remarkably for the time, Lean insisted on shooting on the actual location Charles Dickens had written about in his novel. In *Halliwell's 100*, film critic Leslie Halliwell wrote about 'a breathtaking landscape that is part Romney Marsh, part studio'. But Lean filmed not on Romney Marsh but on St Mary's Marshes, the area Dickens had in mind when he wrote the chilling opening of his book, in which young Pip visits the graves of his parents and five dead brothers and first

Kay Kendall and Kenneth More in Genevieve *(Sirius)*

encounters the escaped convict Magwitch, 'a fearful man, all in coarse grey, with a great iron on his leg . . . a man who had been soaked in water and smothered in mud . . . who limped and shivered and glared and growled'.

Confusion about the location obviously arose because there is a village called St Mary in the Marsh at Romney Marsh on the south coast. St Mary's Marshes is an area, near the mouth of the Thames, that manages to seem remote, while in fact being just 20 miles from London. Pip recounts in the book: 'Ours was the marsh country, down by the river, within, as the river wound, twenty miles of the sea.'

Dickens lived in a house at Gad's Hill, a few miles away, and it was there that he wrote *Great Expectations*, having supposedly been inspired in his opening by the sight of the gravestones of 13 little children in the churchyard at the nearby village of Cooling in the marsh country itself. As well as shooting part of the opening sequences at St Mary's Marshes, Lean used it as the location of Joe Gargery's forge, where Pip lived as a boy. Lean shot Pip arriving in London by coach in front of St Paul's Cathedral, but another scene in which the adult Pip (John Mills) and Herbert Pocket (Alec Guinness's first film role) are picked up from a small rowing boat was shot in the River Medway, just round the corner from St Mary's Marshes, because the Thames was too busy with modern shipping.

At least one critic reckoned it was the greatest British film yet made and Finlay Currie was unforgettable as the convict – even if he was nearing 70 at the time.

HEAVEN'S GATE (1980)

Not only did the ancient city of Oxford figure prominently, if surprisingly, in the western that took United Artists to the point of bankruptcy, but it appeared under the caption Cambridge – Cambridge, Massachusetts, the location of Harvard College, where Michael Cimino's epic western begins. The elegance and sophistication of the opening sequence is contrasted with the grubby brutality of life on the frontier in Wyoming.

The film begins, supposedly in 1870, with a shot of the Tom Tower at Christ Church College before the camera tilts down to Kris Kristofferson, in a formal black suit, running through the Great Gate. The gatehouse dates back to 1526 and the tower was added in 1681 by Christopher Wren to house 'Great Tom', the bell from Osney Abbey.

The *Heaven's Gate* prologue was shot when the body of filming was complete, by which time the original $7.5 million budget had ballooned to $33 million. In a belated attempt to bring the production back under control, United Artists were insisting Cimino stick to a very tight schedule for the final few shots. Executive Stephen Bach recalls in his compelling account *Final Cut* that when Oxford University refused to allow filming at Christ Church on a Sunday, Cimino made his preparations during the night and 'stole' the shot at dawn before the authorities realised what he was doing.

Kristofferson is subsequently seen running to catch up with a brass band and procession, which he does at the Hertford College bridge, an early twentieth-century

Finlay Currie and Anthony Wager in Great Expectations *(Cineguild)*

construction that resembles Venice's Bridge of Sighs, but spans New College Lane rather than a waterway. Graduates assemble on the circular benches of Wren's Sheldonian Theatre for speeches from Joseph Cotten and class orator John Hurt, before dancing the night away on the quad of Mansfield College, which was founded as a Congregationalist training college but is now part of the university. It was built in the Gothic style in the late nineteenth century. All these locations are open to the public.

Heaven's Gate was withdrawn immediately after its American première, re-edited and re-released. It still grossed only $1.5 million.

Cimino had certainly played the Hollywood dictator to the hilt and had ridden roughshod over all attempts to control him and his production. But the film, which was the antithesis of the traditional western, suggesting the West was moulded not by rugged individualists but by corrupt capitalists, has always been rated more highly by European critics. Several have included it in lists of all-time greats. It is at least a highly original film and, for those receptive enough to appreciate it, an incredibly powerful statement about material and spiritual wealth and poverty.

KIND HEARTS AND CORONETS (1949)

One of Ealing's most famous comedies, it boasts a wickedly funny and dark sense of humour and an acting *tour de force* from Alec Guinness – playing no less than eight members of the aristocratic D'Ascoyne family, who stand between Louis Mazzini (Dennis Price) and the title of the Duke of Chalfont. But the film also contains a jarring combination of location footage and studio shots. The use of what are very obviously painted backgrounds in some scenes seems peculiar given that writer-director Robert Hamer and producer Michael Balcon went to the trouble of getting a real castle to represent Chalfont, the object of Mazzini's desires.

The film-makers used Leeds Castle near Maidstone in Kent, an ancient fortress built on two small islands in a lake, surrounded by 500 acres of gardens and parkland. It dates from the ninth century, was rebuilt by the Normans and served as a royal palace for 300 years, beginning in the time of King Edward I. The tall narrow windows, the castellated battlements and the moat effect of the lake make Leeds Castle the very image of what an ancient castle should look like. It is open to the public, with various special events, including open-air concerts and ballooning, which seems ironic given the nature of Lady Agatha D'Ascoyne's death. When Mazzini shot an arrow in the air, she fell to earth in Berkeley Square.

The film took its title from a gentler piece of poetry by Tennyson, including the line 'kind hearts are more than coronets'. The film was a great success and made Guinness a major international star, even though he appears on the credits below not only Price but also Valerie Hobson and Joan Greenwood. Arthur Lowe, who was later to achieve fame through *Coronation Street* and *Dad's Army*, has a small but memorable role as the reporter who asks Mazzini for his memoirs at the end of the film, prompting Mazzini's realisation that he has left the incriminating documents in the prison cell where he had been awaiting execution for a murder he did not commit.

LAWRENCE OF ARABIA (1962)

David Lean's Oscar-winning film about the First World War hero T. E. Lawrence was shot on three different continents, though not in Arabia itself. Most of the shooting was done in Jordan, Morocco and Spain, but there were a couple of scenes in England – the memorial service at St Paul's Cathedral in London and the scene of Lawrence's death, which, although it was the last scene filmed, was part of the sequence that opens the movie.

The shots of Lawrence (Peter O'Toole) preparing to get on his motorbike were done in Almeria, the desert area of Spain where many of the spaghetti westerns were filmed. The scenes of him riding through the English countryside and crashing were done at Chobham in Surrey. O'Toole was filmed sitting on a Brough motorbike on a trailer that was being pulled by the camera car, though he did come off once and narrowly escaped serious injury.

The film took over a year to make and cost a phenomenal $13 million, but it collected more than that at the American box-office alone, made stars of O'Toole and Omar Sharif, and won seven Oscars, including best picture. O'Toole got the first of a record seven nominations as best actor without a single Academy Award.

THE LORDS OF DISCIPLINE (1983)

Hardly a great film, but of passing interest in that the makers deemed it possible to make a film about racial tension in the south of the United States on location in the south of England, substituting an English public school for the American military academy of the story. *The Lords of Discipline* centres on the admission of the first black cadet to Carolina Military Institute in the mid-sixties, but the American military academies apparently refused to allow Paramount on the premises, so they crossed the Atlantic and shot much of the film in England, using Wellington College at Crowthorne, Berkshire, instead.

Although it might seem a giant leap from an American military academy to an English public school, tradition in general and military tradition in particular obviously play major roles at both. Wellington was founded in 1853 for the sons of deceased officers and in memory of the famous duke who sorted Napoleon out at Waterloo. The British monarch is official 'visitor' at the school and the appointment of governors must be approved by Buckingham Palace. Many former pupils have gone into the army and a high proportion of pupils still come from military homes. However, Wellington also counts racing driver James Hunt and comedian Rory Bremner among its old boys. The school is an impressive building, situated in its own estate of over 400 acres.

THE MADNESS OF KING GEORGE (1994)

Several stately homes were used for this film, but none more interesting than Thame Park near Oxford. It was the home of Sophia Wykeham who was briefly engaged to one of George III's sons, the Duke of Clarence.

In the film, George (Nigel Hawthorne) goes to Thame Park for an early course of psychotherapy. Its previous occupant, Sophia Wykeham, was herself 'half-mad', according to diarist Charles Greville. With the royal family going through a series of scandals and

The Lords of Discipline (Paramount). Wellington College, Crowthorne, Berkshire, was used as an American military academy (pictures courtesy of UIP and British Film Commission)

The cast of The
Madness of King
George *outside St
Paul's Cathedral in
London (Goldwyn/
Channel Four)*

serious questions being asked about the king's sanity, it was considered essential that the duke should marry someone of the highest rank and spotless character. Wykeham was considered unsuitable. When the duke became King William IV, he made her Baroness Wenman. She never married and, in fact, the film-makers just missed her when they visited Thame Park.

She had a terrible fear of being buried alive. In accordance with her wishes, her coffin was left open for seven days and it was agreed it should not be buried for 50 years, by which time the estate had been sold. The coffin lay in a vault until 1990 when work was being done on the house and estate and it was thought desirable to finally bury it, 120 years after Wykeham's death.

Thame Park dates back to the twelfth century and its north wing includes the remains of a Cistercian abbey. It is not normally open to the public.

Alan Bennett, who wrote the film's script, based on his play *The Madness of George III*, says: 'I'd no idea myself about the settings or the locations. I wrote the scenes and then they put them in the various settings . . . Thame Park, near Oxford, is this kind of wonderful mixture of houses – eighteenth-century and Tudor and medieval – and it had been bought by a Japanese consortium to turn into a hotel. They'd more or less ruined it really. Then they went bankrupt and it was just left to moulder away; so we took it over to do that scene.'

Bennett says he wanted to show how 'ramshackle' royalty was at the time of George III. 'They were just a rabble really.' A rabble with some splendid houses, nevertheless. Arundel Castle in Sussex, between Worthing and Chichester, served as the exterior of Windsor Castle. It dates from the Norman Conquest and has been the seat of the Duke of Norfolk and his ancestors for more than 700 years. It was besieged and badly damaged by Parliamentary forces in the Civil War and extensively rebuilt in magnificent Gothic style. Its art treasures include Van Dyck, Gainsborough, Reynolds and portraits of the Earls of Arundel and Dukes of Norfolk hung in chronological order. The castle is open from spring to autumn.

Windsor Castle interiors were shot at Wilton House – the Elizabethan home of the Earl of Pembroke – near Salisbury in Wiltshire. It has appeared in several films, including *Barry Lyndon*. The apartments of Queen Charlotte (Helen Mirren) were filmed at Broughton Castle, home of Lord Saye and Sele. This moated medieval castle near Banbury in Oxfordshire was enlarged in the sixteenth century and is noted for its fine panelling, fireplaces and plaster ceilings. There is a secret meeting-room which was used by the Parliamentary side in the Civil War. The meeting between the king and Pitt (Julian Wadham) was filmed at Syon House, the Duke of Northumberland's seat at Brentford. The house was begun by the Duke of Somerset who was executed for treason. His accuser, John Dudley, was created Earl of Northumberland and given Syon. Robert Adam subsequently renovated and decorated the house, designing the Long Gallery which was used in the film. Wilton, Broughton and Syon are all open to the public. Other locations included the Royal Naval College at Greenwich; St Paul's Cathedral in London; and Eton College, in Berkshire, as the Houses of Parliament.

A MAN FOR ALL SEASONS (1966)

Although the locations behind most films remain a complete mystery to the general public, the few magazine and newspaper articles there have been on the subject in recent years invariably mention the Oscar-winning *A Man for All Seasons* and its historic Hampton Court Palace location.

A Man for All Seasons is the story of Catholic statesman Thomas More (Paul Scofield) and Henry VIII (Robert Shaw) and of the clash between church and state. Hampton Court had been given to Henry as the new royal palace by Cardinal Wolsey (Orson Welles). But director Fred Zinnemann insists the production team never shot a single scene at the palace. 'We never set foot in Hampton Court for the purpose of shooting. It was built in Pinewood by my brilliant art director. It was much simpler and cheaper to do it that way and no one could tell the difference . . . The swimming pool at Pinewood was used to play the Thames.'

There was some location shooting, but nowhere near Hampton Court. As More's home, Zinnemann used Studley Priory, at Horton-cum-Studley, near Oxford. An attractive stone building, set in its own wooded grounds, it was founded as a Benedictine nunnery in the twelfth century, used as a private residence after Henry VIII's Dissolution of the Monasteries and converted into a hotel in the 1960s.

For the purposes of the film, it was supposed to be on the Thames and Zinnemann had to find a suitable stretch of tidal river to show Henry VIII arriving and impatiently jumping from his barge to find himself in mud up to his ankles. Zinnemann explained the scene's significance in *Fred Zinnemann: An Autobiography*: 'Furious at first, he suddenly bursts out laughing; his courtiers – the "yes" men of the period – can do nothing other than jump after him, ruining their pretty finery and laughing at the delightful adventure.'

Zinnemann needed a river where the tide would rise and fall, leaving behind deep mud. But modern building and development ruled out virtually every estuary in England. Eventually, the film-makers discovered an unspoilt stretch of the Beaulieu River on Lord Montagu's estate in Hampshire, so the king got out of his boat near Southampton and arrived at a house 60 miles away outside Oxford.

Both Studley Priory and Beaulieu are tangible reminders of the religious upheaval of the sixteenth century, for the Beaulieu estate includes Beaulieu Abbey which was largely destroyed 450 years ago. Beaulieu is also the site of the National Motor Museum. The abbey, museum and house are all open to the public.

A Man for All Seasons won no less than six Oscars, including best picture. Zinnemann won the award for best director, Scofield for best actor and Robert Bolt for best script – an adaptation of his own play. It also won Oscars for cinematography and costumes.

THE MISSION (1986)

Following the success of *Gandhi*, Britain's Goldcrest film company embarked on its most ambitious and expensive project to date, sending Robert De Niro and Jeremy Irons off into the jungles of South America, at a cost of more than £15 million. But at the end of the day, Goldcrest ended up reshooting a vital scene in its local park.

De Niro and Irons play eighteenth-century Jesuit missionaries facing the twin dangers

of hostile Indians and duplicitous church politicians. Associate producer Iain Smith explains that the film-makers were worried about one particular scene. 'It's the scene where Robert De Niro meets the Indians for the first time having dragged this bloody bundle of armour up over the waterfalls . . . We were never very happy with the way it was shot in Argentina and we were unsure about some of the performance at that point so we wanted to give him a second crack at it. It was cheaper to bring three Indians over from Colombia than it was to take a film crew out to Argentina.'

They reshot the sequence in the Black Park country park right next door to Pinewood Studios in Buckinghamshire. 'The trees are really not that different,' says Smith. 'Most people think of jungle as luscious and rich and so on, but we ended up having to bring quite a lot of greenery into genuine sub-tropical jungle. That's because it's all secondary forest nowadays and secondary forest just looks like British forest.' He is confident no one could tell the difference between Argentina and Buckinghamshire. 'It made me think why the hell did we go all the way to South America.'

Black Park and the neighbouring Langley Country Park, on the other side of the A412, are among the most filmed locations in Britain. They were both part of the Langley Park estate of the Duke of Marlborough and have been popular with royalty from Catherine of Aragon to Queen Victoria. Black Park is primarily forest and includes a lake within its boundaries, whereas Langley is traditional English parkland. Hammer and *Carry On* films were regular visitors. More recent productions in Black Park include *Black Beauty* and *First Knight*.

PETER'S FRIENDS (1992)
PRINCESS CARABOO (1994)

Wrotham Park has witnessed some odd goings-on over the years, including visits from Fry and Laurie, Shelley and Byron on drugs, a tramp who convinces everyone she is an exotic princess and an admiral who was shot by his own side. The last example is a true story.

Wrotham was built, at Barnet, in Hertfordshire, for Admiral John Byng in the mid-eighteenth century, but he never got the chance to enjoy it. He was sent to stop the French taking Minorca in 1756, failed, returned to England and was shot for dereliction of duty.

A long, symmetrical building, Wrotham remains the private house of the Byng family and although it is not open to the public, it has probably been seen by more of them than virtually any other stately home in England, for it has appeared in a long list of film and television productions. It was here that Peter (Stephen Fry) entertained his old university friends including Hugh Laurie, Kenneth Branagh and Emma Thompson in a film that managed to be funny and touching, despite many flaws – including an embarrassing drunken scene from Branagh – and a more-than-passing resemblance to *The Big Chill*.

Peter hung a 'welcome' sign over the pillars of Wrotham's rather grand entrance, but that was nothing compared to the outrages of Ken Russell's tenure. He used it as a location for *Gothic*, his 1986 film about Lord Byron and the Shelleys; starring Gabriel Byrne, Julian Sands and Natasha Richardson. Russell returned to Wrotham with Sean Bean and Natasha's sister, Joely Richardson, for a steamy television production of *Lady Chatterley*.

Robert De Niro in The Mission (Enigma/Goldcrest/Kingsmere)

Peter's Friends
*(Renaissance/Goldwyn/
Channel Four). Back
row: Kenneth Branagh,
a stuffed bear, Stephen
Fry, Hugh Laurie.
Middle: Rita Rudner,
Emma Thompson,
Imelda Staunton. Front:
Alex Lowe, Alphonsia
Emmanuel, Tony
Slattery, Phylidda Law*

Wrotham also served as the main location for *Princess Caraboo*, the true story of a young vagrant in the early nineteenth century who manages to pass herself off as an eastern princess who has escaped from pirates. The title role is played by Phoebe Cates and a distinguished cast includes her husband, Kevin Kline, and Stephen Rea. She is adopted by Mr and Mrs Worrall, members of the local gentry, and ends up meeting the Prince Regent (John Sessions) at a ball.

Scenes of the ball were filmed at Luton Hoo, near Luton, in Bedfordshire – a magnificent Robert Adam building in a 1,500-acre park. Both house and grounds are open to the public. Gunnersbury Park Museum in London provided the location for the Worrall kitchen, while the Bishop's Palace in Fulham, London, was used both as the courtroom where Caraboo is tried and for the office of the journalist, John Gutch (Rea).

THE RETURN OF THE SOLDIER (1982)
Captain Chris Baldry (Alan Bates) returns from the First World War to a beautiful wife (Julie Christie) and an elegant home, but all he remembers is the woman with whom he was in love 15 years earlier (Glenda Jackson). A poignant and underrated film, it was based on a short novel of the same name by Rebecca West, who went into great detail to build up an image of Baldry Court and a world of 'brittle, beautiful things' of which Kitty (Christie) is clearly one.

The film-makers shot largely at Firle Place, near Lewes in Sussex. It is an attractive caen-stone, stately home, over 100 yards in length, and has been in the possession of the same family for more than 500 years. It is still occupied by Viscount Gage, one of whose ancestors commanded the British forces at the outbreak of the American War of Independence. Firle Place dates back to Tudor times, though it was largely rebuilt in the eighteenth century. It is open to the public in summer and contains British and European Old Masters, including Rubens, Reynolds, Gainsborough and Van Dyck; Sevres china; Beauvais tapestries and Georgian furniture.

Rebecca West had set the earlier relationship between Chris and Jackson's character, Margaret, at Monkey Island, on the River Thames, near Bray in Berkshire, but by the eighties it was no longer the pleasant countryside West had known, with the M4 passing close by. The film-makers opted instead for the area around Pangbourne, about 20 miles to the west where the River Pang joins the Thames. It is noted for its seventeenth- and eighteenth-century houses and a particularly pretty view across the river to Pangbourne Meadow.

A ROOM WITH A VIEW (1986)
Merchant Ivory's association with the film critic, John Pym, has proved unusually beneficial. For not only has he written two books about their work, but he wound up providing them with their principal English location for the film of E. M. Forster's comedy of Edwardian manners, *A Room with a View*. Pym's family house in Kent served as the home of Lucy Honeychurch (Helena Bonham Carter) and her mother (Rosemary Leach) and it is in his grounds that Simon Callow, Julian Sands and Rupert Graves are discovered frolicking naked by Mrs Honeychurch, Lucy and her stuffy fiancé, Cecil Vyse (Daniel Day-Lewis).

Julian Sands, Simon Callow and Rupert Graves at Foxwold in Kent in A Room with a View *(Merchant Ivory)*

The first half of the story is set in Florence, where Lucy arrives for a holiday with her cousin, Charlotte (Maggie Smith), only to discover their rooms have no view. Their friend, the Reverend Mr Beebe (Callow), encourages them to accept an offer to exchange rooms with Mr Emerson (Denholm Elliott) and his son, George (Sands). But Lucy and Charlotte cut short their holiday after George kisses Lucy.

Director James Ivory and producer Ismail Merchant used John Pym's home, Foxwold, near Brasted, as the Honeychurch residence Windy Corner. Pym says: 'I wrote a book on Merchant Ivory in the early eighties, entitled *The Wandering Company*, and I became friends with them. They had been here before, and the house is, in fact, fairly close in period and location to the house as described by E. M. Forster, so it was suitable.'

Foxwold is a half-timbered, many-gabled mansion house, built by a London solicitor, Horace Noble Pym, in 1883. It has remained in the family ever since. Merchant Ivory's decision to film there was also influenced by the possibility of creating a lake for Callow and company's naked horseplay in a disused sunken garden within Foxwold's extensive grounds. 'It's not open to the public, although local people do walk through certain tracks,' says Pym.

There are, however, other places nearby that were used in the film and which are open. The tiny National Trust village of Chiddingstone served as the local village in the film. It is a single street of picture-postcard, half-timbered, sixteenth- and seventeenth-century houses, with a thirteenth-century church, which was Mr Beebe's church. The village was used by Merchant Ivory for both interiors and exteriors. It takes its name, Chiddingstone, from an ancient stone, where, according to local lore, nagging wives were taken to be publicly chided or scolded.

Emmets Garden, another National Trust property in the same area, was used in the film for a garden party. It is a four-acre arboretum on a hilltop site, begun late in the last century without any particular plan or design. Each tree and shrub has been planted on its own merit.

Reviewing *A Room with a View* in the *Monthly Film Bulletin*, Philip Strick said: 'The first impression is of near-perfection.' It was nominated for eight Oscars, including best picture, and won three – for script, costumes and art direction. It won the British Academy Award for best picture and did much better at the box-office than any previous Merchant Ivory film, grossing more than $60 million worldwide.

THE SECRET GARDEN (1993)

The Secret Garden became the Secret Gardens, plural, in the film of Frances Hodgson Burnett's popular children's book.

Burnett had lived at Great Maytham Hall in Rolvenden, Kent, in the 1890s and it is thought that she based her overgrown hideaway on a neglected high-walled garden there. The building has now been converted into flats, with carefully tended grounds. Finding the right garden turned out to be something of a nightmare for the film-makers and they wound up with a combination of gardens from the north and south of England, and at Pinewood Studios.

They shot at both Allerton Park, near Knaresborough, in Yorkshire, and Luton Hoo, near Luton. Luton Hoo was built by Robert Adam in the mid-eighteenth century, but was subsequently gutted by fire and reconstructed. The building is considered less interesting than its contents – which include Fabergé jewellery, Renaissance bronzes and medieval ivories – or its park, which was the work of Capability Brown and is open to the public. A third garden was laid out at Pinewood Studios, where, if the weather prevented filming, everyone could retire indoors and shoot interior scenes.

In the film, the garden is the secret play area for Mary, who has been orphaned in India and is sent home to live with her uncle, Lord Craven, at Misselthwaite Manor – represented in the film by Allerton Park, the ancestral home of Lord Mowbray and the finest Gothic revival stately home in England. It is open to the public. Mary is seen walking across the lawns with the impressive house filling the screen behind her. But the film-makers also took some exterior shots at Luton Hoo and at Fountains Hall, near Ripon in Yorkshire. A handsome Jacobean mansion open to the public, it stands close to Fountains Abbey.

Several other locations provided various rooms, including St Pancras Chambers, at St Pancras Station in London. Two of England's most famous public schools were also used – Eton College, in Berkshire, and Harrow, in Middlesex.

SUPERMAN IV (1987)

It is impossible to tell whether one English critic was being ironic at the time of the film's release when he said that Metropolis, where Superman lives, looked just like Milton Keynes. But the truth of the matter is, it is Milton Keynes. The sprawling new town in Buckinghamshire was used to double for Metropolis in close-ups, while long shots and backgrounds for flying sequences were shot in North America.

Superman's alter ego, Christopher Reeve, blamed Milton Keynes for the failure of the film – which turned out to be the last of the series – ignoring the awfulness of the script, the weak characterisation and the generally poor acting. It is, however, possible to enjoy *Superman IV* if you are familiar with Milton Keynes and enter into the spirit of the town's elevation to superstardom.

At the prompting of a small boy, Superman goes to the United Nations to tell them that he has decided to destroy the world's entire arsenal of nuclear weapons, except he does not go to the United Nations, he goes to Milton Keynes Central railway station – an easy mistake to make, even for a superhero. Superman is seen a couple of times outside the modern, mirrored-glass building in Station Square. *The Daily Planet*, the newspaper where he works as Clark Kent, is located in a neighbouring office block.

Kent and Superman go on a double date with Margot Kidder and Mariel Hemingway's characters at Hemingway's hotel, with much mayhem and confusion ensuing as Kent and Superman keep switching places. Hemingway gushes about the romantic view from her balcony and Kent gives her the slip just as she enters the glass-sided lift. This sequence was shot not at a top hotel, but at the head office of the Argos retail group in Avebury Boulevard – another futuristic building, but not futuristic enough for some critics.

TOMMY (1975)

A street was demolished and a theatre and pier were burned down during the filming of the quintessential rock opera, *Tommy*. The street was demolished deliberately, but the fire on the pier was an accident that brought unwanted headlines to the production. As if that was not enough bad publicity, the film-makers came under attack from local clergy for transforming a former Christian church into a church for the worship of the goddess Marilyn Monroe. The man behind all this? It had to be Ken Russell, who had already scandalised decent society with *The Music Lovers* – his no-holds-barred biopic of homosexual composer Tchaikovsky – and *The Devils* – portraying sexual fantasy and demonic possession among the nuns of seventeenth-century France.

Tommy had been a milestone for rock music when it appeared as a double album by The Who in 1969. A series of songs related the story of a deaf, dumb and blind kid called Tommy, who becomes first a champion at the arcade game called pinball – playing, it is suggested, by sense of smell – and secondly a prophet; before his followers finally reject him and in the process set him free. The Who performed the entire rock opera live on tour for two years, taking in several opera houses. The band's singer, Roger Daltrey, was the obvious choice for the title role in the film version, with the drummer, Keith Moon, playing his sleazy Uncle Ernie. Ann-Margret played Tommy's mother, Russell regular

Oliver Reed was his stepfather, Frank; Elton John was the Pinball Wizard and Tina Turner was the Acid Queen. There were also parts for Eric Clapton, Jack Nicholson, Robert Powell and the remaining Who members, John Entwistle and Pete Townshend, who was the principal composer.

The film was shot mainly at Shepperton Studios and in and around Portsmouth, including Southsea and Hayling Island. For one of the early scenes, Russell needed a street that he could literally knock holes out of. It is a scene where Tommy's parents (Ann-Margret and Powell) are seen running through a street during the blitz. Russell was lucky that there was an area in Portsmouth currently being demolished and he was able to take over part of the Cumberland Road in Fratton for his own personal blitz.

Tommy's mother meets her new husband, Frank, at Bernie's Holiday Camp, which utilised shots of Hilsea Lido and the beach huts at Southsea. Bernie's Holiday Camp ballroom was really the theatre on South Parade Pier, Southsea. During filming, a fire broke out and the beautiful old wooden theatre and the pier on which it stood burned down, which did not endear the film-makers to their host community.

Filming of the pinball duel between Roger Daltrey and Elton John took place over three days, with 1,500 local extras, at Southsea's Kings Theatre, which happily survived the experience and continues in use as a theatre. There was further trouble, however, over the use of St Andrew's Church at what was the Royal Marines barracks at Eastney. Russell turned it into the Church of Marilyn Monroe, with graven images of the actress supposedly offering cures to the afflicted. The building had been deconsecrated, but that did not deter local protests.

Tommy becomes a messiah himself, with his own holiday camp, which was, in fact, Pound's scrapyard at the bottom of Portsmouth's Twyford Avenue. Pound's were a firm of ship-owners and ship-breakers and there was all sorts of decommissioned naval hardware in the yard.

If nothing else, Russell has always been one of Britain's most imaginative directors and he utilised the mounds of buoys that were just lying around. He got his staff to scour Hampshire for silver paint and turn the buoys into giant silver pinballs. They continually needed repainting because the actors had to climb over them and the paint came off. Fire breaks out – as it is supposed to do – in the rebellion at Tommy's Holiday Camp and Russell managed to insert some of the footage he had taken of the fire at the pier. The pier has now been rebuilt. Pound's had several yards, but they are no longer involved in ship-breaking and they left the site of Tommy's Holiday Camp vacant; empty land except for the memories.

The film included the songs 'See Me, Feel Me', 'I'm Free' and, of course, 'Pinball Wizard'. Ann-Margret was nominated for the best-actress Oscar and Pete Townshend was nominated for the music. Critic Alexander Walker rated the film Russell's best of the seventies. He wrote in his book, *National Heroes: British Cinema in the Seventies and Eighties*: 'Russell seized all the opportunities for visual wizardry: Tommy resembled a phantas-magoria of Dali, Bosch, Tanguy and Yves Fuchs. A skeleton crawls with slugs, lizards and snakes . . . huge iron canisters litter the amusement parks like the spawn of monstrous fishes.'

Some of the sites are now forgotten even in Portsmouth, but *Tommy* has secured its place in rock history.

WISH YOU WERE HERE (1987)

Emily Lloyd shot to fame as a foul-mouthed, independently-minded teenager whose behaviour outrages the population of the seaside town where she has grown up.

Although it is not named in the film, the principal location was Worthing, a sedate Sussex resort and popular retirement destination. The hairdressing school, where Lynda (Lloyd) trained, was specially kitted out for the film, but the bus depot where she subsequently works, is the real thing. And the Dome cinema, where her lover, Eric (Tom Bell), was projectionist, is next door in Marine Parade. The film is set in the early fifties and the Dome not only had the right architecture and decor, but even suitably vintage projection equipment. 'Our projectors are about mid-thirties,' says Glyn Owen, the Dome projectionist who acted as technical consultant, played a non-speaking role in the film and even wound up in the trailers. 'We've probably got the oldest projectors in England.'

The Dome was built at the beginning of the century and was a roller-skating rink before becoming a cinema shortly before the First World War. A listed building, retaining the deep red carpets and chandeliers that were characteristic of the period, it continues to operate as a cinema and was still using the same ancient projectors the best part of ten years after *Wish You Were Here* was made.

Owen says: 'I helped in the projection box and made it appear more authentic and showed Tom Bell how to stand in the right position and handle the right levers and knobs. And I played a bus conductor in the bus garage scene when she's showing her new French-style knickers. I'm one of the leering conductors. I didn't say anything – just grunted once.'

Although Lynda moves to another town in the film, the reality was more complex, for director David Leland continued to use footage shot in Worthing for the other town as well, with occasional shots from neighbouring towns stitched into the film at various points. Seafront scenes were shot at both Worthing and nearby Bognor Regis, whilst Rustington's village hall was used for a dance scene and the bowling scenes were filmed in Brighton.

Emily Lloyd in Wish
You Were Here
(Zenith/Channel Four)

LES LEÇONS DE LA VIE
(THE BROWNING VERSION)

CHAPTER THREE
Locations Far From the Madding Crowd
THE WEST COUNTRY

THE BROWNING VERSION (1951, 1994)
GOODBYE, MR CHIPS (1969)
THE GUINEA PIG (1948)

Sherborne School in Dorset has played host to a series of films in its illustrious history, including both adaptations of *The Browning Version*. In the more recent one – a subtle updating of Terence Rattigan's one-act play – Albert Finney gives a monumental performance as the fearsome classics master who is forced to come to terms with his failings as a teacher and a husband. Director Mike Figgis explains: '*The Browning Version* is the story of a man and his wife and the school – a triangle set in a beautiful prison.'

Figgis needed a monumental setting to complement Finney's performance and to provide an atmosphere of history and tradition, discipline and scholarship; an elegant setting for the cricket, the garden party and the prize-giving.

Finney's character (Andrew Crocker-Harris) is pressured into early retirement from the Abbey School, for which Figgis used a combination of two public schools in Dorset. Exterior shots were filmed at Milton Abbey School in the village of Milton Abbas. The main part of the school is a large eighteenth-century Gothic mansion, though the school incorporates the medieval abbey church and some of the buildings of the monastery founded by Athelstan in 938. The mansion itself was built for the first Earl of Dorchester in the eighteenth century and the school was founded as recently as 1954. It stands in extensive parkland and is open to the public during spring and summer holidays.

Interiors were filmed about 12 miles away at Sherborne School, which was also used for the 1951 version, with Michael Redgrave in the main role. It, too, has close links with a local abbey, but they go back much earlier than those of Milton Abbey School. Sherborne School traces its history back to the eighth century and St Aldhelm. Like Milton Abbey, it incorporates some monastic buildings, though, in this case, not the abbey church itself.

Both Milton Abbey and Sherborne are traditional Anglican schools and Finney watched classics taught in a 300-year-old schoolroom at Sherborne. He would later teach his own class of young actors in that same classroom where many famous former pupils have pored over their textbooks. The roll of former pupils includes David Sheppard, Nigel Dempster, the King of Swaziland and Jeremy Irons, who might have made a very fine Crocker-Harris himself. Figgis also filmed among the old inns and the handsome sixteenth- and seventeenth-century houses in the small town of Sherborne.

The school lies at the heart of the film and at the heart of Crocker-Harris, but it is in the town that his wife (Greta Scacchi) and another teacher (Matthew Modine) conduct an

Albert Finney, Matthew Modine and Greta Scacchi in The Browning Version *(Paramount)*

affair, and where one of Crocker-Harris's boys finds an old copy of Robert Browning's translation of the Greek tragedy *Agamemnon*, in which the king is killed by his wife. It is a gift that deeply moves 'the Hitler of the Lower Fifth' and renews his faith in human nature.

A quarter of a century earlier, Peter O'Toole had filmed at Sherborne School when he appeared in the musical remake of *Goodbye, Mr Chips*, along with Petula Clark. The film made extensive use of the school and O'Toole and his wife, Sian Phillips, who also appears in the film, took a cottage in the local area. O'Toole plays Mr Chipping who is passed over for the headmaster's job at Brookfield School, but remains popular with the boys until his final goodbye. The screenplay, curiously enough, was written by Terence Rattigan and was based on James Hilton's novella. O'Toole said later that the idea of a musical *Goodbye, Mr Chips* filled him with horror and the only reason he read the script was that it was by Rattigan. O'Toole thought Rattigan pulled it off; the public thought otherwise – though O'Toole was nominated for the best actor Oscar.

A fourth school drama to shoot at Sherborne was the 1948 film, *The Guinea Pig*, in which Richard Attenborough plays a scholarship boy who finds it tough going at a public school. Attenborough was actually in his mid-twenties at the time.

Although the school is a working school, it is possible for visitors to see round the grounds.

DOCTOR DOLITTLE (1967)

Rex Harrison might have been well advised to consider the old adage about not working with animals or children before he undertook this role. He was surrounded by not one, but dozens of animals every day. He had to pat them, lift them and even kiss them. He was pecked, scratched and bitten by everything from a chimpanzee to a squirrel – which needed a couple of gins before it would calm down and stay in place long enough to be filmed. Then there was the continual distraction of animals relieving themselves in the middle of speeches or songs. As if all that were not bad enough, it rained on 51 out of the 56 days *Doctor Dolittle* spent on location in the Wiltshire village of Castle Combe. And to cap it all, the film-makers had to deal with a local resistance movement that did not want them in the village and even went so far as plotting to blow up the sets.

When the film finally did come out it got nowhere near recouping 20th Century-Fox's $20 million budget. The project started promisingly enough. Harrison's previous musical *My Fair Lady* had been a big hit and Alan Jay Lerner and Andre Previn, who had both worked on *My Fair Lady*, were to write the songs for this adaptation of Hugh Lofting's children's stories about a doctor who can talk to animals – including a two-headed llama called a pushmi-pullyu. But during its lengthy development period, Lerner and Previn left to be replaced by Leslie Bricusse. Michael Flanders and Donald Swann, composers of clever but sedate comic songs, came and went and it was Bricusse who finally wrote the songs. Meanwhile, Harrison was replaced by Christopher Plummer only to rejoin the project later.

Filming began in the summer of 1966 in Castle Combe, a small and ancient village of stone cottages. Many consider it the most beautiful village in England. It represented Puddleby-on-the-Marsh, the little fishing village where Doctor Dolittle lives in the mid-nineteenth century. Castle Combe met all the requirements of the film, except one. It is old, it is scenic, but it is about twenty miles from the sea. The village had changed little in centuries and St Andrew's Church and other familiar features should be readily recognised at the beginning of the film by anyone who knows Castle Combe – though viewers may be puzzled by the presence of a lagoon and fishing boats in the foreground, deep in the heart of the Wiltshire countryside.

Undaunted by Castle Combe's lack of a waterfront, director Richard Fleischer and his crew dammed the village brook and created one. Many people liked Castle Combe just the way it was and were bitterly opposed to the modifications, even if they were temporary. There was even a plot to dynamite the waterfront. In his autobiography, *Rex*, Rex Harrison claims that the plot involved 'one gallant military gentleman'. The gent in question was the young Ranulph Fiennes – the exploit ended his military career, though he later became famous as an explorer.

It was not gunpowder, treason or plot, but the weather that finally drove Fleischer and Harrison away, though not before they had filmed numerous scenes in and around the village, using the seventeenth-century Dower House as Doctor Dolittle's home. Interiors of his house were shot on a cramped set in California, where there was a better supply of trained animal actors. Hollywood's professional animal talent had been prevented from coming to Britain by quarantine regulations and Harrison had his worst fears about British animals confirmed when a supposedly tame squirrel emerged battling from its cage. Sets were built on a ranch, which was considered better able to accommodate the animals than the studios.

The production subsequently moved to the West Indies, where once again it was plagued with rain. It should have taken six months to film. It actually took a year and when it came out audiences stayed away in droves. It is certainly not a classic, but some of the performances and songs, and certainly the colour of the locations, costumes and characters, rise above Fleischer's flat direction. *Doctor Dolittle* won Oscars for special effects and for the song, 'Talk to the Animals'. It was nominated for best picture and it remains popular whenever it is shown on television.

DRACULA (1979)

This version has been overshadowed by Hammer and Coppola, although it adheres more faithfully to Bram Stoker's original story than most. It also boasts Laurence Olivier as Van Helsing and has Frank Langella reprising the role of Count Dracula that he played successfully on Broadway.

Stoker's story was set in the north-east of England, though the film-makers actually shot in the south-west, using King Arthur's Castle Hotel at Tintagel, Cornwall, as their main location. It is a bleak mock-Gothic building, built in the style of a castle at the turn of the century, and situated on a dramatic site overlooking the sea. As the name suggests, it is a site long associated with King Arthur. Movies normally bring a little glamour to locations and boost tourist business. However, the Castle Hotel's appearances have not been as a romantic castle, but as a mental hospital in one film, *Dracula*, and a remand home in another, the 1986 film, *Lamb*, starring Liam Neeson.

King Arthur's Castle Hotel, used as an asylum in Dracula *(Universal/Mirisch) and a reformatory in* Lamb *(Cannon/Flickers/Limehouse/Channel Four)*

In *Dracula*, Van Helsing's daughter, Mina (Jan Francis), is staying at the asylum run by Jack Seward (Donald Pleasence) — the father of her friend, Lucy (Kate Nelligan) — when Count Dracula turns up as the only survivor of a shipwreck.

As Dracula's home, the film-makers used St Michael's Mount, a picturesque castle dating back to the Middle Ages, located on a small island, near Penzance. The island is owned by the National Trust and accessible by causeway at low tide. The castle is privately occupied, but open to the public.

The scene when Dracula boards a ship in an attempt to return to Romania was shot at the Cornish fishing village of Mevagissey. Nearby Crinnis Beach in Carlyon Bay was used for part of the shipwreck sequence.

Interestingly, when the film was released, critic Richard Combs wrote in the *Monthly Film Bulletin* that it was a 'triumphantly lurid creation that seems bound to be either under-valued for its circus effects or over-valued for the stylishness with which it steers between the reefs of camp and theatrical indulgence'.

FAR FROM THE MADDING CROWD (1967)

The people of the Dorset village of Sydling St Nicholas were delighted when their thirteenth-century church was chosen to appear in *Far From the Madding Crowd* and determined that church and churchyard should look their best. A band of volunteers went to work on tidying up the churchyard, only for the vicar to receive a distraught phone call from one of the production team asking him to stop at once. Director John Schlesinger wanted the churchyard to look neglected.

'That is why it looks as it does — a disgrace to the parish,' wrote the Revd Harry Brayford, vicar of Sydling St Nicholas, in the handbook for the 1968 Thomas Hardy Festival. The tale underlines the point that locations are not always chosen for their prettiness. The main reason Sydling St Nicholas was chosen as Weatherbury Church was, apparently, because of its gargoyles. In one scene, water pours from a gargoyle's mouth on to the grave of young Fanny.

Despite Brayford's shame, the West Country does look superb on film, with Schlesinger making use of numerous locations in Dorset and Wiltshire — ranging from the historic town centre of Devizes to the quaintly-named Scratchy Bottom, where Gabriel Oak's sheep plunge over the cliff near the beginning of the film.

Oak was played by Alan Bates, who had previously starred in Schlesinger's *A Kind of Loving*. He was one of three very different types of men vying for the attention of Bathsheba Everdene, played by Julie Christie, who had recently won an Oscar under Schlesinger's direction for *Darling*. Peter Finch was gentleman farmer William Boldwood and Terence Stamp was the soldier Sergeant Troy.

Scriptwriter Ferderic Raphael stuck very closely to the book, but although the film was shot on location in Hardy's Wessex, Schlesinger did not feel constrained by the exact locations the novelist had in mind and intercut shots from various places as if they were one and the same. Bathsheba's home, shown at the beginning of the film, was a derelict dairyman's building at Bench, just beneath the National Trust's Hardy Monument and near Waddon House, which serves as Boldwood's home later in the tale. When Oak visits

Bathsheba and proposes, the viewer gets the impression that he lives just a field or two away, though his farm in reality was more than ten miles from there: Scratchy Bottom is on the Dorset Coast Path, very close to Durdle Door, which later serves as the location where Sergeant Troy does a Reggie Perrin, taking off his clothes and swimming out to sea. Some of the most magnificent scenery in the film was shot on this area of coastline.

After he loses his flock, Oak has to seek work and attends the hiring fair in Casterbridge – Hardy's name for Dorchester. Schlesinger opted instead for Devizes, an ancient market town across the county boundary in Wiltshire, with some additional shots from Shaftesbury. Schlesinger shot in the Market Place in Devizes, in front of the Bear Hotel, which dates from at least the sixteenth century and still operates as a three-star hotel, and its next-door neighbour, the Corn Exchange, which was used as a corn exchange in the film, though it has subsequently been redeveloped and sub-divided inside, with uses ranging from conferences to discos. There is a cross in the Market Place which records that during a quarrel over money one Ruth Pierce asked Heaven to strike her dead if she were lying. 'She instantly fell and expired,' says the inscription.

Nearby is St John's Church, a twelfth-century church used in the sequence where Sergeant Troy is meant to marry Fanny Robin (Prunella Ransome). She, however, has gone to the wrong church. She realises her mistake and hurries to St John's where she meets Troy coming out. He accuses her of making a fool of him and they never do marry, though she remains his one great love.

In the 1968 Hardy Festival handbook, Norman Boothroyd, warden of St John's, recalled that when Schlesinger came to film the interior scenes where Troy and the parson wait for Fanny in the Norman sanctuary, Schlesinger found the church pews full of local people who had come along to spectate. They were asked to leave, but Boothroyd refused to go, insisting that he was responsible for the church and if the film-makers wanted to make an issue of his presence it was they who would have to go. He was allowed to stay. Boothroyd enthused about the transformation of the Market Place for filming. 'Parking outside the restricted area, I walked to the centre of town, straight into the past of one hundred years ago . . . Market stalls on four-wheeled carts, people dressed as a century ago; ill-clad youngsters sitting on the steps of the Cross, whilst long-skirted women with bonnets and shawls, moved amongst the stalls; a farmer and wife rode sedately in pony and trap; a coach deposited passengers outside the Bear.'

In charge of hiring 300 extras in Devizes was Daniel Baber, a Wiltshire man who has managed to combine farming with professional dancing. He wrote and volunteered his services when he heard about the film. 'I held auditions,' he says three decades later. 'The Swindon car industry was going through a poor time and the workers all came down, but they weren't Hardy characters at all. They were all pale and wan. We wanted people of the land. So it was great fun finding character faces . . . John Schlesinger was so delighted with the people I provided that he gave me a speaking part in the film.'

At the hiring fair, Baber is the bewhiskered gent who suggests to Boldwood that he might want to hire an old shepherd. 'There's work in him yet . . . and you would get him cheap.'

Baber remembers sharing a dressing-room with Finch at the Bear and later dancing at

Gold Hill in Shaftesbury appeared in Far From the Madding Crowd *and Hovis commercials*

the party where Boldwood shoots Troy. 'I could afford to pay someone to look after the farm and I went off and danced for them for 12 days in Thornhill House, near Sturminster Newton.'

The scene where Gabriel Oak first arrives in Casterbridge and passes Sergeant Troy's men, and the one in which the pregnant Fanny struggles up the hill to the poorhouse at night were filmed on Gold Hill in Shaftesbury, a steep cobbled street, lined with a colourful variety of old cottages. It subsequently reached new heights of fame when it was used in a nostalgic television advert for Hovis bread, with a soundtrack of Dvorak's 'New World Symphony'.

The other town that features in the film is Weymouth, where Bathsheba and Troy are seen at the beach. The first bathing-machine was reputedly used at Weymouth and King George III came to try it in 1789 while a band played 'God Save the King'. Georgian terraces overlook the wide esplanade and sands.

In one of the film's most memorable sequences, Troy displays his skills with a sabre, repeatedly charging Bathsheba and flashing his sword around her. The curious, steep, grassy ravines in which it was filmed are part of Maiden Castle, a pre-Roman fortress whose flat hilltop is surrounded by a maze of little valleys. It was stormed by the Romans in the first century and was subsequently abandoned, though it was the site of a pagan temple in the fourth century.

The cockfight which Troy attends was shot at Horton Tower, a 120-foot tower, built by the lord of the manor for locating deer herds. The house at Weatherbury, which Bathsheba inherits, was represented by Bloxworth House, near Bere Regis. A brick Jacobean house, extensively altered in the eighteenth and nineteenth centuries, it is privately owned but may be visited by arrangement. The barn that was used for the all-night party was the old Tithe Barn at Abbotsbury, which now houses a country museum. Exteriors of Boldwood's house were shot at Waddon House and interiors at Thornhill, neither of which are open to the public.

Far From the Madding Crowd marked a departure from the gritty social realism of Schlesinger's previous films, which had focussed largely on the industrial north of England. *A Kind of Loving* was shot in Stockport and *Billy Liar* in Bradford. *Far From the Madding Crowd* was an unhappy production at times. Terence Stamp, who played Sergeant Troy, recalls in his volume of autobiography, *Double Feature*, that disagreements began at the initial reading of the script where it became apparent that some actors had mastered West Country accents and some had not. Stamp had learned his part in a Dorset accent, but Schlesinger decided that none of the principals should use an accent. Schlesinger later praised the performance of Bates and Finch, who was to work with him again on *Sunday, Bloody Sunday*, but remarked that 'some' of the others were 'uneven'. Schlesinger decamped to America and promptly won an Oscar for *Midnight Cowboy*.

Far From the Madding Crowd clearly went against the grain of sixties' fashion and suffered for it with hostile reviews, though it did reasonable business at the British box-office. Viewed afresh, it compares favourably with other period dramas. There is nothing wrong with the fact that different actors bring different approaches to very different characters. And the scenery and look of the production are stunning.

Roman Polanski's *Tess* (1979), starring Nastassia Kinski, was filmed, not in England, but in France, to which Polanski had fled to escape a prison sentence for having had sex with a 13-year-old in the United States.

THE FRENCH LIEUTENANT'S WOMAN (1981)

Meryl Streep and Jeremy Irons were filmed in the historic and scenic town of Lyme Regis in Dorset, on some of the locations used in John Fowles's novel, including the Undercliff and the Cobb, the old harbour wall on which Streep's character stands looking out to sea awaiting the return of her lover from France. 'They are quite specifically described in the book and it would have been ridiculous not to use them,' says director Karel Reisz.

Lyme was a busy port back in the Middle Ages and the first skirmish between Drake's fleet and the Spanish Armada took place in its bay. It was granted a royal charter by King Edward I, but was strongly Parliamentarian in the Civil War and withstood a two-month Royalist siege in 1644. The Duke of Monmouth disembarked at the Cobb in 1685, leading 80 men in an abortive rebellion against James II. In the eighteenth century, Lyme Regis became one of the first seaside resorts in the south-west of England and was one of the settings for Jane Austen's novel, *Persuasion*, as well as for Fowles's book, which is set in the mid-nineteenth century. Austen's character, Louisa Musgrove, suffers a dramatic fall on the Cobb. It is here that Fowles's Charles Smithson (Irons), a fossil collector, first sees Sarah Woodruff (Streep) being buffeted by stormy winds. He is told by his fiancée, Ernestina (Lynsey Baxter), that Sarah is mad, and he becomes fascinated by her and her history.

Reisz says: 'We were there for about four weeks, I think, and the plan was – when a storm came, wherever we were, we upped sticks and went quickly down to the Cobb. I knew the sequence I wanted and I had it all mapped out. I knew exactly where the cameras were going to go, and, in fact, shot that sequence in about an hour and a half or two hours – we just took advantage of the storm that came.'

He insists no one, actors or stand-ins, was ever in any danger, though locals advise against venturing on to the Cobb in rough weather.

Reisz also shot extensively in the area of the Undercliff – the slopes between Lyme and Axmouth caused by the erosion of the vertical cliff-faces. The strange nature of the place and the many springs sustain a rich variety of flora, including bracken taller than a man. Fowles says in his book that it is the closest England comes to a tropical jungle.

Several locations were used in the town itself, including Broad Street, which runs down to the sea and contains many old buildings including the Royal Lion Hotel, a coaching inn dating back to the beginning of the seventeenth century.

After being dismissed from her position as a lady's companion in Lyme, Sarah is installed in a hotel in Exeter by Charles. He visits her there and they make love. 'That's actually not in Exeter,' says Reisz. 'I forget where that is. It's somewhere on the south coast. Exeter is very urban now. In Exeter itself, we didn't film at all.' His production designer Assheton Gorton recalls it as being Kingswear – a village at the mouth of the River Dart, opposite Dartmouth.

Charles is seen arriving at Exeter Station, which in reality was Kingswear Station, on the picturesque Torbay Steam Railway that runs from Kingswear to Paignton. The line was

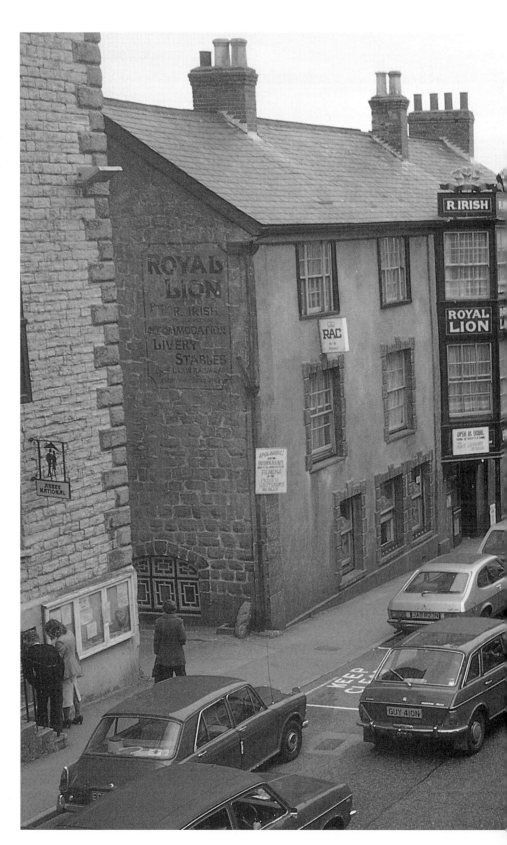

The French Lieutenant's Woman *(UA). Road markings and modern signs disappeared as the film-makers moved Broad Street, Lyme Regis, back through time from 1981 to 1867 (picture courtesy of director Karel Reisz)*

The French
Lieutenant's Woman
*(UA). Picture courtesy of
director Karel Reisz*

taken over by the Dart Valley Light Railway Company in the early seventies and trains still operate on it throughout the summer.

Endicott's Family Hotel, where Sarah stayed, was represented by the Steampacket Inn just up the hill from the station on Fore Street. It was built in the middle of the nineteenth century and would have been quite new at the time of the story. Although film fans can sleep in the room Hugh Grant and Andie MacDowell used in *Four Weddings and a Funeral*, on this occasion a drink in the bar will have to suffice. The Steampacket does not have accommodation and the bedroom scenes were shot elsewhere.

In the film, Sarah disappears and Charles tracks her down years later in the Lake District. Reisz recalls: 'The long shots are in Windermere and then we pan up the hill and we cut to the house, which is a Voysey house somewhere in Surrey.' Charles Voysey was a late-nineteenth/early-twentieth-century architect renowned for long, low houses with specially designed furniture. 'We wanted the house of an avant-garde architect,' says Reisz, 'because she changes into a different world there.' It was one of several private houses used in the film.

Streep and Irons are actually playing Anna and Mike, two actors who, in turn, are playing Sarah and Charles. Anna and Mike's story parallels that of Sarah and Charles and obviously shares some of the same locations. The film also shot on locations in London and at Twickenham Studios.

Meryl Streep, writer Harold Pinter and production designer Assheton Gorton all won Oscar nominations.

THE REMAINS OF THE DAY (1993)

It took four English stately homes to create on film Darlington Hall, the setting for Merchant Ivory's poignant story about duty and responsibility, love and loss among the ruling and serving classes of England before and after the Second World War.

Anthony Hopkins gave one of cinema's great performances as Darlington Hall's butler, Mr Stevens – a man who takes a personal pride in the smooth running of the international conferences and top-level political meetings that take place there as international tensions mount during the thirties. He believes that being a butler is a vocation and hires his aged father as under-butler, sparing him little attention on his deathbed because of important events elsewhere in the house.

Stevens never questions his station in life or his master's apparent Nazi sympathies. Nor does he approve of romantic involvements among senior domestic staff and so he cannot bring himself to admit his own feelings, kept hidden over many years, for Miss Kenton, the housekeeper played by Emma Thompson.

The film was based on a Booker Prize-winning novel by Kazuo Ishiguro, a Japanese writer who grew up in Britain. It was a brilliantly constructed first-person narrative. *Newsweek* called it 'quietly devastating'.

Stevens's true feelings leak out from the incidents and conversations he relates, even though he refuses to admit them openly. Therefore, the film called for, and got, an extremely subtle performance from Hopkins. Producer Ismail Merchant said a twitch on Hopkins's face delivered a mile of emotion. He was nominated for an Oscar as best actor, should have won, and might well have done had he not won the award just two years earlier for *The Silence of the Lambs.*

The nature of the book also left a lot of scope for the film-makers in their vision of Darlington Hall. There is little descriptive detail in the book, though a sense of grandeur permeates it.

Dyrham Park, near Bath, was used for the exterior views of the house. It is a magnificent building situated at the end of a long, winding drive in the cleft of a valley, with unspoiled scenery clear to the horizon. It was comprehensively rebuilt in the late seventeenth century for William Blathwayt, who was no stranger to affairs of state. At a time of war with France and bitter divisions between Protestant and Catholic in England, he served as Secretary of State to King William III. Dyrham Park's east front is one long wall of Bath stone with rows of tall, narrow windows. Dyrham Park is now owned by the National Trust.

Lord Darlington's library and dining-room were shot at Corsham Court, near Chippenham in Wiltshire – a sixteenth-century mansion which was altered in the eighteenth century by Capability Brown and is now home of Lord Methuen. Merchant Ivory also filmed in the famous picture gallery, which measures 72 feet by 24 feet and is considered one of the most impressive of all Georgian domestic interiors – the ceiling is by Brown, the display mirrors by Robert Adam and the furniture by Chippendale. The art collection includes Van Dyck's *Betrayal* and many Italian, Flemish, Dutch and English Old Masters.

Anthony Hopkins and Emma Thompson in The Remains of the Day *(Merchant Ivory / Columbia)*

Several key scenes in Darlington's staircase hall were shot at Powderham Castle, near Exeter, which has been the seat of the Courtenays, Earls of Devon, since the end of the fourteenth century. The staircase hall, which dates from 1754, is notable for its elaborate carving and rococo plasterwork. The film also used the eighteenth-century neoclassical music room; the twin-roomed, Regency period library; the anteroom, which is furnished with Baroque bookcases from the 1740s; and the state bedroom, containing a giltwood four-poster with crimson velvet drapes and an earl's coronet surmounting the tester.

Badminton House, Gloucestershire, was used principally for its servants' quarters – the 'downstairs' area. Finding luxurious state rooms is easy for film-makers compared with finding authentic period servants' quarters. These days they have often been turned into cafés, souvenir shops or caretakers' flats. Unlike the other houses used for *The Remains of the Day*, Badminton House is not routinely open to the public. It remains first and foremost the home of the Duke of Beaufort and his family and, although largely unoccupied, the servants' quarters remain much as they were half a century ago. It was at Badminton House that the seeds of the personal tragedy of this great film were sewn.

The concluding scenes were shot in Weston-super-Mare, on the Bristol Channel, which grew from a little fishing village in the nineteenth century to become one of England's major seaside resorts in Edwardian times. The Highbury Hotel served as Miss Kenton's guest-house; she met Mr Stevens for tea in the Winter Gardens Pavilion and they stroll together on the Grand Pier as night falls and they prepare to say goodbye.

SCANDAL (1989)

Britain was rocked in the early sixties by revelations that the Secretary of State for War, John Profumo, had been sharing the attentions of showgirl Christine Keeler with the Soviet naval attaché. It was a story that had everything – class, sex and power.

The film-makers wanted to shoot at Cliveden, Lord Astor's former estate, where Profumo (Ian McKellen) first meets the naked Keeler (Joanne Whalley-Kilmer). Cliveden estate is now owned by the National Trust and the house operates as a luxury hotel. Other films, including *Help!* and *Chaplin*, have shot there, but permission was refused on this occasion. According to sources involved in the film, the hotel was ready to allow filming – subject to the approval of the Astor family – but some family members did object.

Instead, director Michael Caton-Jones used Wilton House, the Earl of Pembroke's Elizabethan mansion near Salisbury in Wiltshire. It is famous for its splendid state rooms, designed by Inigo Jones, and its art treasures, which include Van Dyck, Rembrandt, Rubens and an eighteenth-century statue of Shakespeare who is reputed to have acted in *As You Like It* at Wilton in 1603. Wilton House was used extensively, though Caton-Jones also shot at Longleat House. Both houses are open to the public.

The film centres on Keeler's friend, Stephen Ward (John Hurt), who introduces her to high society. Caton-Jones used Bathurst Mews in Paddington, London, for Ward's home – which was really in Wimpole Mews. It is at Ward's flat that Keeler's West Indian boyfriend, Johnnie Edgecombe (Roland Gift), starts shooting when she refuses to let him in. London's County Hall and Nottingham's Shire Hall were used for the Old Bailey scenes. The latter is now a law museum.

In the wake of the scandal, Profumo resigned, Ward committed suicide at the end of his trial for living off the earnings of prostitution and the Conservative Government was voted out of office, ending more than a decade of Tory rule.

Joanne Whalley-Kilmer and Bridget Fonda in Scandal *(Palace/British Screen/Miramax)*

SLEUTH (1972)

Laurence Olivier and Michael Caine both won Oscar nominations for this compelling thriller, which might have been sub-titled *Two Men and a House*, for there are really only two characters in the film and the action takes place in the otherwise empty country house belonging to one of them.

Olivier plays Andrew Wyke, a detective novelist, while Caine is Milo Tindle, who owns a chain of hair salons and is having an affair with Wyke's wife, Marguerite. The wife never appears in the film. Her portrait was modelled on Joanne Woodward and Marguerite appears in the credits as being played by Margo Channing – the name of the Bette Davis character in another Joseph L. Mankiewicz film, *All About Eve*.

Wyke invites Tindle to his home, where he explains a devious scheme that will benefit them both. He proposes that Tindle should break into the house, dressed as a clown, and steal his wife's jewels. Tindle can then sell them while Wyke claims the insurance money. At least that is the plot as outlined by Wyke, but there are many unexpected twists before the final credits.

Athelhampton House in Dorset was used for this battle of wits, along with interior sets at Pinewood Studios in Buckinghamshire. Michael Caine is seen arriving at the house

*Michael Caine arrives
at Athelhampton House,
Dorset, in* Sleuth
*(Palomar).
Picture courtesy of
Patrick Cooke*

Sabu in The Thief of
Bagdad *(London)*

at the beginning of the film in a red MG sportscar, which remains at Athelhampton. The house itself features in scenes where Caine breaks in and where he tries to break out, and finally at the film's conclusion with the arrival of the police. Rooms modelled on Athelhampton were constructed at Pinewood and a maze was specially erected in Athelhampton's great court as if to symbolise the twists and dead-ends within Anthony Shaffer's script.

One of the finest fifteenth-century stately homes in the south of England, Athelhampton is privately owned but it is open to the public from March to October. Its location sounds as if it must have been dreamt up by film scenarists, situated as it is just outside Puddletown, on the Piddle. A strangely irregular stone building, with tall narrow windows, the house itself looks like the product of film production designers. It was built in 1485 for Sir William Martyn, a Lord Mayor of London, on the site of the palace of Athelstan, the tenth-century king of West Saxons and Mercians, and subsequently of all England. The Martyn family estates were divided between four daughters at the end of the sixteenth century and thereafter Athelhampton entered a period of decline. It was restored in the nineteenth century and Inigo Thomas was employed to create a new garden and replace the cowsheds with graceful Renaissance 'outdoor rooms'.

Athelhampton's 20 acres include eight walled gardens, fountains, pavilions and topiary pyramids. The gardens are regarded as being among the finest of their type. The east wing of the house was badly damaged by fire in 1992, but most of the contents were saved, and it is now open again. Athelhampton was also used for the 1976 *Doctor Who* adventure *The Seeds of Doom*, now out on video, in which Earth is threatened by an alien species of plants called Krynoid.

THE THIEF OF BAGDAD (1940)

This spectacular film adaptation of *The Arabian Nights* began at Denham Studios, near London, planned to film in Bagdad itself, and ended up in Hollywood, changing directors several times *en route*. Michael Powell is one of three directors whose names appear on the credits, though that list is certainly not exhaustive.

Somewhere near the beginning of this process, Powell went off to Cornwall with Sabu, who plays the street boy, Abu, and Rex Ingram as the genie to shoot the scene in which the genie comes out of the bottle. They went to Sennen Cove, one mile north of Land's End, a location that had been selected by one of the assistant directors. 'Sennen Cove is a delightful little spot, a smugglers' haunt,' wrote Powell in his book *A Life in Movies*. Unfortunately, 'it was unsuitable in every way . . . What we needed for the encounter between Sabu and the genie was a landscape and seascape like the Persian Gulf . . . vast quantities of sand and sea, with plenty of room for a forty-foot-high genie to move around in; and that was what we finally settled for on the coast of Pembrokeshire, South Wales. What I found at Sennen Cove was a picturesque natural landing between low cliffs, where the tide came right up to the steps and where there was only a beach of golden sand when the tide receded.'

Powell goes on to note that Sennen Cove did, however, make it into the final film, crediting Osmond Borradaile's photography.

The outbreak of war scuppered hopes to shoot in Bagdad itself and caused the transfer of the film to Hollywood so Denham Studios would be free for propaganda films. But all the various problems do not seem to have affected the quality of the finished product. It won Oscars for cinematography, art direction and special effects, and is described by *The Virgin Film Guide* as 'perhaps the most splendid fantasy film ever made'.

THE TITFIELD THUNDERBOLT (1953)

The Titfield Thunderbolt was a celebration of the great days when steam railways linked little villages across the length and breadth of the British countryside – and the film is all that remains now of the Limpley Stoke-Hallatrow line, near Bath. The railway is under threat in the film but, led by the squire (John Gregson) and the vicar (George Relph), the villagers of Titfield take it over and run the train themselves.

As Titfield Station, director Charles Crichton used Monkton Combe Station, which has now disappeared beneath the playing fields of Monkton Combe School – though visitors to the village can still walk down Brassknocker Hill as the commuters did in the film on their way to catch the train to Mallingford. Crichton shot at various points along the line, opening the film with a shot of the local Titfield train chugging backwards beneath the Midford Viaduct while an express whizzes overhead. He used a variation on the same theme when he shot the Titfield train going under a bridge at Combe Hay, while

The Titfield
Thunderbolt *(Ealing)*

the rival bus goes over it. The battle between the train and Sid James's steamroller was shot at Radstock.

One station that features in the film does survive, for Crichton used Bristol Temple Meads as Mallingford.

The whole enterprise is financed by a wealthy alcoholic (Stanley Holloway), who is attracted by the idea that bars on trains do not need to observe the normal opening hours. His house was not in Monkton Combe, but in the nearby village of Freshford.

Although most of the location filming was done on or near the Limpley Stoke line, Crichton did shoot some location sequences elsewhere. When the bus-owners sabotage the train, the villagers replace it with a nineteenth-century engine, the *Titfield Thunderbolt*, from the local museum. The museum was, in fact, the Imperial Institute in Exhibition Road, London, on a site now occupied by Imperial College. Dozens of extras manhandled a replica of the Liverpool and Manchester *0-4-0 Lion* down the steps one night in August 1952 to the amazement of people coming out of a concert at the nearby Royal Albert Hall.

The Titfield Thunderbolt was the first Ealing comedy in colour, reworking the familiar theme of the triumph of community spirit over bureaucracy. Many railway enthusiasts would cite it as their favourite film, though it lacks the bite of Ealing's best comedies.

TOM JONES (1963)

The history of Nettlecombe Court, one of the principal locations for *Tom Jones*, is about as colourful as the plot of Henry Fielding's eighteenth-century comic novel and Tony Richardson's Oscar-winning film, starring a young Albert Finney as the lusty hero.

In his memoirs, *Long Distance Runner*, Richardson recalls an owner who thought he was a bird, lived in a tree and descended once a day to be fed crumbs off a silver platter by his butler. At the time of the film, Nettlecombe was being used as a girls' school, but has subsequently become a centre once again for people obsessed with birds. It was taken over in the late sixties by the Field Studies Council, which runs short residential courses on bird-life and other environmental subjects there.

Nettlecombe Court is a part-Elizabethan mansion, situated in Somerset in a secluded valley between the Brendon Hills and Bristol Channel. The great hall and one of the more ornate bedrooms (No. 23) were used in the film. And if birds are a recurring theme in the history of Nettlecombe, then bars provide the theme for the courtyard. It now serves as the centre's beer garden, but appeared in the film as Newgate Jail.

Cranborne Manor House in Dorset provided another location and Richardson enthuses in his memoirs about the gardens, describing them as 'a labyrinth of garden succeeding garden, glimmering with white and yellow roses'. The owners discourage publicity, though the gardens do regularly open to the public from March to September.

Richardson also filmed on Exmoor, probably the most beautiful and varied moorland in England, and in the old port town of Bridgwater in Somerset. Castle Street, which features in the film, dates back to the early eighteenth century.

Tom Jones was a great success at the box-office, costing $1 million and taking $17 million in North America alone. It was nominated for ten Oscars, including no less than

*Max Rennie, Helen
Pearce and Paul Scofield
on the Scilly Isles for*
When the Whales
Came *(Golden Swan/
Central Television/
American Continental)*

three nominations in the category of best supporting actress, with Diane Cilento, Edith Evans and Joyce Redman all short-listed. Redman shared the famous scene with Finney in which they stare into each other's eyes and tear into a banquet, with ever-increasing passion. The film ended up with Oscars for best picture, director (Richardson), adapted screenplay (John Osborne) and music (John Addison).

WHEN THE WHALES CAME (1989)

Bryher, the smallest of the inhabited Scilly Isles, provided the setting and locations for the film version of Michael Morpurgo's story about the life of two children, Daniel (Max Rennie) and Gracie (Helen Pearce), in the early part of this century, and of their relationship with the mysterious old man called the Birdman (Paul Scofield). He turns out to have been the last person to leave the neighbouring island of Samson, uninhabited since the well ran dry after the locals killed a herd of narwhals. Seventy years later, a narwhal is stranded on one of Bryher's beaches and again the locals want to kill it.

Popplestones was the beach in question, though other beaches were used for other scenes. The children play on Rushy Bay beach and the net-making and boat scenes were shot at Great Par. Nothing remains of the Birdman's house, which was built on top of Samson Hill, but the children's houses were traditional islanders' cottages near Great Par.

The film-makers also shot on the island of Samson. It is possible to visit the island and its deserted cottages. There are regular boat trips from Bryher during the summer. The schoolroom scene was shot in the Methodist Chapel on the island of St Martin's.

Marian Bennett, one of Bryher's 80 residents, acted as local co-ordinator for the film. She believes that it was a very positive experience for the island. 'Everybody on the island was fully consulted at every point and everybody who wanted to be employed was employed,' she says. 'People enjoyed the company of the crew.' It has also helped tourism. 'A lot of the people who come here have seen the film. The book on which it's based is on a lot of school curricula, so children in particular, I think, are very interested in visiting and will often then bring their families with them.'

The island has subsequently been used for BBC Television's *Chronicles of Narnia*.

CHAPTER FOUR
Brando, Bond and Public School Revolution
CENTRAL ENGLAND

THE GO-BETWEEN (1971)

'The past is a foreign country: they do things differently there,' wrote L. P. Hartley at the beginning of his novel, translated to the screen by director Joseph Losey and writer Harold Pinter.

The Go-Between is set at the turn of the century and change is in the air. The old order is under threat, a threat crystallised in the affair between Marian Maudsley (Julie Christie), a daughter of the manor, and Ted Burgess (Alan Bates), a local farmer. The original story was recounted by the young boy, Leo, played in the film by Dominic Guard, who is enlisted as their go-between. He is invited to spend the summer at Brandham Hall by his schoolfriend, Marcus (Richard Gibson, who became Herr Flick in *'Allo, 'Allo*), though it is clear that Leo is not quite of the same class as his friend. Of course, it all ends tragically. Pinter had been reluctant to write the script at first, saying he found the book so powerful that it had him in tears.

The film was shot largely on location at Melton Constable Hall, a seventeenth-century country house in Norfolk. It was owned by a local farmer and, as it was unoccupied at the time of filming, an air of decay had already set in. Losey paid little for the use of the estate but had to redecorate the house before filming commenced. He also had the lawns sprayed with green paint because they had been neglected for so long that when they were cut the grass was yellow. Cinematographer Gerry Fisher reckoned the paint job was 'a bit dodgy, what with people wandering around in crinolines'.

As if it somehow embodied the collapse of the old order, Melton Constable stood empty for many years after filming and was described by conservationists as 'the finest empty country house in England'. The Save Britain's Heritage group complained that it was scandalous that it had been neglected for so long. It was subsequently used as an art and cultural centre and was finally sub-divided into separate properties. It is not normally open to the public.

The public can, however, see the green on which Ted's cricket team play a team of gentlemen led by Marian's fiancé, Viscount Trimingham (Edward Fox), in one of the key scenes of the film. Ted proves an outstanding player but the match is settled when Leo makes a decisive catch for the gentlemen. The game was played on the green at Thornage, a little village between Melton Constable and Holt. The film-makers also shot on Norfolk Broads and in Norwich, including Tombland, a part of the city which was used as a market place back in Saxon times.

The famous opening words – 'The past is a foreign country: they do things differently there' – are spoken by Michael Redgrave in the film, playing the small role of the grown-up Leo. Losey, an American who settled in Britain at the time of Hollywood's Communist witch-hunts, so enjoyed Norfolk that he continued to rent the same cottage for several years.

The Go-Between won the Palme d'Or at the Cannes Film Festival, in preference to Visconti's *Death in Venice*, and the eminent American critic Judith Crist called it 'a masterpiece of incredible delicacy, visual elegance and extraordinary intelligence'.

IF . . . (1968)

Many are the schoolboys who have dreamed of killing a teacher or prefect, but Lindsay Anderson got the chance to go back to his old public school and machine-gun the lot of them. Malcolm McDowell plays the senior pupil who leads a violent revolt on speech day in a film that is a disturbing mix of realism, surrealism and anarchism.

When it came to finding a location, Anderson approached the headmaster at Cheltenham College, an exclusive boarding-school in Gloucestershire, which Anderson had himself attended as a pupil. It is housed in handsome Victorian buildings on extensive grounds on the edge of town. The headmaster asked if the film would be anything like *Tom Brown's Schooldays* and Anderson assured him that the two stories shared 'certain features'. He did not point out that the feature they most obviously shared was that of ritual flogging or that the main difference is that Tom Brown does not actually kill anyone. There was a furore when the film appeared and for years afterwards Cheltenham went out of its way to stress that it was not at all like the film. There is no corporal punishment now, of course, and it even admits girls.

If . . . would have been a sweet revenge for unhappy schooldays, except Anderson himself insisted that he remembered his schooldays with affection. David Sherwin and John Howlett wrote the script. Anderson wrote in *The Movie* magazine: 'I responded to the story, then entitled *Crusaders*, because I approved of its romantic and rebellious spirit, and because there was so much of my own experience that could relate directly to the subject; and not just my experience of school but my experience of society in the years that had followed.' Anderson had first seen the script in 1966 but the film had the good fortune of appearing two years later when international student unrest, particularly in America and France, was at its height. So, although *If . . .* is, perhaps, the definitive portrait of the English public school, its themes of oppression and revolution appealed to a much wider audience.

JANE EYRE (1995)

Charlotte Brontë's story of Jane Eyre and Edward Rochester is brought to life at Haddon Hall, near Matlock in Derbyshire, where the relationship between the Italian director Franco Zeffirelli and his American star, William Hurt, proved as tempestuous as that in Brontë's novel. 'Difficult?' says Zeffirelli. 'He's a madman . . . Stars think they're the only thing that matters and we'd better leave them their illusion as long as they give a good performance . . . I think that despite his efforts to destroy himself, William Hurt is fantastic.'

The film has an international cast with Hurt as Rochester, France's Charlotte Gainsbourg as Jane Eyre, New Zealand's Anna Paquin, Australia's Elle Macpherson and England's Joan Plowright.

*Malcolm McDowell in
If... (Memorial)*

Zeffirelli had seen old prints of Haddon Hall, the imposing, castellated manor house of the Duke of Rutland, but was surprised to find how well preserved it was. 'It's a magnificent place – extraordinary,' he says. 'It's miraculous how this house has been kept for centuries intact. They haven't done any alterations.'

It dates back to the eleventh century and, although most of it is of later origin, there has been little change over the last 300 years or so. Haddon Hall seems to have sprung from the pages of a period romance, with its greystone walls, battlements and turrets. *The New Shell Guide to England* claims that 'it is possibly the most authentic and complete example of a medieval and manorial house to be seen in the country.' House and gardens are both open to the public, who can wander from the banqueting hall, with its fifteenth-century tapestry and antlers which have been on the wall since Charles II was king, to the enormous kitchens, with old water-storage troughs.

Zeffirelli considered the terraced gardens magnificent. He was at Haddon Hall for three weeks and amended his shooting script to maximise use of the location. 'The scenery is not a backdrop behind your story – you better make your story be part of the overall vision, otherwise you might as well have front projection in the studio like they did in Hollywood in the thirties.'

In the novel, Rochester's house, Thornfield Hall, burns down and Zeffirelli even had a fire on location at Haddon Hall – though most of that sequence was filmed in Ealing Studios in London.

Other locations included Brimham Rocks, near Pateley Bridge in north Yorkshire. Dozens of large, millstone grit rocks have been sculpted by ice, frost and storm over many centuries into weird shapes reflected in names like Dancing Bear and Druid's Skull. They lie scattered across a site of more than 50 acres in the care of the National Trust and make a popular picnic spot and adventure playground for families. It is here that Rochester and Jane Eyre meet.

LADY CAROLINE LAMB (1972)

Robert Bolt, writer turned film director, was able to shoot this star-studded historical drama at Chatsworth House in Derbyshire, which has historical connections with Lady Caroline Lamb, and where Elizabeth I kept Mary Queen of Scots prisoner 250 years earlier. Lady Caroline Lamb moved in the highest echelons of society. Bolt cast his wife, Sarah Miles, in the title role and his supporting cast included figures from the highest echelons of British acting talent – Ralph Richardson, John Mills and Laurence Olivier as the Duke of Wellington.

Caroline marries William Lamb (Jon Finch), but their incompatibility is soon obvious and she begins an obsessive and highly demonstrative affair with the poet, Lord Byron (Richard Chamberlain), threatening to make all three seem ridiculous. She dresses as a topless black servant to be near him and slashes her wrists when he rejects her.

Much of the filming was done in Italy, but the production team spent two weeks in Derbyshire, at Chatsworth – the grand classical mansion of the Duke of Devonshire. Lady Caroline Lamb was a niece of the fifth Duke and her portrait still hangs at Chatsworth. The house is set in extensive grounds, with fountains and ornamental gardens. The park runs to about 11,000 acres. In her book, *Serves Me Right*, Sarah Miles described it as 'a backdrop to end all backdrops'. The house, which is open to the public, contains paintings by Van Dyck and Rembrandt and ceiling artworks by Laguerre and Verrio, though the *Blue Guide to England* dismisses them as 'pompous'.

Miles did her own riding for the film and was badly hurt in a fall from her horse in front of Chatsworth. She had to wear a brace for eight weeks. However, despite the opulence of the location and Miles's efforts in the main role, critics complained about the film's failings both as drama and as history.

LADY JANE (1985)

Moving from theatre to cinema, director Trevor Nunn grasped the chance to use a whole series of fine historical locations, installing the tragic short-lived monarch, Lady Jane Grey (Helena Bonham Carter), and her husband-of-convenience, Guildford Dudley (Cary Elwes), in Compton Wyngates in Warwickshire, while others plot the future of the country.

Compton Wyngates is a Tudor house of stone, wood and pink brick, with battlements and picturesque long, narrow windows. It is located in a hollow in the hills between Banbury and Stratford-upon-Avon and is rated by *The New Shell Guide to England* as 'one of the most visually satisfying houses' in the country. It has been in the ownership of the Marquess of Northampton's family since it was built in the late fifteenth century and is occasionally open to the public.

Dover Castle, which featured in Franco Zeffirelli's *Hamlet* as Elsinore, was used as the Tower of London, where Jane is executed. Other locations included Leeds Castle and the magnificent Hever Castle in Kent (see the entries for *Kind Hearts and Coronets* and *Anne of the Thousand Days*); Broughton Castle, near Banbury, Oxfordshire (see *The Madness of King George*); Haddon Hall, near Bakewell, Derbyshire (see *Jane Eyre*); and the grounds of nearby Chatsworth House – a very grand seventeenth-century house whose gardens include elaborate waterworks and are surrounded by a great park (see *Lady Caroline Lamb*).

Chastleton House, near Chipping Norton in Oxfordshire, was used as Princess Mary's house. The present Jacobean building, with five gables and two towers, was built by a Cotswold wool merchant, Walter Jones, and includes a secret room where Arthur Jones, a supporter of Charles I, hid after the Battle of Worcester.

Another secret hiding place in the National Trust's ornate timber-framed Little Moreton Hall, near Congleton in Cheshire, was used by the film-makers – or, more specifically, by moonlighting firemen who were working on *Lady Jane*. Their boss, who had reportedly banned freelance work on the film, paid a surprise visit. 'We hurriedly hid the "moonlighting" firemen – still carrying their cups of tea – in a secret room in the house and greeted the fire chief in complete innocence,' says production manager Malcolm Christopher. 'I was unable to accompany him on his inspection of the house, which was carried out by one of its permanent staff. In his enthusiasm to show off the house to its fullest extent, this member of staff revealed the secret room complete with its guilty occupants.' It is thought Little Moreton's secret room behind the chimney-breast may have been a ruse, because there is a second, less obvious room at the end of an underground passage beneath the moat.

Little Moreton Hall, which was used as a brothel in the film, is an extraordinary building, like something out of an *Alice in Wonderland* cartoon. It is built in sections reminiscent of Roses sweets' boxes – narrower at the bottom than at the top. The walls are divided into squares of brown and white stripes and patterns, giving the impression of some giant chocolate cake. *The New Shell Guide* says it is unquestionably one of the finest specimens of black-and-white architecture in England.

All these properties are open to the public at least occasionally.

MAURICE (1987)

Merchant Ivory followed in novelist E. M. Forster's footsteps to Cambridge University, where he studied and which he used as one of the principal settings of *Maurice* – the only novel in which he confronted his homosexuality. It was written in 1913, but was published only after his death more than half a century later, and it was widely regarded as one of his weaker books.

The rights to *Maurice* lay with the fellows of King's College, Cambridge, who had serious reservations about a film version. Not only did Merchant Ivory manage to talk them into allowing a film, but also persuaded them to allow filming at the college itself, where Maurice's (James Wilby) sexuality is awakened by another student, Clive Durham (Hugh Grant). Merchant Ivory recruited staff and students at the college to play staff and students in the early part of the century.

King's College is one of Cambridge's most famous colleges and one of the most prominent features of the city skyline. It was founded by Henry VI in 1441 and includes the poet, Rupert Brooke, and the economist, Maynard Keynes, among its former students. The chapel, which took more than 50 years to build, is considered one of the finest Gothic buildings in Europe. It has no less than 25 stained-glass windows and a high fan-vault ceiling. The chapel and college grounds are normally open to the public, and the world-famous choir, which is heard in the film, sings Evensong on most days. The Backs – the open land behind the colleges in King's Parade – offers a pleasant walk and a different, more distant perspective.

Maurice and Clive continue their friendship at the Durham family seat, Pendersleigh, for which director James Ivory and producer Ismail Merchant used the home of an acquaintance, just as they had done for *A Room with a View*. On this occasion they used Wilbury Park in Wiltshire, home of the actress Maria St Just and one of England's most notable neoclassical Palladian houses.

MEMPHIS BELLE (1990)

Forty-six years after the Second World War ended the skies over the south of England were once again dotted with B-17 bombers, Mustang fighters and German Messerschmitt ME-109s as producers David Puttnam and Catherine Wyler and director Michael Caton-Jones recreated the final flight of the famous B-17 called the *Memphis Belle* – the plane that was to become a symbol of the Allied war effort.

The B-17 Flying Fortress was a major advance on previous bombers. It could carry twice as many bombs and go twice the distance before refuelling. Nevertheless, the 75-foot-long plane was a big, slow-moving target for anti-aircraft guns and fighter planes. Most of the airmen were scarcely out of their teens and one in three died in action. The *Memphis Belle* flew 24 successful missions over enemy territory and if it completed one more, the crew would return to the safety of the United States as heroes and as part of a public relations drive to boost morale and increase the sale of war bonds.

Hollywood director William Wyler shot historic action footage while flying five missions in the original *Memphis Belle*. Four decades later, during a brief spell as head of Columbia, David Puttnam was watching a clip of Wyler's documentary with Wyler's daughter, Catherine Wyler, Columbia's senior vice-president of production, when they hit on the notion of a feature-film account of the final flight.

Most of the surviving B-17s were in the United States and the original intention was to shoot there. Hundreds of airfields were considered, but none were deemed suitable. 'You have to keep in mind that we needed not only land space but enormous traffic-free air space as well for the shooting of the film,' said Puttnam. It was at this point that they switched their attention to England.

They were keen to use Duxford, Cambridgeshire; home of the Imperial War Museum's collection of aircraft, which included the only serviceable B-17 in England. It was less than ten miles from Bassingbourn, where the original *Memphis Belle* was based during the war. Two B-17s were available from France and if two more could make the flight from America, the film would be viable. It took the pilots six days to make the journey, via Nova Scotia, Greenland, Iceland and Scotland. The services were secured of three of the last four operational German Messerschmitt ME-109s, out of the 33,000 that were built. The film-makers also had the use of eight Mustangs. Nicknamed 'little friends' by the B-17 crews, they escorted the bombers until their limited fuel supplies ran low.

There were three weeks of aerial photography at Duxford, involving as many as 17 planes, including the camera plane, at any one time. Aircraft enthusiasts came from all over Britain to photograph the meticulously choreographed overhead battles.

Duxford has 130 aircraft, the biggest collection of historic planes in Europe, from flimsy First World War biplanes to Gulf War jets. The public has the chance to see the Spitfire, Lancaster, U-2 spy-plane and, of course, the B-17. Duxford is open daily and there are regular displays. The film-makers brought the original crew over to England to meet the actors, including Matthew Modine and Eric Stoltz, and they visited the museum at Bassingbourn which is dedicated to the American airmen who were stationed there.

While aerial photography was shot at Duxford, the art department were turning a huge empty airbase at Binbrook, Lincolnshire, into a busy 1943 bomber station. Binbrook had ceased operational flying in 1988 and was subsequently classified as a 'relief landing-ground'. After three weeks of location shooting at Binbrook, production moved to Pinewood Studios, where the interiors of the planes had been reconstructed. Caton-Jones had the opportunity to fly in one of the B-17s and described the experience as terrifying. The plane was freezing cold and constantly vibrating. 'You can't imagine how frightening it must have been for the boys who actually flew these raids,' he told *Empire* magazine. 'Half of the danger was encountered long before they ever got near Germany. They'd take off loaded with fuel and bombs and then have to circle over Norfolk for ages waiting to form up, at 25,000 feet with the windows open. They had no radar and once they got into the cloud they couldn't tell which way was up. So it was quite common for them to crash before actually setting off.'

One of the film-makers' B-17s crashed during what seemed like a very straightforward sequence. 'I was coming back from lunch with Harry Connick Jr (one of the cast) across the airfield and there was this plane going down the runway at about 150 miles per hour and it began to veer off and spin out of control,' said Caton-Jones. 'It ended up in a cornfield, blazing. I just got this terrible feeling that somebody was going to die.' But on this occasion the most serious injury was broken limbs.

Memphis Belle appeared to mixed reviews. It was an old-fashioned film from a time when causes were just and heroes were ordinary guys in extraordinary situations. Perhaps the world had become more cynical since then.

THE NIGHTCOMERS (1972)

It was while shooting this film with Michael Winner and Stephanie Beacham, near Cambridge, that Marlon Brando, whose career had been going through a difficult phase, heard he had won his battle for the lead role in *The Godfather*. While *The Godfather* was to mark a new beginning for Brando, *The Nightcomers* was devised to lay some distinguished literary ghosts from the past.

It was inspired by Henry James's nineteenth-century novella, *The Turn of the Screw*, in which a governess on an isolated English estate discovers that her two young charges are under the evil influence of the ghosts of a previous governess, Miss Jessel, and the estate steward, Peter Quint. *The Nightcomers* is a sort of prequel with Quint (Brando) and Miss Jessel (Beacham) involved in an intense sado-masochistic relationship.

They had several steamy scenes together and Brando would break the tension with practical jokes. During rehearsal for a bondage scene he had to tie Beacham up, which he did and then went off for lunch. But he did such a good job that no one could get the knots out until Brando himself came back.

It seems appropriate that *The Nightcomers* should have been filmed at Sawston Hall, which reputedly has several ghosts of its own, including that of Queen Mary Tudor. Sawston Hall is mentioned as early as 1086 in *The Domesday Book* – William the Conqueror's survey of his kingdom – and it played an important role in the Catholic-Protestant conflicts of the sixteenth century. Sir John Huddleston sheltered Queen Mary at Sawston in 1553 when she was being pursued by anti-Catholic conspirators. He smuggled her out in the disguise of a dairymaid and when Mary was told that her enemies had set fire to the house, she promised to build a better one, which she duly did using stones from Cambridge Castle. It is a solid and imposing, slightly sinister, brownstone building, standing in extensive walled grounds which include rare trees and medieval fishponds.

During Elizabeth's reign, when harbouring a priest could lead to torture and death, several hiding holes were constructed in the house. Sawston was temporarily the home of at least two Catholic martyrs, John Rigby, who was Sawston's steward, and Nicholas Owen, who built one of the hiding places.

During the Second World War, Sawston was taken over by the RAF and the great hall used as an operations room. Sawston is now a language school.

Winner recalls: 'Marlon Brando stayed there a couple of nights until he found the owner kept waking him up, telling him there were calls from America, which he didn't want to receive anyway.' In his autobiography, *Brando – Songs My Mother Taught Me*, Brando says he enjoyed the film and noted Winner's arch sense of humour and characteristic British sense of class. He says Winner had one room laid out with expensive china and linen which was reserved for use by themselves and a few others. Brando said he wanted to eat with the cast and crew. With a fine ear for vocal mannerisms, Brando recalls Winner saying: 'Marlon, I am sorry to say this, but the crew do not wish you to eat with them. They are much happier in the next-door canteen eating on their own and not worrying about the overpowering presence of their employers and a major star.'

Brando went into the canteen but no one would sit beside him, and when he later managed to have lunch with actress Thora Hird, he could not make out a word she said because of her strong northern accent.

OCTOPUSSY (1983)

The James Bond films have used many memorable locations, though most of them have been abroad. The most spectacular one in *Octopussy* – one of the best of Roger Moore's Bond films – was certainly the title character's white marble palace that seems to rise straight out of the blue waters of Pichola Lake in India. It was built by the Maharana of Udaipur in the eighteenth century and is now the luxury Lake Palace Hotel.

The climax of the film was also set overseas, with Bond in a race against time to stop an atomic explosion in Germany, but it was filmed in England. Octopussy (Maud Adams) has been using a circus troupe as a front for smuggling imperial Russian jewels to the west. Bond boards her circus train and discovers that she has been set up by her fellow villain, General Orlov (Steven Berkoff), who has planted a bomb timed to explode after the circus arrives for a show at the US Air Force base at Feldstadt in West Germany. Bond is forced to disguise himself as a clown to infiltrate the circus troupe. RAF Upper Heyford in Oxfordshire stood in for the American base and the train sequence was done at the Nene Valley Railway in Cambridgeshire.

Phil Kohler, regular production manager on the Bond films, cites *Octopussy* as the most interesting for locations in Britain. 'The whole of the Nene Valley Railway was turned into the east/west border of Germany,' he says. 'That was a big sequence – with the station, and the train hitting the Mercedes. That was all done at Nene Valley at Wansford.'

The line is maintained by a preservation society, with steam trains running between Wansford and Peterborough.

The film's opening sequence, in which Bond flies a 12-foot AcroStar plane, with folding wings, was shot partly in England. The plane comes out of the back of a horse-box. 'That was shot near Oxford,' says Kohler. 'All the aerial stuff was done over Florida. It was filmed in three places: in America, in Oxfordshire and the other part of it was shot at the studios [Pinewood, near London]. And then we had to match it all.'

Bond is under attack from a heat-seeking missile; he flies into the enemy base, turns his plane and flies out, leaving the missile behind. Then he runs out of gas and lands at a filling station. And that is all before the opening titles. There is a long way to go before the adventures in Udaipur and Nene Valley.

REVOLUTION (1985)

Goldcrest, the British film company that scored a major success with *Gandhi*, took an enormous gamble with this film, investing £16 million in it and bringing Al Pacino and Donald Sutherland to England for an epic historical drama set in America.

As New York, director Hugh Hudson used the Norfolk port of King's Lynn, which has many seventeenth- and eighteenth-century buildings and numerous physical signs of its links with the Netherlands. The waterfront area around the seventeenth-century Custom House was used as New York harbour, where trapper Tom Dobb (Pacino) arrives

Marlon Brando and
Stephanie Beacham in
The Nightcomers
(Scimitar/
Kastner-Kanter-Ladd)

at the beginning of the film and has his boat requisitioned for the campaign against the British. King's Staithe Square was also used. Hudson told *Films and Filming* magazine: 'Williamsberg and the other preserved towns in America are just too immaculate. Even the bricks are scrubbed.'

The main battle scene was shot on the Devon coast south-east of Plymouth, the British camp was on Dartmoor, near Burrator Reservoir, and the American Valley Forge camp was on Army land at Thetford in Norfolk. For war-ravaged Philadelphia, the film-makers used the Cambridgeshire town of Ely, at the southern edge of the Fens, and Melton Constable Hall, the seventeenth-century Norfolk country house that had been used in *The Go-Between*.

John Mollo, *Revolution*'s costume designer and historical consultant, recalls: 'It was absolutely derelict when we were there . . . We needed it to look like the state buildings in Philadelphia had been stripped out . . . It looked like they had taken away the wood panelling and everything else, so we made a point of it.'

It may have been a revolution that made the United States the great nation it is today, but for Goldcrest it was a revolution that failed. The film opened in America to terrible reviews, confirming the worst fears of many in the British film industry who had seen the project seemingly spiral out of control. *Time* said it was a chaotic mess, the *LA Daily News* said it was easily one of the worst films of the year and television critic Robert Osborne said it was one of the worst films ever. Goldcrest lost £10 million and was left virtually bankrupt.

SATURDAY NIGHT AND SUNDAY MORNING (1960)

When turning Alan Sillitoe's powerful novel of working-class life into a film, director Karel Reisz used the neighbourhood in Nottingham where the author had grown up and the factory where Sillitoe himself had worked.

The novel was published in 1958 and its success established Sillitoe as one of English literature's foremost Angry Young Men, alongside John Osborne, whose play, *Look Back in Anger*, appeared the previous year. Sillitoe wrote the screenplay of *Saturday Night and Sunday Morning* himself and collaborated with Reisz on a documentary about Nottinghamshire miners so Reisz could get a feel for the place before beginning work on the feature film.

In his first major role, Albert Finney was cast as Arthur Seaton, possibly cinema's greatest working-class anti-hero – a man able to articulate his anger at the social injustices in his life and his dependency on a boring, dead-end job in a simple, seven-word philosophy – 'Don't let the bastards grind you down.'

They filmed in the Raleigh bicycle factory where Sillitoe himself had resisted any attempt to be ground down. Sillitoe later said: 'It gave me a wonderful emotional shock to see Albert Finney standing at exactly the same place at the bench in the Raleigh factory where I had worked.'

Reisz thought the factory had closed years ago, but it is still there in the Nottingham suburb of Radford, producing more bikes than ever – up to 6,000 a day – with a much smaller workforce. The number of employees fell from about 8,000 to under 2,000

Shadowlands
(Spelling/Price/Savoy)

between the sixties and nineties. The factory is not normally open to the public. 'The street scenes were all done in Radford,' says Reisz, 'actually, in the street where Alan Sillitoe's mother still lived at the time . . . stone terrace houses, with those backs that are surrounded by stone walls.' The area has now been extensively redeveloped.

SHADOWLANDS (1993)

As Richard Attenborough's film builds to its emotional climax, the writer, C. S. Lewis, is inspired by a painting he has had since childhood to take his dying wife, Joy Gresham, in search of its idyllic setting – the Golden Valley. But when the film-makers visited the valley they got something of a shock. 'The real Golden Valley is in Herefordshire on the border with Wales and it's pretty scrubby-looking,' says location manager Nick Daubeny. The film, which is set in the fifties, demanded 'unspoilt' and 'stunning', not 'scrubby'.

Lewis has finally admitted to himself that he is in love with Gresham only after he discovers that she is dying of cancer. The couple are on honeymoon, treasuring their final days together. The setting had to be just right. Daubeny found it about 30 miles south-east of the real thing at a point on the meandering River Wye near Goodrich. It was at Symond's Yat Rock, alongside the Wye Valley Walk, that Anthony Hopkins (Lewis) and Debra Winger (Gresham) found their Golden Valley with its lush green countryside rolling away into the distance. At the end of the film, Lewis returns to the valley and is seen walking with Gresham's young son, Douglas, at Bicknor Court Farm, a short distance from Symond's Yat Rock.

Attenborough says: 'Everybody has moments within their lives when they have had to face up to circumstances of loss, of death, of illness. The way such an experience is presented in this film script touched a chord and the marvellous thing about it, of course, is that you don't come out of the cinema feeling anything but elation. You feel life is wonderful, life has something tremendous to offer, something magical.'

Shadowlands is unique in its progression from a one-off BBC drama in 1985 to a West End and Broadway play and, ultimately, a Hollywood film. The original BBC production, written by William Nicholson and starring Joss Ackland and Claire Bloom, won BAFTA and Emmy awards. Nigel Hawthorne won a Tony award for his performance in the New York stage production and might have expected to get the lead in the film, but Attenborough likes to work with actors with whom he has worked before. Eight-year-old Joseph Mazzello, who plays Douglas, had worked with Attenborough on *Jurassic Park* and Attenborough had done five films with Hopkins, who has to show the gradual development and emotional thawing of his character under Gresham's influence.

C. S. Lewis's work ranged from religious essays to children's novels, most notably *The Lion, the Witch and the Wardrobe*. He also taught at Oxford University and was a bachelor in his fifties when Gresham entered his life.

Much of the filming of *Shadowlands* was done in Oxford itself. Magdalen College (pronounced Maudlen), where Lewis was a fellow, features prominently, with important scenes in the fifteenth-century chapel and carved oak dining-hall, as the very intimate and human drama is played out against a severe backdrop of pomp and history. Magdalen dates back to 1458 and is one of Oxford's most beautiful and spacious colleges, as well as one

ANTHONY HOPKINS

DEBRA WINGER

He thought that magic
only existed in his books,

and then he met her.

RICHARD ATTENBOROUGH'S FILM

SHADOWLANDS

Based on a true story.

SHADOWLANDS is the tender and deeply moving true story of the love affair between C.S. Lewis and J
as C.S. Lewis, professor of English literature and language at Magdalen College, Oxf
Lewis, known to his friends as Jack, lives a life of quiet routine, teaching and writing amid the all-male fellow
intellectually; a man more in touch

Debra Winger portrays American poetess Joy Gresham, the prickly and outgoing woman who walks
Only when Joy returns to the United States, does Jack begin to discover the depth of his feelings for her, ye
summon – or face – his long-sublimated emotions. He does, howe
When Joy is threatened with deportation, Jack secretly marries her so that she can obtain citizenship. For
denial. Her denunciation of his emotional dishonesty finally strikes a nerve in Jack, but, before he can voic
her, Jack finally proposes and they marry again,
For months the cancer miraculously stays in remission, though both know the future is uncertain. When Joy
time, his faith is severely tested. Out of his love for Joy he promises to adopt Douglas and pass on to him t

Certificate: U   Running

SPELLING FILMS INTERNATIONAL in Association with PRICE ENTERTAINMENT and
In RICHARD ATTENBOROUGH'S FILM "SHADOWLANDS" Music Composed and Conducted by GEORGE FE
Production Designed by STUART CRAIG Director of Photography ROGER PRATT B.S.C. Co Producer DIANA HAWKINS
Produced by RICHARD ATTENBOROUGH and BRIAN E

SAVOY PICTURES

...land in 1952, this timeless tale about the power of love stars Anthony Hopkins ...med for his poetry, children's books, and religious essays.

... surrounded himself with friends who rarely challenge him, either emotionally or ... heart.

...ife, bringing a totally new perspective to his carefully ordered existence.

...months later, he still resists becoming romantically involved, seemingly unable to ... shy son, Douglas (Joseph Mazzello).

... of convenience, but she has fallen deeply in love and can no longer accept his

...is admitted to hospital suffering from advanced bone cancer. Faced with losing ... God and the world.

...es again, Jack must face the painful reality of life without her, and, for the first ...ed – that being open to the joy of love entails vulnerability and the pain of loss.

...RD ATTENBOROUGH'S FILM

SHADOWLANDS

...nts ANTHONY HOPKINS · DEBRA WINGER
...BB Costumes Designed by PENNY ROSE Editor LESLEY WALKER
...G Screenplay by WILLIAM NICHOLSON Based on His Stageplay
...ATTENBOROUGH

Angel Eastman Eastman Color Films DOLBY STEREO 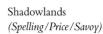 SPELLING FILMS INTERNATIONAL

Shadowlands
(Spelling / Price / Savoy)

of the richest. Oscar Wilde, Compton Mackenzie and Dudley Moore are among its famous 'members'.

Other Oxford locations included Christ Church Meadow; Duke Humphrey's Library, built in the fifteenth century to house the books of Henry V's brother, Humphrey, Duke of Gloucester; the eighteenth-century Radcliffe Camera, a baroque rotunda and the earliest example of an English circular reading-room; and the seventeenth-century Sheldonian Theatre, based on the Theatre of Marcellus in Rome – semi-circular in front and rectangular behind – and the first work of Christopher Wren, who served as professor of astronomy at Oxford. The Great Central Railway's Loughborough Station was used as Oxford station and the tea-room of Oxford's sedate nineteenth-century Randolph Hotel was used as the setting for the first meeting between Lewis and Gresham, when Gresham embarrasses the writer with her forwardness.

Pengethley Manor Hotel, near Ross-on-Wye, was used as the hotel in which Lewis and Gresham stay on their journey in search of the Golden Valley, and it was where Hopkins, Winger and Attenborough themselves stayed for several nights in June 1993. Lewis and Gresham were also shown driving through the Monnow Valley, near Garway, looking for the Golden Valley.

Attenborough says he had never come across so moving a story as *Shadowlands*. 'Sixty pages in, almost everybody who read it had to put it down. They could not continue reading without taking a break to compose themselves. It is a very human story. ' Angie Errigo, writing in *Empire* film magazine, called it 'a wonderfully affirmative tale of love'. Debra Winger was nominated for the Oscar for best actress, losing out to Holly Hunter in *The Piano*, and Hopkins would surely have been Oscar-nominated for this film if he had not won a nomination for *The Remains of the Day*.

CHAPTER FIVE
Misplaced Encounters
THE NORTH OF ENGLAND

BACKBEAT (1994)

Location filming included the Liverpool street where John Lennon shared a flat with Stuart Sutcliffe, the ill-fated fifth Beatle, who died of a brain haemorrhage at the age of 21. But Lennon (Ian Hart) and Sutcliffe (Stephen Dorff) did get a better view this time round. Location manager Jeff Bowen considered the actual flat, at 3 Gambier Terrace, where they had stayed in 1960. Bowen says it was 'not in a very good state of repair' – though it was hardly a palace in Lennon and Sutcliffe's time either. The squalor in which they lived featured as part of an exposé of 'Beatnik' lifestyle in the *People* newspaper before the Beatles became famous. Bowen says: 'I moved it along about ten houses so we had the view of the Anglican Cathedral bang outside the window.'

The scene in which Lennon and Sutcliffe look out over Liverpool and discuss the future was shot on top of one of the tower blocks at Aigburth Drive, and their departure for Germany was shot on the other side of the Mersey at Victoria Dock, Birkenhead, using one of the Isle of Man ferries.

The film-makers also shot in Hamburg, where the Beatles served their apprenticeship, though the clubs were reconstructed in England. Some were in vacant premises, but the Dome, at 178 Junction Road, Tufnell Park, London, was used as Hamburg's Top Ten Club and the National Club, 234 Kilburn High Road, London, served as the Star Club.

The poignant scene in which Sutcliffe's girlfriend, Astrid Kirchherr (Sheryl Lee), tells Lennon she loves Sutcliffe, and the usually cynical Lennon hints that he loves them both, was filmed at Talacre Beach and Point of Ayr Lighthouse in north Wales on the opposite side of the Wirral from Liverpool.

BRIEF ENCOUNTER (1945)

It started with a speck of dirt in Celia Johnson's eye and ended with a grand unconsummated passion, in one of the classics of English cinema.

Laura Jesson (Johnson) is at Milford Junction waiting for her train home after her weekly shopping trip when she encounters the fateful speck. Alec Harvey (Trevor Howard), a doctor who has regular surgeries in Milford, comes to her assistance. They meet again by chance and the relationship develops from there, with trips to the cinema and the Kardomah café before they catch their trains home to their respective spouses. The third important character in this very English drama, adapted from Noel Coward's one-act play, *Still Life*, is, of course, the railway station itself Milford Junction – played by Carnforth Station in Lancashire.

The north of England was determined not merely by dramatic requirements, but by

the fact that the film needed a location far enough away from the south coast for the film-makers to be given sufficient warning of air-raids. Writer-director David Lean said: 'The war was still on and the railway people said, "There may be an air-raid at any moment and you'll have time to put out the lights in that remote part up in the north. You'll know when the planes are coming." We were a blaze of lights from filming.'

Lean also wanted a station that had local trains, for Laura to get on, and fast, non-stopping express trains, for Laura to consider throwing herself under. It was reported, however, that drivers slowed down to see what the bright lights were all about and had to be instructed to speed up so Lean could catch the rush and roar of the expresses as background atmosphere. Lean also shot footage of fast trains at Watford Junction. Another requirement for Milford Junction was a buffet, where the relationship between Laura and Alec Harvey begins and ends.

Lean found what he was looking for at Carnforth on the London, Midland and Scottish line between London and Glasgow. It had been an important junction since the line to Ulverston opened in the middle of the nineteenth century. Before the First World War nine mail trains went through Carnforth every night. Most of the film was shot at Denham Studios, near London. They closed down many years ago, but Carnforth Station remains. The west coast main line platforms have gone, the buffet building was boarded up and there have been proposals in the past to close local services. But the historic station survives – a monument to Laura and Alec's romance through which thousands of rail travellers speed just as they did in the film half a century ago, probably oblivious to the passionate drama unfolding on the platforms.

The area of England in which *Brief Encounter* is set is never made entirely clear in the film. It has the feel of the Home Counties, though northern place-names, such as Giggleswick and Hellifield, can be seen on the destination board.

The film was premièred outside London, not in Lancashire, but in Rochester, where one loud woman burst into laughter at the first romantic scene and others joined in until the whole place was in uproar. Lean feared he had a disaster on his hands, but the film did reasonable business elsewhere, with Lean noting that it tended to do well in 'better-class halls'. It was much less successful than other romantic melodramas of the time, including the now-forgotten *Piccadilly Incident*. The Germans, apparently, could not understand Laura and Alec's anguish and wondered why they just did not get on with their affair.

The film is very much a portrait of a particular time and place, and one might add class, but although it was mocked and satirised in the sixties it continued to find new fans in the AIDS-conscious eighties and nineties when fidelity became fashionable again. It has appeared regularly in critics' polls of the best films of all time. A 1974 TV remake was shot in Winchester, with Richard Burton and Sophia Loren.

CUL-DE-SAC (1966)

Roman Polanski wrote the script for this strange, absurd thriller shortly after leaving his native Poland for Paris. A transvestite lives with his nymphomaniac wife in a small castle on an island. As if their existence is not fragile enough, an escaped convict turns up and imposes himself upon them.

*Backbeat
(PolyGram/Scala/
Channel Four)*

Celia Johnson and Trevor Howard in Brief Encounter *(Cineguild)*

*Francoise Dorleac and
Donald Pleasence in
Cul-de-Sac (Sigma)*

Polanski was inspired by a sense of humiliation at the bitter failure of his marriage to the actress Basia Kwiatkowska. He even hoped she might play the nymphomaniac and he would play the transvestite. But he had no idea where he might find his island castle. Yugoslavia was considered, before Polanski hired a light plane and flew up the east coast of England in search of locations. He found what he was looking for on Holy Island, with its small but dramatic Lindisfarne Castle sitting on top of a steep rock by the sea. The female role was eventually played by Francoise Dorleac, elder sister of Catherine Deneuve who had just starred in Polanski's *Repulsion*. Donald Pleasence played the transvestite and Lionel Stander the convict.

It was a distinctly odd film and they were a distinctly odd crowd, descending on the little island with all the trappings of stardom. Pleasence came in an enormous Lincoln car. Dorleac arrived with 17 cases and a hairless chihuahua which nipped the ankles of anyone who came near.

Polanski was a hard task-master. Dorleac had a long nude scene. The problem was not that she was naked, it was that she was naked in the freezing North Sea and Polanski wanted it done again and again – ignoring protests from her colleagues – until Dorleac passed out from the cold. The location doctor thought she had had a heart attack.

Dorleac never fulfilled her promise as she was killed in a car crash in 1967. Pleasence kept his head shaved when he played James Bond's adversary, Blofeld, in *You Only Live Twice* and Stander went on to fame as Robert Wagner's sidekick in the television series *Hart to Hart*. Polanski was to use Lindisfarne again (see page 146) for *Macbeth*.

DIAMOND SKULLS (1990)

There is a certain irony in the fact that a study of élitism and the vicious self-preservation of the upper classes should choose as its principal location an estate that was formerly known as the home of the richest commoner in England – not a National Lottery winner, but seventeenth-century banker Sir Charles Duncombe.

Gabriel Byrne plays Lord Hugo Buckton who knocks down a young woman in Belgravia in London after a dinner with the officers of his former regiment. His friend, Jamie (Douglas Hodge), is alarmed by his failure to report the accident to the police. The next day, Jamie accompanies Buckton when he goes to see his parents, Lord and Lady Crewne (Michael Hordern and Judy Parfitt), at Crewne Hall. The film-makers used Duncombe Park, near Thirsk in Yorkshire.

In 1695, banker Charles Duncombe bought the Helmsley estate, with its medieval castle, from the Duke of Buckingham, prompting Alexander Pope to write:

'Helmsley once proud Buckingham's delight,

Slides to a scrivener or a City Knight.'

In 1713 Duncombe's nephew began work on an elegant and sturdy new limestone house, to the design of the local amateur architect William Wakefield, on a site which commands a magnificent view of the countryside. It was used for both exterior and interior shots on *Diamond Skulls*, though interiors were also shot at Wrotham Park and High Canons in Hertfordshire.

Jamie tries to discuss the accident with Buckton but Buckton is more concerned with the possibility that his wife, Ginny (Amanda Donohoe), is having an affair. The accident victim dies but it was Jamie's car that Buckton was driving and the police turn up at Jamie's barracks to check it. The film-makers used various London clubs and military establishments, including the Duke of York's Barracks in Chelsea.

Jamie eludes the police, turns up at Crewne Hall, but the following morning his car is found abandoned on the clifftops and his body on the beach below – a scene shot at Fan Bay, near Dover in Kent, almost at the opposite end of the country from Duncombe Park.

The house has been described as 'a smaller and plainer Castle Howard'. For most of this century it has been used as a girls' school, but it has been restored to use as the family home of the Duncombes, Lord and Lady Feversham, and was recently opened to the public for the first time.

A HANDFUL OF DUST (1988)

Not only did the Duke of Norfolk have his home taken over by film people for this faithful adaptation of Evelyn Waugh's bitter mix of comedy and tragedy, but he found his station in life reduced from that of nobleman to gardener. The duke, dressed in decades-old gardening clothes, can be seen in the film standing alongside a bonfire and tugging at his cap as a mark of respect when Mrs Rattery (Anjelica Huston) approaches the house, having just landed her biplane outside.

Director-writer Charles Sturridge said at the time that he regarded the house as being as important to the story as any of the characters. Tony Last (James Wilby) is a thoroughly decent chap. Faced with the adultery of his wife, Brenda (Kristin Scott Thomas), he is

Michael Hordern at Duncombe Park, Yorkshire, in Diamond Skulls *(Working Title/British Screen/Channel Four)*

Kristin Scott Thomas
and James Wilby in
A Handful of Dust
(Stagescreen)

prepared to pretend that it is he who has been guilty of adultery and go on providing for his wife. It is only when her demands escalate to the extent that he would have to sell his beloved home that he finally decides to take a stand – not that Evelyn Waugh made the place seem particularly attractive. He said Hetton was 'formerly one of the notable houses of the county, [it] was entirely rebuilt in 1864 in the Gothic style and is now devoid of interest'.

Sturridge used Carlton Towers in Yorkshire, a strangely square mansion that looks as if it has been built entirely of Lego. In 1066 one of William the Conqueror's knights was given the manor of Carlton and it was subsequently owned by the Stapeletons, whose elaborate family crest includes a Saracen's head to commemorate heroics in the Crusades. The crest can still be seen over the fireplace in the drawing-room. Carlton Hall was rebuilt in the seventeenth and eighteenth centuries and was transformed into a Gothic mansion in the nineteenth. Brickwork was covered with cement to look like stone, turrets and battlements were added and the name was changed to Carlton Towers. Sturridge said: 'Strangely enough, Carlton Towers was the first place we saw, but we felt we had to test it against almost every other Gothic house we could find. When we went back to Carlton at the end of the search, we knew at once that it was the perfect location. It has nearly everything that Waugh described in the book.'

The Duke of Norfolk was not the only one in his family to appear in the film. His daughter, Marsha Fitzalan, is a professional actress. She played society hostess Polly Cockpurse.

A Handful of Dust also filmed at the old railway station at Windsor in Berkshire and at the Café de Paris in London's Coventry Street, just off Leicester Square. It was a fashionable nightclub in the thirties and, although it had become a disco, it retained its period decor and furnishings, and was considered ideal for Brenda Last's dinner-date with her lover.

The film ends far from London society, with Last stuck in the South American jungle – a sequence which necessitated a trip to Venezuela. The contrast between stately England and some remote and primitive corner of Venezuela reflects the various violent contrasts at the heart of this under-rated and surprisingly powerful film.

LET HIM HAVE IT (1991)

The story of Derek Bentley, the 19-year-old who was hanged for a murder committed by his 16-year-old accomplice, was set in the London area in the early fifties, but filmed largely on Merseyside, with the New Brighton seaside resort doubling for the London borough of Croydon.

The film begins with an air-raid in which the eight-year-old Bentley is buried under the rubble. The sequence was shot in Toft Street, Liverpool. Lynn Saunders of the Liverpool Film Office says: 'A house was due for demolition, so the film company, with a local demolition company, partly demolished the house, added gas pipes with SFX (special effects), did the scene and then completed demolition after filming. This scene was shot during the Gulf War and a senior citizen, close by, thought Saddam Hussein was bombing his street.'

As a teenager, Bentley (Chris Eccleston) becomes involved with Chris Craig (Paul Reynolds) and his elder brother, Niven (Mark McGann). Director Peter Medak, who also made *The Krays*, shot scenes of the young gangsters at Liverpool Docks and around Falkner Square, where Niven Craig is arrested and where Bentley and Chris Craig sleep on a park bench. The same location was subsequently used when Daniel Day-Lewis slept rough in *In the Name of the Father*. And, as in *In the Name of the Father*, *Let Him Have It* used St George's Hall in Liverpool as the Old Bailey.

The scene on the warehouse roof, where Craig shoots dead a policeman, was filmed in London. The film-makers checked various possible locations. They phoned one company and spoke to the civil engineer responsible for the site. He asked what the film was about and was duly told. 'Oh my God,' he said, 'I was on the jury.'

Much of the prosecution case against Bentley hinged on his alleged instruction to Craig 'Let him have it' and whether it was an order to shoot or hand over the gun. Bentley was under arrest at the time. The jury found Bentley guilty but recommended mercy. The judge formally sentenced him to death, but also supported the mercy plea. Craig was too young to hang. But there were fears about teenage crime getting out of control and the Government appeared to want to make an example of someone. So Bentley hanged for a murder, which by any normal definition, he did not commit.

MACBETH (1971)

Fifteen months after his heavily pregnant wife, Sharon Tate, was slaughtered in their villa in Los Angeles by the deranged disciples of Charles Manson, the gifted Polish film-maker Roman Polanski took himself off to the windswept coasts of Northumberland and the remote mountains of Snowdonia for a very violent and highly personal adaptation of Shakespeare's *Macbeth*, with its treachery and madness, its ghost of murdered Banquo and the slaughter of Lady Macduff's family in their own home. So, Shakespeare's 'Scotch play'

Paul Reynolds and Chris Eccleston in St George's Hall, Liverpool, in Let Him Have It *(Vivid/Le Studio Canal Plus/ British Screen)*

was filmed entirely outside Scotland – in England and Wales.

Polanski had hoped to make his comeback with an adaptation of Henri Charriere's best-selling book about escape from Devil's Island, *Papillon*. But that project fell through and was later filmed by Franklin J. Schaffner, starring Dustin Hoffman and Steve McQueen. Instead, Polanski began collaborating with the famous theatre critic, Kenneth Tynan, on an adaptation of *Macbeth*. Tynan had just put on his notorious nude revue *Oh! Calcutta!*.

Previous stage and film productions of *Macbeth* had found little scope for nudity. But Tynan determined that Lady Macbeth should do her sleepwalking scene naked. It would certainly symbolise her somewhat dodgy state of mind. Only a mad person would walk around a Scottish, or Northumbrian, castle, without at least a couple of pairs of long johns on. Curiously, or perhaps not so curiously, *Playboy* put up most of the money for the film.

It was a relatively lightweight cast with Jon Finch as Macbeth; Francesca Annis as Lady Macbeth; Martin Shaw, who would become a household name in TV's *The Professionals*, as Banquo; and a young, chubby-cheeked Keith Chegwin as his son, Fleance.

Filming began with four weeks of freezing rain in Snowdonia National Park. While shooting one of the scenes with the witches, a cameraman was blown off his perch into a crevice and was lucky to survive. The opening scenes were shot on the wide, expansive beach at Morfa Bychan, near Porthmadog. The production then moved to Northumberland for two weeks of filming at Lindisfarne Castle on Holy Island – where Polanski had directed *Cul-de-Sac* – and at Bamburgh Castle, which was also used as the Scottish royal residence in another film of the early seventies, *Mary, Queen of Scots*, with Vanessa Redgrave and Glenda Jackson.

Left: Lindisfarne Castle and
Right: Bamburgh Castle, Northumberland: principal locations for Macbeth *(Playboy/Caliban)*

Lindisfarne Castle represents Macbeth's original castle. He begins the play as Thane (Lord) of Glamis, a village north of Dundee. Glamis Castle was, in fact, the childhood

home of the Queen Mother. However, Shakespeare's text stipulates Macbeth's castle to be in Inverness. Macbeth subsequently becomes Thane of Cawdor, which is indeed near Inverness, though it seems odd that he should have a castle in Inverness before acceding to the title.

Lindisfarne Castle is the very picture of a medieval castle – a small fortress atop a steep rock that rises suddenly out of the flat land by the seashore. It can be seen for miles around. It was built in the sixteenth century, about 500 years after Macbeth's death, to defend the nearby harbour. In the nineteenth century it served as a coastguard station and it was converted into a private house by the architect Sir Edwin Lutyens at the beginning of the twentieth for Edward Hudson, the wealthy publisher of *Country Life*. Lytton Strachey was a house guest and described the castle as 'very dark, with nowhere to sit, and nothing but stone under, over and round you'. Lindisfarne Castle is now owned by the National Trust and is open to the public.

Bamburgh Castle, just five miles down the coast, plays the king's palace, which Shakespeare specifies as Forres in the North-east of Scotland. Bamburgh, which is also open to the public, is a much grander building than Lindisfarne. Actually, it is several buildings behind protective stone walls. Again it is very dramatic, set behind a long and popular beach. The ramparts offer a superb view of the coast and countryside. The castle's keep dates back to Norman times and much of the curtain walling was there by the middle of the thirteenth century. Bamburgh was indeed a royal residence for several generations, but it was acquired by the Newcastle arms tycoon, Lord Armstrong, who initiated extensive reconstruction work in the late nineteenth century.

Polanski made various temporary alterations of his own to both Lindisfarne and Bamburgh, putting a roof – shaped like a witch's hat – on a section of the former. Polanski and Tynan wanted to highlight the difference in scale between the two castles in order to represent the change in Macbeth's fortunes when he becomes king. It certainly seemed like a good idea, but Tynan felt the two castles blurred into each other in viewers' perceptions.

Polanski actually preferred the studio work at Shepperton, where he had more control over various elements, including the weather, though there were still problems with his accent. One complicated courtyard scene was worked out involving sprinklers to simulate the beginning of rain. If anything went wrong, it would take a couple of hours for everything to dry out. It seemed to be going fine until, much to Polanski's surprise, everyone stopped. Reportedly jumping up and down with rage, he demanded to know why. The assistant director ventured that Polanski had said 'Cut.' Polanski said: 'No, no, I said "Cut. Bring in the cut."' Of course, he meant cut as in horse and cut.

Certain lines and episodes in the film obviously reminded Polanski of his own tragedy, particularly the killing of Macduff's wife and children – 'Your wife and babes savagely slaughtered'. Tynan later wrote that he had not been looking forward to the scene. 'A difficult moment arrived when I queried the amount of blood that would be shed by a small boy stabbed in the back. Polanski replied bleakly: "You didn't see my house last summer. I know about bleeding."' That was the only time Polanski alluded to his wife's murder in Tynan's presence during filming.

*Timothy Dalton and
Vanessa Redgrave in
Mary, Queen of Scots
(Universal)*

The greatest strengths of the film are visual – the castles, the hills, those beach battle scenes at the beginning. However, writing in *Monthly Film Bulletin*, Philip Strick said: 'In adapting Shakespeare to suit (*Playboy* owner) Hugh Hefner and themselves, Polanski and Tynan have served *Macbeth* extremely well.' Most of the critics liked it and it has been released on video as part of Columbia's Hollywood Collection.

MARY, QUEEN OF SCOTS (1971)

It might have been more accurately named *Mary, Queen of Northumbrians*, for most of the location filming took place on the other side of the border.

Producer Hal Wallis reckoned Holyrood Palace in Edinburgh was 'too modern' and 'too restored' for his purposes, so he used Bamburgh and Alnwick Castles in Northumberland. And instead of sailing from France to the port of Leith after the death of her first husband, Mary (Vanessa Redgrave) steps ashore at Seahouses, a village a few miles from Bamburgh. 'We turned an old tug into a wonderful galleon and she landed on the beach and it was a terrific scene,' says Simon Relph, who was assistant director on the film.

Bamburgh Castle is one of the most dramatic castles in England – several buildings grouped behind a protective wall, on a site that dominates the surrounding countryside and commands a fine view of the North Sea coastline. Bamburgh was the seat of the kings of Northumbria and there has been a castle there for 1,400 years. The keep survives from Norman times, though there was considerable restoration and extension of the castle in the eighteenth and nineteenth centuries.

In the eighteenth century, after it was acquired by the Bishop of Durham, it housed a boarding-school for servant girls, a surgery and dispensary for the poor, and a refuge for shipwrecked sailors. It was bought by the arms tycoon, Lord Armstrong, at the end of the last century. It remains the Armstrong family home and now includes the Armstrong Museum.

Alnwick Castle, just 16 miles away, dates from the eleventh century. It has been in the possession of the Percy family – the Dukes of Northumberland – since the beginning of the fourteenth century and its outward appearance has remained much the same since then. It is a picturesque, medieval brownstone fortress, with tall, narrow windows, more or less enclosed by a defensive wall. In contrast, the interior state rooms are a picture of opulence in the style of the Italian Renaissance.

Both castles also appear in Hal Wallis's 1964 historical drama, *Becket*, with Richard Burton and Peter O'Toole. Bamburgh was used for Ken Russell's *The Devils* and Roman Polanski's *Macbeth*, and Alnwick for Disney's *The Spaceman and King Arthur* and Rowan Atkinson's popular television sitcom *Blackadder*.

Some of the castles Mary visited are no longer in existence. Dunbar, where she took refuge from hostile Scottish lords, was destroyed after her surrender; and Fotheringhay in Northamptonshire, where she was beheaded in 1587, is now only a mound.

No less than 25 major sets were built at Shepperton Studios near London, but the film-makers did shoot at Hermitage Castle, a grim, square thirteenth-century stronghold about ten miles south of Hawick. Relph recalls cast and crew going off to buy Pringle's sweaters from the town during breaks in filming.

Mary stayed at Hermitage, which was the castle of the Earl of Bothwell (Nigel Davenport), her third husband, though their relationship pre-dated the murder of her second, Lord Darnley, played in the film by the future James Bond, Timothy Dalton. Although the use of Hermitage Castle was an authentic touch, Hal Wallis declared that his intention was entertainment rather than documentary. The film, for example, has Mary meeting her cousin, Elizabeth (Glenda Jackson reprising a role she had already played on television in *Elizabeth R*), though historians believe they never met. They were filmed together at Parham House, a restored Elizabethan mansion at Pulborough in Sussex, with a 158-foot-long gallery and a noted collection of Elizabethan and Stuart portraits.

Bamburgh, Alnwick, Hermitage and Parham are all open to the public.

MOUNTAINS OF THE MOON (1990)

The film-makers spent 11 weeks in Kenya recreating the historic expeditions of the nineteenth-century explorers, Richard Burton (Patrick Bergin) and John Hanning Speke (Iain Glen). But one of the biggest location headaches occurred in Britain when it came to finding somewhere to represent the headquarters of the Royal Geographical Society – the London society which sponsored the men. It is the setting for the climactic debate after the two explorers fall out over the source of the Nile. 'We wanted to do the scenes in London, but there is so little standing due to the property developers that it was impossible,' said art director Norman Reynolds.

Eventually, his own voyage of discovery took him to Liverpool Town Hall. 'It is exactly of the period and quite wonderful, with a curved gallery almost like an amphitheatre,' he

Patrick Bergin in
Mountains of the
Moon *(Carolco)*

said. 'That's how Bob (writer-director Bob Rafelson) had described it in his screenplay. But by the time we found it, we'd have been happy with any suitable period building.'

It was used for interiors, while another Merseyside town hall was used as the Royal Geographical Society exterior. It is located just across the river in Birkenhead, where twin flights of steps lead up to a grand, pillared entrance. Liverpool Athenaeum provided the Royal Geographical Society's map room for a memorable scene in which Burton compares scars with Dr Livingstone (Bernard Hill). London dock scenes were also filmed on Merseyside.

The south of England did manage to come up with some suitable stately homes for the film. Stratfield Saye, seat of the Duke of Wellington, near Reading, was Lord Houghton's home where Burton meets his future wife and partner in adventure, Isabel Arundell (Fiona Shaw). The Arundell family home was Milton Manor in Oxfordshire, while Dorney Court, outside Windsor, Berkshire, served as the Speke home. All three are open to the public.

THE RAILWAY CHILDREN (1970)

Keighley and Worth Valley Railway Preservation Society, one of England's leading rail heritage groups, provided the key locations for the film of E. Nesbit's popular story about three Edwardian children who move from London to the Yorkshire countryside and have a succession of adventures around the local railway.

The family is forced to move when the father (Iain Cuthbertson), a Government official, is wrongly imprisoned for spying. The mother (Dinah Sheridan) pretends to the children – Bobbie (Jenny Agutter), Phyllis (Sally Thomsett) and Peter (Gary Warren) – that they are pretending to be poor as a game. The children quickly settle down in their new surroundings, are attracted by the passing trains and befriend the local railway porter, Perks (Bernard Cribbins).

The railway that was used by Lionel Jeffries, who wrote and directed the film, was Keighley and Worth Valley Railway and the children's local station was Oakworth in the middle of the five-mile line. Keighley and Worth Valley Railway opened in 1867 and carried normal passenger services until 1962 when the preservation society was constituted. Its volunteers run steam trains at weekends and daily during the summer. They have worked towards preserving the best aspects of a 1950s' branch line, though the Oakworth station has been restored to the condition it would have been in before the First World War. It never had electricity; the platform and waiting-room are lit by gas.

Oakworth Station was also used for the television version of *The Railway Children* prior to the film. John Schlesinger's wartime drama *Yanks* and various television productions, including *Last of the Summer Wine*, have used Oakworth or other parts of the line, which has six stations, two tunnels, two level-crossings and two signal boxes. The valley itself consists of peat and heather moors, woods and hillside pastures divided by dry-stone walls.

The Mytholmes tunnel, between Oakworth and Haworth, was another key element in the film of *The Railway Children*. It was the setting for the paper chase and landslide.

Haworth, one of the stops on the line, is, of course, best known as the village where the Brontë sisters lived in the first half of the nineteenth century, before the railway opened. In 1848 Charlotte and Anne Brontë walked through a thunderstorm from Haworth to Keighley to get a train to London to reveal the true identity of the authors of their books, which they had published under pseudonyms. Their home, the Brontë Parsonage Museum, was used in the film as the house of the doctor (Peter Bromilow), and the village's cobbled main street also figures in the film.

The railway children's home, 'Three Chimneys', is a private house at Bents Farm, near Oxenhope. It is not open to the public but can be seen on the Railway Children Walk, which goes through what is known as the Top Field. The film remains extremely popular today and still attracts visitors to the railway.

Both Jenny Agutter and Sally Thomsett became successful adult actresses. Agutter appeared in numerous films including *Walkabout, Logan's Run* and *Equus*. Thomsett is best known as one of the main characters in the television situation comedy *Man About the House*.

ROBIN HOOD (1991)

Although Robin Hood is supposed to have lived at the time of Richard the Lion-heart and his brother, the scheming Prince John, in the twelfth century, the makers of the Patrick Bergin version of the legend chose a castle built in the middle of the nineteenth century as their principal location. Peckforton Castle, near Chester, was intended as a reconstruction of a medieval fortress and its well-maintained appearance was exactly what director John Irvin wanted. 'After all, in medieval England medieval castles would not have been old and crumbling,' he said.

In the film, Peckforton is the castle of Baron Daguerre (Jeroen Krabbe), erstwhile friend of Robin (Bergin), and of Daguerre's ward, Maid Marian (Uma Thurman). Peckforton is regarded as the most ambitious and authentic imitation medieval castle in England, an extensive, red sandstone stronghold with battlements and turrets, surveying the Cheshire plain from the top of a wooded hill. It has a large interior courtyard, entered through a gatehouse complete with drawbridge and portcullis.

Peckforton was built for the first Lord Tollemache, who had large estates in Cheshire and Suffolk and was widely respected as a progressive landlord. He provided estate workers with a cottage and three acres. The Tollemache family lived at Peckforton until the Second World War when the castle was abandoned. It stayed empty until it was bought by the present owners in 1988. It is now open to the public throughout the summer.

The caves at nearby Beeston Castle were also used in the film, but although Beeston is owned by English Heritage and open to the public, the caves are considered dangerous and are closed off.

For outdoor scenes, the film-makers were careful to use only woods with the sort of trees that would have been found in medieval England. Several sequences, including the opening conflict in which Robin Hood comes to the defence of a poacher, were shot at Tatton Park, Cheshire – a 2,000-acre estate that includes woodland and deer park. It is the National Trust's most visited property, with more than 700,000 visitors a year. The Georgian mansion house was not used in the film, though it provided interior locations for television's *Brideshead Revisited* and *The Adventures of Sherlock Holmes*. Other outdoor scenes for *Robin Hood* were shot in Wales around the village of Betws-y-Coed.

STORMY MONDAY (1988)

Newcastle is undoubtedly one of the main attractions in this thriller starring Sean Bean, Melanie Griffith, Sting and Tommy Lee Jones. The city's waterfront area provided both the locations and the plot.

Tommy Lee Jones plays Cosmo, an American businessman who is buying up waterfront properties as part of a crooked deal. Sting plays Finney, the owner of a jazz club who refuses to sell. Bean is Brendan, a young drifter who overhears a couple of heavies planning a visit to Finney. Brendan throws in his lot with Finney by going to warn him. The thugs are subsequently seen leaving from Newcastle Central Station, one of them nursing a broken arm.

Mike Figgis wrote the screenplay and music and directed the film. *The Virgin Film Guide* says: '*Stormy Monday* draws its strength from subtle shadings of character and a vivid evocation of its setting.' Associate producer Alan Wands recalls: 'At the time, the waterfront in Newcastle was basically hanging in rags. We moved in, found an office, set up and did various deals with this one property company who had all these empty properties. We used the interior of what had been warehouses or some kind of market or whatever, and we put sets up in them. We built the Key Club in an old warehouse in a street called the Side. We also had what we called the Hopper Bar – it was the bar where Melanie Griffith and Sean Bean go for a drink after work. Again, that was a derelict building that had been a bar. It was just off the Side, underneath the Tyne Bridge . . . And there was another

place on the Side which we called the Weegee Bar (both bars were named after American photographers). It was the café or diner that Melanie Griffith was supposed to be working in, which was exactly the same deal. It was derelict.'

The film also used the Royal Station Hotel and made particularly dramatic use of the city's bridges. There is a car chase on the low-level Swing Bridge; Griffith and Bean are accosted by Cosmo's men at the Tyne Bridge and the final showdown between Sting and Tommy Lee Jones takes place on the dramatic High Level Bridge, with the rail track above the road, and a pedestrian route alongside. Wands suggests Figgis was paying homage to *Get Carter*, a 1971 Tyneside thriller with Michael Caine. 'Quite a lot of *Get Carter* was also set on the High Level Bridge.'

WUTHERING HEIGHTS (1992)

Juliette Binoche and Ralph Fiennes filmed on location on the North Yorkshire moors as literature's great ill-fated lovers, Cathy Earnshaw and Heathcliff. Emily Brontë set her novel above the village of Haworth, where the Brontës lived in what is now a museum.

However, Haworth is so busy with tourists that the film-makers dismissed any notions of attempting to capture the desolate and eerie atmosphere of the novel in the immediate vicinity. Instead, they chose a location about 15 miles away, just north of the village of Grassington, as the site of Wuthering Heights – the house where Heathcliff and Cathy grow up. Dramatic licence was used in erecting a Gothic façade right up against the skyline, rather than in a more sheltered spot, as common sense would have dictated.

A real house was used for Thrushcross Grange, home of the Linton family into which Cathy marries, having rejected Heathcliff as her social inferior. The film-makers used Broughton Hall, at Skipton – a 70-room mansion which has been in the Tempest family since it was built in 1597. Broughton Hall, which was also used for the television production, *A Woman of Substance*, was suggested by Ralph Fiennes, who went to art school with one of the family.

The glass dome in the conservatory was restored, chimneys repaired, the front of the house sand-blasted and new gravel laid in the drive – all at Paramount film company's expense. The house is open to the public on certain days.

The film team also used the barn and outhouses at the National Trust's East Riddlesden Hall to film Heathcliff at work in the carding shed, where wool is combed before spinning.

Other locations included the moors themselves. Standing stones were erected on Boss Moor, while Heathcliff and Cathy declare their love near Aysgarth Falls. But Yorkshire locations hardly compensate for a very French Cathy.

The 1939 version, with Laurence Olivier and Merle Oberon, was shot in California, where a section of Californian hills was turned into Yorkshire at enormous cost. The tumbleweed was dusted purple for long shots and 1,000 heather plants were used in the close-ups.

CHAPTER SIX
Under Milk Wood and Up the Khyber
WALES

CARRY ON UP THE KHYBER (1968)

When the film opened, an old soldier who had served on the North-West Frontier wrote to the producer, Peter Rogers, saying that he had immediately recognised the Khyber Pass – the famous mountain route linking Afghanistan and Pakistan, or India as it then was. Since the time of Alexander the Great countless troops have marched through the pass, beneath the dangerous mountains of the Hindu Kush, and many have died there.

Of course, the punchline is – and you can always spot the punchline in a *Carry On* story – that it was not the Khyber Pass at all. It was the Pass of Llanberis in Wales, which was about the farthest the *Carry On* team ever got from Pinewood Studios. The French Foreign Legion adventure *Carry On . . . Follow that Camel* was shot on location on Camber Sands in Sussex, and Maidenhead Town Hall was regularly used as the films' hospital set.

In the book, *What a Carry On*, Peter Rogers wrote: 'Every film in the series has been shot at Pinewood – on the stages, on the back-lot, in the garden, in the paddock, in the carpark, in the boardroom, in the restaurant, and in the bar.'

The films were enormously successful at the box-office and by the time they got to *Carry on up the Khyber*, they obviously felt they could splash out a little, with a trip across the border to the boulder-strewn pass that runs beneath Mount Snowdon. Llewelyn the Last held his brother, Owen the Red, prisoner here for 23 years. Good names, but not quite as wacky as those in *Carry on up the Khyber*, one of the funniest and most satirical of the series, with the Third Foot and Mouth defending the British residency against the Burpas of the Khazi of Kalabar (Kenneth Williams). In an admirable demonstration of British resolve, Sir Sidney Ruff-Diamond (Sid James) refuses to let the battle disrupt his dinner party, even when the walls start crumbling around him.

Private Widdle (Charles Hawtrey) was the soldier detailed to guard the gate to the Khyber Pass, which looks like a very ordinary farm gate and has a sign on it saying 'Please Shut the Gate'.

Rogers wrote in *What a Carry On* that he was recalled from Wales to meet Princess Margaret, who was visiting the studio. She asked where the director Gerald Thomas was. 'He's up Snowdon,' Rogers supposedly replied. It is clear that an auteur is at work in this film.

THE DRUM (1938)

Although set in India, Zoltan Korda's colonial yarn was filmed on location in the Rhinog mountain area near Harlech, beginning a long cinematic association between Wales and Asia.

The film's star, Sabu, had been a stable boy in Mysore when the director Robert Flaherty discovered him and cast him in *Elephant Boy*, a year before *The Drum*.

In *The Drum* he plays an Indian prince who helps the British army resist an attack by his duplicitous uncle, Ghul (Raymond Massey). Korda used various locations in the rugged countryside of boulders and scree-covered slopes around the Rhinog Fawr mountain. He filmed in the area of the Roman Steps – a strange ascent of flat slabs that has been attributed to the Romans and various other possible builders.

Wilym Hughes, an expert on film-making in Gwynedd, says: 'They say that's why we've got so many wild goats in the area, because they brought their goats and elephants for the film.' The absence of wild Rhinog elephants suggests the film-makers kept tighter control of them.

Sabu went on to star in *The Thief of Bagdad*, which was begun in Britain but ended in Hollywood (see separate entry). And he played an intense Mowgli in Korda's live-action version of *The Jungle Book*, shot in America. He never outgrew juvenile roles and died while still in his thirties.

THE ENGLISHMAN WHO WENT UP A HILL BUT CAME DOWN A MOUNTAIN (1995)

Chris Monger was inspired by local folklore that he had heard as a boy to write this story about English map-makers who, in 1917, declare that one of Wales's mountains does not come up to scratch – it is 15 feet too short – and will be omitted from future maps. The local villagers determine to raise the mountain by their own labours.

'The film uses one of the old Ealing conventions of a community that galvanises together to beat an outsider,' said Monger, who also directed the film. 'The outsiders are two English map-makers (Hugh Grant and Ian McNeice) who visit a village in Wales to declare that its beloved mountain is really just a hill.'

The village was represented by Llanrhaeadr-ym-Mochnant, in Montgomeryshire, and the mountain by the nearby Gyrn Moelfre; though the area is as well known for its waterfalls and its importance to the Welsh language as it is for its mountains. The Pistyll Rhaeadr falls, which drop 240 feet in total, are regarded as one of the Seven Wonders of Wales. And it was at Llanrhaeadr that William Morgan translated the Bible into Welsh in the sixteenth century – the basis for the modern language.

For the film, diggers and bucket-carrying extras built two giant mounds of earth on the Gyrn Moelfre. 'They are fantastic,' Monger told the *Daily Telegraph*, 'They work much better than professional extras. They "method" it and, when they have to react to something, they just go with it.' Monger also shot just along the road at Penybontfawr.

FIRST KNIGHT (1995)

King Arthur was Scottish; Lancelot, American and Camelot, Welsh, in this £50 million version of the story of the knights of the Round Table. Sean Connery played the legendary king, Richard Gere was Lancelot, Julia Ormond was Guinevere and Arthur's ancient stronghold of Camelot was built in the Welsh hills.

Production designer John Box tells how Camelot represented a major location

problem. 'In the script Camelot had to be approached across water, and how the hell do you do that?' Box had to construct a huge set in plaster and plywood – the film required a location that combined scenery, water and means of access. Eventually, the film-makers found what they were looking for at Trawsfynydd Lake, near Ffestiniog in north Wales. 'There's a power station there and the atomic energy boys had built this road across the lake. That was our saviour and we built our set on the other end of it,' says Box.

The building of Camelot employed about eighty joiners and construction workers, and about eight hundred paid extras were taken on in an area where unemployment had been high even before the closure of the nuclear power station a few years earlier. The valley had, in fact, been dammed to supply water to another, non-nuclear power station – the Maentwrog hydro-electric station – creating an enormous reservoir that turned hills into small islands.

The lake and small town of Trawsfynydd probably take their name from an ancient road, for the word means 'that which spans the mountain'. The road south from the town runs in a straight line for about ten miles across the moors towards Dolgellau, parallel to the old Roman road, Sarn Helen.

At the time of filming, the *London Evening Standard* reported dismay in the village when Richard Gere appeared in the Gader Café, ordered tea and then proceeded to drink it while eating cakes he had bought at the baker's down the street. 'If he had been a local, he'd never have got away with it,' one teenager was quoted as saying. But the café manageress was apparently left speechless.

Journalists were banned from locations but that did not stop newspapers reporting that Connery needed step-ladders to get on his horse.

The 1953 Alan Ladd film, *The Red Beret*, shot in the Trawsfynydd area too. The makers of *First Knight* also filmed in the hills around the town of Blaenau Ffestiniog, north of Trawsfynydd, and at other locations in the area. There was further location shooting in England. A thatched village was built on the National Trust's Ashridge Estate in the Chilterns in Hertfordshire, Arthur and Guinevere's wedding was filmed at St Albans Cathedral, which dates back to Norman times, and other scenes were shot at Burnham Beeches and Black Park – two popular locations for film-makers because of their proximity to Pinewood Studios in Buckinghamshire.

THE INN OF THE SIXTH HAPPINESS (1958)

This big-budget feature, starring Ingrid Bergman as missionary Gladys Aylward, was to have been shot on location in China until director Mark Robson fell out with the Nationalist Chinese leader, Chiang Kai-shek, on the question of the film's portrayal of Chinese feet. It was left to a young British production designer to conjure up a walled Chinese city on the hillsides of north Wales. 'We were going to shoot it all in Taiwan,' says John Box, the production designer who went on to win Oscars for *Lawrence of Arabia, Doctor Zhivago, Oliver* and *Nicholas and Alexandra* in the sixties and seventies. 'But there was a confrontation between Chiang Kai-shek and the director. Chiang Kai-shek didn't want any reference to past China, he was trying to build a new China, and "bound feet" upset him.'

It was the Chinese practice to break and bind girls' toes to give them the distinctive teetering walk that Chinese men found attractive.

Box continues: 'Mark Robson said he wasn't changing the script because it was based on fact . . . Chiang Kai-shek would not give way . . . It was down to me – how the hell do you make this bloody movie? I was very young. I was in my late twenties or something and it was a huge film and there was a huge amount of money involved with Ingrid Bergman's salary. I just had a feeling that Wales and Chinese water-colours had an affinity; so I went to Wales and, well, it happened there. '

It did not just happen, a Chinese walled city had to be recreated at Nantmor, at the foot of Cwm Bychan valley, near Beddgelert.

'We built this huge set,' recalls Box. 'We built the outer walls of a Chinese town. What was behind the walls, all the close-up stuff, was done back in the studio. But the Welsh scene was quite something. All the bombers going in and all the rest of it was all done in Wales, quite tricky, a bit old-fashioned now, but still pretty good.'

During the Japanese war, Aylward, a British parlourmaid turned Chinese missionary, led a hundred children to safety across the Yellow River. 'We took Ingrid Bergman all over Snowdonia singing "Nick-nack-paddy-wack, give the dog a bone" and all that,' says Box. *Halliwell's Film Guide* described it as a 'romanticised biopic . . . with lots of children, a happy ending, and everyone sensationally miscast. Somehow it all works'.

Ingrid Bergman in The Inn of the Sixth Happiness *(20th Century-Fox)*

The Inn of the Sixth Happiness *(20th Century-Fox). A Chinese walled city was built on farmland at Nantmor, near Beddgelert in Wales (picture courtesy of British Film Commission)*

The Inn of the Sixth
Happiness *(20th
Century-Fox).
Picture courtesy of
British Film
Commission*

Robert Donat, star of *The 39 Steps* and *Goodbye, Mr Chips*, played the Chinese mandarin. He was very ill during filming and died soon after, adding an extra poignancy to the final words of his screen career: 'We shall not see each other again, I think. Farewell.'

Snowdonia served as the Sino-Soviet border area in *The Most Dangerous Man in the World*, a 1969 spy film with Gregory Peck, while John Box returned to the area in 1982 for *The Keep*, a supernatural Second World War film set in the Carpathian Alps, directed by Michael Mann and starring Scott Glenn and Jurgen Prochnow. The film-makers were denied permission to shoot in Eastern Europe and opted for a combination of Spain, Shepperton and a disused Snowdonian slate quarry.

A KISS BEFORE DYING (1991)

Although set in America, James Dearden's thriller was filmed largely in Britain. The skyline of Philadelphia and a Caribbean honeymoon cabin were constructed at Shepperton Studios, near London, and other key scenes were shot on location in Cardiff.

The film opens with a small boy watching the freight trains of the Carlsson Copper Company. Jonathan Corliss (Matt Dillon) grows up determined to break into the company at the top by marrying Carlsson's daughter, Dorothy (Sean Young). His plans go wrong and he ends up killing her. He subsequently woos and marries her identical twin, Ellen, though she eventually discovers the truth and the film reaches its climax at the Carlsson plant, represented by the Allied Steel and Wire company's Tremorfa steelworks in Cardiff. They are fully operational and not normally open to the public.

There was two weeks of location work in New York, but most of the filming was done in Britain because it was cheaper and the English writer-director, James Dearden, was able to call the shots after the success of his previous thriller *Fatal Attraction*.

ON THE BLACK HILL (1988)

One of the most celebrated films of Welsh landscape, *On the Black Hill* shot in the Black Mountains, the Brecon Beacons and Mynydd Epynt. Based on a novel by Bruce Chatwin, it tells the story of two twins and their farm on the Black Hill of the title over a period of almost one hundred years.

Director Andrew Grieve shot on top of the Black Hill itself, on the edge of the Black Mountains, about fifteen miles west of Hereford and just west of the village of Craswall. But the farm he used was about twenty miles away at Llanfihangel Nant Bran in the Mynydd (Mount) Epynt area.

The farm in the novel and the film is called The Vision and there is a farm near the Black Hill of that name. But, although Chatwin used its name, he had in mind another farm on the Black Hill itself when writing the book. 'It wasn't really big enough for filming purposes,' says Grieve. 'The one that we found had had very little done to it. It had been lived in by a 90-year-old couple, and when their children had put them into an old people's home it was all closed up, but it had been kept up absolutely beautifully in the old way with hedges properly laid and everything, so it was just a wonderful find . . .

'The main town that we used was Hay-on-Wye, with a little bit of Brecon. We filmed

Sean Young and Matt Dillon in A Kiss Before Dying *(Universal/Initial)*

on the Brecon Beacons as well for some of the scenes. So, sometimes, you come out of a farm on the Epynt, straight on to the Brecon Beacons and then finish up in the Black Mountains. It was all a combination of places.'

RESTORATION (1995)

Caerphilly Castle played host to the recreation of the Great Fire of London in Michael Hoffman's costume drama *Restoration*. starring Robert Downey Junior and Meg Ryan. Caerphilly Castle is reckoned to be the second largest castle in Britain, after Windsor – Tennyson believed it was more accurately considered a ruined town than a castle. It is used in *Restoration* as the Cheapside area of seventeenth-century London and the water around it served as the Thames waterfront.

The castle dates back to the thirteenth century, though the Romans had a fort there around AD 75.

Despite its size and brief importance in Welsh history, as various figures struggled for

power, Caerphilly Castle had fallen into decay by the early sixteenth century. The towers were blown up or partially blown up during the Civil War, resulting in the 'Leaning Tower of Caerphilly', which is 80 feet high and leans 13 feet off the perpendicular. Restoration work began on the castle in the nineteenth century; houses were demolished, moats and lakes refilled and the property is now in the care of Welsh Historic Monuments.

The film's title refers to the restoration not of a building, but of the monarchy after Oliver Cromwell's death. Downey plays Robert Merivel, a young doctor who is appointed Royal Physician to the King's Dogs and is required to marry one of the King's mistresses. He is given a title and the Bidnold estate on condition that he does not attempt to consummate his marriage.

For Bidnold exteriors, the film-makers used Forde Abbey and Gardens, near Chard, on the Dorset–Somerset county boundary. It was founded as a Cistercian monastery in 1140 but was converted to a private house in the mid-seventeenth century by Sir Edmund Prideaux, who served as Cromwell's Attorney-General. Its mixture of medieval, Tudor and seventeenth-century architecture is considered striking rather than beautiful, but Merivel is intended as a rather vulgar nouveau riche character with more wealth than taste.

The gardens are open throughout the year and the house in the summer.

The gardens and seventeenth-century fish-ponds of Mapperton House, a Tudor manor house, near Beaminster, Dorset, were also used; while interiors were shot at the seventeenth-century mansion, Brympton d'Evercy, near Yeovil in Somerset. It reputedly has the longest straight staircase and the smallest legal distillery in England, producing Brympton apple brandy. The house at Brympton d'Evercy and the gardens at Mapperton are both open to the public.

Merivel falls from favour with the king and spends some time with a friend who runs a Quaker asylum, for which the film-makers used Tretower Court, another Welsh Historic Monuments property, near Crickhowell. Tretower is remarkable for its completeness, with late medieval buildings grouped around a central courtyard. It was considered suitably austere for the asylum. There is a Norman castle alongside.

UNDER MILK WOOD (1972)

Lower Town, Fishguard, became Dylan Thomas's fishing village of Llareggub in this unusual project, which is essentially a film of a poem, though Dylan Thomas wrote it as a 'play for voices', with the radio in mind. There is no plot, but a wealth of Welsh characters, brought to life in funny and inventive prose by Thomas.

The film was clearly a labour of love for the Welsh actor Richard Burton, who plays one of the narrators. Elizabeth Taylor is Rosie Probert, Peter O'Toole, the blind Captain Cat, and the supporting cast includes Vivien Merchant, Sian Phillips, Victor Spinetti and Ruth Madoc, star of television's *Hi-De-Hi!*

It is generally believed that the village of Llareggub was inspired by Laugharne, a small town on the Taf estuary, where Dylan Thomas lived and where he is now buried. The name Llareggub had quite a different inspiration, which becomes apparent when it is read backwards.

The film-makers opted to shoot in Lower Town, Fishguard, a picturesque little fishing village, on the north coast of Pembrokeshire. They built Captain Cat's home on the quay and used one of the cottages, the Bear's Cave, as the Sailors Arms. The narrators (Burton and Ryan Davies) wander around observing life in the village.

Fishguard itself is a small town set back from the sea. The ferry port, where there are regular sailings to Ireland, is located just over a mile away at Goodwick. The Fishguard area was the scene in 1797 of the last invasion of Britain when three French frigates landed an army of 1,400 convicts under the command of the Irish–American General Tate. Legend has it that the local women gathered to resist them, the convict army mistook their red petticoats for red military uniforms, rebelled and forced Tate to sign an unconditional surrender.

CHAPTER SEVEN
Rob Roy, Hamlet and Other Local Heroes
SCOTLAND

BRAVEHEART (1995)

One day in the summer of 1993, an American tourist walked off the street into the Edinburgh offices of the Scottish Screen Locations agency. He announced his name was Wallace, that he had learned about the Scottish freedom fighter of the same name during a previous holiday in Scotland, that he had written a film script about him and now he wanted advice on locations.

Randall Wallace was a novelist, though none of his novels had made it into print in Britain. In short, no one had ever heard of him. Shortly after that visit to Scotland, Wallace told me: 'I know it may seem as if I'm like some little old lady from Virginia who wants to write a history of an ancestor . . . I assure you that's not the case. I've just come across a story that, to me, is possibly the greatest adventure story in history.'

It was a story set in thirteenth-century Scotland about the son of a small landowner who leads an uprising against the English and drives their armies from his native land. Although Wallace is ultimately defeated and executed, Robert the Bruce, who had previously collaborated with the English, subsequently leads the Scots to victory and independence.

Within a year of Randall Wallace's unscheduled visit to Scottish Screen Locations, his project had begun filming with a budget of over £40 million and Mel Gibson as director and star. But it was Ireland that was ultimately chosen for the bulk of the filming – not only because it could offer tax incentives, studio facilities and suitable castles in convenient locations, but also because it supplied real soldiers for the big battle scenes.

Filming began in June 1994 in Scotland, where the film-makers constructed a medieval village in Glen Nevis, beneath Britain's highest mountain and close to one of the principal locations for *Rob Roy* which arrived just a few weeks later.

There was considerable controversy when it was announced, just prior to production, that most of the shooting would be done in Ireland. Dunsoghly Castle, a modest fifteenth-century tower just outside Dublin, stood in for Edinburgh Castle, possibly the most famous ancient fortress in the British Isles, but it was reckoned that international audiences would never know the difference. The use the film-makers made of Trim Castle was even more audacious. The castle, about 25 miles north-west of Dublin, was used to represent both York and London. 'We just used two sides of the castle,' says production manager Mary Alleguen. 'We did York one side and London the other side.'

Trim dates back to 1173 and is the largest Anglo-Norman castle in Ireland. There are extensive ruins, including a keep 21 metres high and an outer wall incorporating no less

Mel Gibson in Braveheart (20th Century-Fox)

than ten towers, behind a moat. The Earl of Ulster held court here and King Richard II used it to confine his cousins, Humphrey of Gloucester and Henry of Lancaster, later Henry IV.

Braveheart also used Bucktive Abbey, seven miles north-east of Trim, for London scenes. The ruined abbey dated back to 1146, though it was subsequently rebuilt.

The scene of Wallace's greatest triumph, the Battle of Stirling Bridge, was restaged on the Curragh Plains, in County Kildare. With victory, Wallace briefly assumed the modest title of Guardian of Scotland. The Battle of Falkirk, which in reality took place only about ten miles from Stirling and just six months later, was fought not far from the Curragh at Ballymore Eustace.

Wallace's army was defeated, but through his example he had sown the seeds for a more lasting triumph under Robert the Bruce at Bannockburn in 1314.

THE EDGE OF THE WORLD (1937)

The film was inspired by the evacuation in 1930 of the remote islands of St Kilda in the Atlantic Ocean, one hundred miles west of the Scottish mainland. But writer-director Michael Powell was refused permission to film there as St Kilda had been turned into a nature reserve. He went instead to Foula, an island that shared many of the features of St Kilda, including high cliffs and a sense of bleak isolation.

Although Foula is only 16 miles south-west of the mainland of Shetland, there was no airstrip at the time and crossing by boat was uncomfortable and often impossible. The island, which is really the tip of an underwater mountain, is only three miles long and the population has fallen dramatically from over 200 at the beginning of the century to a few dozen spread around scattered crofts. But the fact that there were some inhabitants meant Powell had a ready supply of extras, which he would not have had on St Kilda.

Powell's story centres on two families – the Mansons (John Laurie, Eric Berry as his son and Belle Chrystall, his daughter) and the Grays (father Finlay Currie and son, Niall MacGinnis) – and on the debate over possible abandonment of the island for a potentially easier life elsewhere. Strangely, it is decided that the two young men should have a race up the cliffs and the winner will decide the fate of the island. One dies in the attempt.

Powell filmed along the Kame, the 1,200-foot cliffs on the west side of Foula, recording in his memoirs how he had Eric Berry sprawled on the tip of a waterfall where the Hoevidi Burn plunges into the sea. 'It occurred to me that I might be taking advantage of his amiable nature,' Powell wrote in *A Life in Movies*. He also wrote a book specifically on the film called *200,000 Feet on Foula*, reissued under the title *Edge of the World*.

Powell met Emeric Pressburger soon after filming *The Edge of the World* and they went on to make such classics as *The Life and Death of Colonel Blimp* and *The Red Shoes* together.

GREGORY'S GIRL (1981)

Just when Gregory's school football team is at its lowest ebb, it discovers a new star in Dorothy (Dee Hepburn), but then Hepburn has had the benefit of training with Partick Thistle and their international goalkeeper, Alan Rough.

Gregory's Girl was Bill Forsyth's second film, after the success of *That Sinking Feeling*, which is recorded in the *Guinness Book of Movie Facts and Feats* as the cheapest British feature film to get an international release. *That Sinking Feeling* cost £6,000 and most of the actors came from Glasgow Youth Theatre.

Gregory's Girl was shot on location – not in Glasgow, but in Cumbernauld, a new town established in the fifties, 14 miles outside Glasgow. The gawky youth of the title was played by John Gordon Sinclair, or Gordon John Sinclair as he styled himself at the time. He strikes up an awkward relationship with Dorothy in the school football team. The school in question was Abronhill High School and much of the filming took place in the Abronhill area.

Cumbernauld is divided into a number of self-contained districts, dissected by the new town's main roads, which, in theory, keep cars and pedestrians well apart, though Gregory's route to school subverts the intentions of the town planners and brings him into rare contact with his driving instructor father.

Most of Cumbernauld's early population relocated from Glasgow and the big clock in the modern indoor town centre, where Gregory arranges to meet Dorothy for a date, was the 100-year-old clock from St Enoch's Station in Glasgow. 'It was one of the most difficult scenes to get right because they didn't like us stopping that clock,' says Paddy Higson, production supervisor on the film.

They had further problems on the final scenes, as several girls have a sort of mini-date with Gregory before passing him on, leading to the famous 'horizontal dancing' sequence with Sinclair and Clare Grogan dancing while lying down. 'Everywhere we set up, another ice-cream van started up and made life extremely difficult for us,' says Higson.

Forsyth was to make ice-cream an integral part of the plot a few years later in *Comfort and Joy*.

GREYSTOKE – The Legend of Tarzan, Lord of the Apes (1984)

For Tarzan's ancestral residence, the film-makers chose one of the finest homes in Scotland, Floors Castle, near Kelso in the border country. A couple of years after romance had blossomed here between Tarzan and Jane, Prince Andrew would propose to Sarah Ferguson in the very same chambers.

Much of the filming for *Greystoke* was done in Cameroon (and at Elstree Studios); but Tarzan (Christopher Lambert) returns to Britain for a while to live with his grandfather, the Earl of Greystoke, and the earl's ward, Jane Porter, before eventually returning to the jungle alone. Lord Greystoke was played by Ralph Richardson – in his final film – and Jane by Andie MacDowell, though such was the dissatisfaction with her that her voice was dubbed by Glenn Close.

There is a place called Greystoke, near Penrith, in the Lake District. Lord Howard of Penrith suggested to the writer, Edgar Rice Burroughs, that he could use the Greystoke heritage as Tarzan's family background. But when it came to filming, Lord Howard's granddaughter, Joanie Richards, said: 'Our little castle wasn't grand enough for them.'

Floors Castle, on the other hand, is reputedly the largest occupied stately home in Britain, with a total of 365 windows. It was built in the eighteenth century as the seat of the Duke of Roxburghe, though it was extended by William Playfair early in the nineteenth. Although still the residence of the duke, Floors does open to the public. A long, imposing structure, it is set in its own extensive grounds, overlooking the River Tweed.

It was here that King James II of Scotland was killed when a cannon exploded in 1460. Although he was besieging Roxburgh, which had been in English hands for a century, he apparently ordered that the cannon be fired, not in an assault, but to mark the arrival of his queen with a royal salute. So, all in all, Floors has not been a very lucky setting for love matches.

As well as exterior shots, Floors was the location in the film for a grand ball and its staircase figured prominently. The Earl of Greystoke is fatally injured sliding down the stairs on a tea-tray.

Some interiors were done at Hatfield House, near London. The Natural History Museum in London appears as itself in the film; Tarzan finds his adoptive ape father, Silverbeard, and accompanies him into Kensington Gardens, near the Albert Memorial, where the ape is shot dead and Tarzan determines to return to the simpler life of the African jungle.

HAMLET (1990)

Castles from all over Europe were considered for the Franco Zeffirelli/Mel Gibson version of Shakespeare's great tragedy before the film-makers settled on Dunnottar and Blackness in Scotland, along with Dover Castle in Kent, to represent Hamlet's castle, Elsinore.

At this point I should declare an interest in the choice of Dunnottar – an extensive medieval ruin on cliffs 160 feet above the North Sea, about fifteen miles south of Aberdeen. In May 1989, I suggested Dunnottar in an article in *The Scotsman*. On a flying visit to Scotland four months later, Zeffirelli told me: 'I have not seen anything like it in the world. Now that I have seen it, I am falling in love with it. The whole place is quite extraordinary. There are rocks you have never seen and there is not one tree, not even a bush. It looks like something from another planet.'

Dunnottar is surrounded on three sides by sea and on the fourth by a deep natural cleft. Zeffirelli had already considered the real Elsinore, Kronborg Castle in Denmark, but felt it lacked the menace he wanted. 'It must be a castle where you get familiar with the idea of a tragedy, something rotten in Denmark. There has been a murder and there is the ghost of his father. It just cannot be pleasant at all.'

Dunnottar has a long history of violence and bloodshed. There had been a Pictish fort there in the Dark Ages, replaced by a primitive castle in the thirteenth century. William Wallace stormed the English garrison in 1297, burned the church down but failed to take the castle. It was greatly extended by the time the Earl Marischal withstood the Marquis of Montrose's siege in 1645. During Cromwell's Civil War, the Scottish crown jewels were taken to the castle for safety and the governor held out against attackers until the crown jewels had been smuggled away. In 1685, 167 Covenanters were imprisoned at Dunnottar, many of them in a vault with one window overlooking the sea. Many died there.

Zeffirelli had an artificial façade added to the castle ruins when he returned to Dunnottar the following year. Dunnottar is used when Elsinore appears in long shots or in the background behind Hamlet.

Dover Castle is located on a hill within the busy port of Dover itself and was used for closer shots. The artificial façade that was added to Dunnottar was modelled on the battlements at Dover – another castle with a long and bloody history. The keep was built by Henry II in the twelfth century – with walls up to twenty-two feet thick – and in 1216 the castle just managed to hold out against French attack. During the Second World War the evacuation from Dunkirk was planned in Dover Castle. Dating from the first century, the Pharos, the only surviving ancient Roman lighthouse in the world, is situated within the grounds.

Blackness is a much more modest castle built on a headland about twenty miles west of Edinburgh in West Lothian. A cold, inhospitable place, with a peculiarly uneven and rocky courtyard, Blackness was built in the fifteenth century and for many years was used as a prison. Zeffirelli filmed inside the castle, using the courtyard and several rooms – although most of the film's interiors were shot at Shepperton Studios in Middlesex.

To give the three locations the same dark and weathered look, the film-makers mixed tons of coal dust with water and sprayed it over them. All three castles are open to the public.

There were many doubters when Zeffirelli announced a new adaptation of Shakespeare's play with Mel Gibson – a man best known for the *Mad Max* and *Lethal Weapon* action films – as the ill-fated Prince of Denmark. But the film got excellent reviews and some now regard it as one of the best film adaptations of Shakespeare's work, ranking alongside Olivier and Branagh.

Lunch on a film location often consists of coffee and sandwiches, but over oysters and steak *au poivre* in an impressive little restaurant in the town of Stonehaven, near Dunnottar, Zeffirelli said: 'Whenever I have tacky material, I am not good at that. I must have great situations, great characters, great texts and then I bring out my best work.'

For Zeffirelli, that first visit to Scotland the previous year was an emotional affair, for as a young man he had served alongside Scottish soldiers in his native Italy during the Second World War. He was fighting with the partisans when he ran straight into a detachment of what he thought were English soldiers. He asked if they were English and they indicated in no uncertain terms that they were not. Zeffirelli thought he was about to die. Long seconds passed before they told him: 'We're not ✳✳✳✳✳✳ English, Jimmy. We're ✳✳✳✳✳✳ Scottish.' 'It was a nasty trick,' said Zeffirelli. 'They were the longest five seconds of my life.' Nevertheless, he never forgot that there is a difference between the English and the Scots.

HEAVENLY PURSUITS (1986)

This is the film in which the Pope moved to Glasgow, with the city chambers standing in for the Vatican and the Clydesdale Bank head office in St Vincent Street representing the Vatican Bank. Tom Conti plays remedial teacher, Vic Mathews, in this gentle comedy co-starring Helen Mirren and made entirely on location in Glasgow.

Vic has been achieving small miracles with his pupils at the Blessed Edith Semple School, but he is rushed off to hospital after collapsing, and X-rays reveal an incurable brain cancer. Meanwhile, the authorities' main concern is seeking canonisation for Edith

Mel Gibson at Dunnottar Castle, near Aberdeen, in Hamlet *(Marquis)*

Semple, who has one authenticated miracle to her name. They send Father Cobb to the Vatican/city chambers. Cobb is played by Brian Pettifer, who would subsequently put some distance between himself and the Holy Spirit by becoming one of Rab C. Nesbitt's sidekicks.

The Blessed Edith Semple School was a combination of two Glasgow schools. Most of the shooting was done at the old Queen's Park Secondary between Grange Road and Prospecthill Road. It was no longer functioning as a school and was used for both interiors and exteriors, though some exteriors were done at Notre Dame Primary in Victoria Crescent. It was at Notre Dame Primary that Vic made his spectacular rooftop leap to save a pupil and wound up in hospital for a second time, at which point it is revealed that the incurable cancer has miraculously cleared up. The hospital used was Glasgow's Western Infirmary.

Other locations were the exterior of St Mungo's Church, Townhead; the interior of St Alphonsus', London Road; the Mitre Bar, Brunswick Street,; the *Herald* building in Albion Street; and Queen Street Station. Vic's flat was in Bentinck Street.

HIGHLANDER (1986)

The castle at the heart of the film *Highlander* says it all. Eilean Donan (pronounced ale-ann donn-ann) is one of Scotland's most dramatic and one of Britain's most photographed.

A plain, high-walled castle, it occupies a little island in Loch Duich – linked to the mainland by a causeway – beneath the heights of the West Highlands. It is a dreamy, misty, romantic vision of what a medieval castle should look like. And yet the present castle was built less than one hundred years ago, albeit on the ruins of earlier fortifications. It is history as illusion, like the film itself.

Highlander opens in modern New York where Conner MacLeod (Christopher Lambert) is confronted by a mysterious swordsman, whom he decapitates in the ensuing duel in the carpark of Madison Square Garden. A metallurgist discovers that fragments of the swords are hundreds of years old. Flashbacks to the Scottish Highlands 400 years ago reveal that MacLeod is one of a race of people who are virtually immortal. They can only kill each other, but ultimately only one can survive.

Loud, flashy, violent and intellectually empty, the film was panned by the critics at the time. It is undeniably rubbish, but as rubbish goes it is excellent. It works on its own terms, a hotch-potch of ideas. Hero and villain battle through the centuries in a high-energy amalgam of swashbuckler and urban thriller. It ruthlessly mixes genres, which is something critics rarely like. *Highlander* is in many ways the perfect representation of video-age cinema, with no respect for history, using only those details that suit it and making up the rest. Well, after all, it is about people who are immortal. Central to the mix of reality and fantasy is the image of the proud, fierce, kilted Highlander and the vision of Eilean Donan, from which we see Conner MacLeod and his clansmen set out for battle over the causeway in 1536.

There has been a fort at Eilean Donan in Wester Ross since the mists of time. A castle was built in 1230 and held by the MacRaes as constables for the MacKenzie Earls of Seaforth. In 1719 it was garrisoned by Spanish troops who came to fight for the Jacobite cause Bonnie Prince Charlie would spearhead 26 years later. The castle was reduced to a pile of stone by English guns and remained a ruin until 1912 when restoration began, using plans of the original medieval castle. It took 20 years and cost a quarter of a million pounds. Eilean Donan is now owned by a charity and opens to the public. Timbered roofs support iron chandeliers, and bare stone walls contrast with the opulence of Chippendale and Sheraton furniture.

Far from Eilean Donan, beneath dark foreboding skies, the MacLeods meet their enemies in Glen Coe, the wild glen where, in February 1692, the MacDonalds extended hospitality to Government soldiers under the command of Captain Robert Campbell, and in return were murdered in their beds for being late in swearing an oath of allegiance to King William in London. The two countries had come under a single monarch since James VI of Scotland became James I of England in 1603. Glen Coe is a cold desolate place, where hillwalkers are often lost and frequently perish in the mist and snow. It is easy to imagine the ghosts of past ages still wandering the bare hillsides.

For the battlefield, the film-makers used a site just off the A82, which runs through the glen. Heading east from Glencoe Village and past the area known as 'The Study', the battle scenes were shot beside the large lay-by (with the AA phone box) on the right-hand side of the road. MacLeod is seemingly mortally wounded and when he recovers he is driven out of his village – referred to in the film as Glenfinnan, though Glenfinnan is really well to the south of Eilean Donan. Eilean Donan is referred to in the script as Glamis Castle, which is near Dundee, well over one hundred miles away.

MacLeod is next seen living in a keep, constructed by the film-makers at The Study in Glen Coe. The mountaineer Hamish MacInnes, who lives in the area and worked on the film, says: 'It gets its name from a place where Queen Victoria stopped and admired the view, and she said "What a study". There's also another interpretation that it's derived from the Gaelic meaning the anvil. So you can take your pick.'

MacLeod acquires a wife, Heather (Beatie Edney), and a mentor, Ramirez (Sean Connery), who trains him for immortality amid some of the best scenery in Britain. MacLeod goes swimming in Loch Shiel, at Glenfinnan, and running on an expanse of deserted beach at Refuge Bay at Cuartaig, Morar, very close to the location used by Bill Forsyth in *Local Hero*. Training in swordsmanship takes him all over the place, from Mossy Wood at Arisaig, near Morar, to dizzying precipices in Glen Coe, from Glen Nevis to the island of Skye. MacInnes says: 'On *Highlander*, I got that very spectacular photograph of the sword-fight on top of the Cioch, the pinnacle on Skye . . . There were doubles doing it for Connery and Lambert.'

Cioch is a Gaelic word for a woman's breast, which the rock is thought to resemble. While they are at a market, Ramirez advises MacLeod to avoid heartache by leaving Heather, a scene shot in Glen Nevis, near the youth hostel. The script called it Jedburgh Market, though Jedburgh is in the Borders.

There is a powerful scene where Heather comes towards MacLeod and the viewer realises she has aged while MacLeod remains the same. And there is the added poignancy of hearing the late Freddie Mercury sing: 'Who wants to live forever?'

Sean Connery and Christopher Lambert in Highlander *(EMI/Highlander)*

Highlander is rubbish, but it is truly compelling rubbish and rarely, if ever, has a film used Scottish scenery so effectively. *Highlander II* was shot in Argentina, but *Highlander III* shot partly in Scotland, including Glen Coe, Glen Nevis and Ardnamurchan.

I KNOW WHERE I'M GOING (1945)

Michael Powell searched the coasts of England and Wales, considering and rejecting Bardsey Island, Holy Island and the Farne Islands, before finally looking in Scotland for a location for Emeric Pressburger's tale about a headstrong young woman who is on her way to marry a rich industrialist only to be stopped by bad weather within sight of the island where he is staying and where the wedding is due to take place.

Powell found what he was looking for on Colonsay and Mull, which was to be the principal location where Joan Webster's (Wendy Hiller) journey comes to a premature halt. She is taken in by Catriona Potts (Pamela Brown) and stays at her house, Erraig, which in reality is Carsaig House, a private house in a village of the same name on the southern coast of Mull. Joan is befriended by the local laird, Torquil MacNeil, but is determined to resist her feelings for him and continue with her marriage plans.

Torquil MacNeil was to have been played by James Mason, but according to the account in Michael Powell's book, *A Life in Movies*, Mason did not like Powell's idea of using Carsaig not only as a location but as the film unit's base, enabling them to work from dawn to dusk. According to Powell, Mason demanded first-class accommodation, as per contract, and was replaced by Roger Livesey, though in the end Livesey never went near Mull at all. He was appearing in a play in London and although Powell spent six weeks on Mull, all the location scenes of Torquil were done in long-shot with a double, intercut with studio close-ups of Livesey.

Torquil shows Joan Moy Castle, which is a few miles from Carsaig at Lochbuie. He explains that an ancient curse prevents him from entering the ruins.

Joan moves out of Erraig and joins the Robinson family in the castle they have rented, Sorne in the film, Torosay in reality. A Victorian castle in the Scottish baronial style, it and its 12 acres of Italian terraced gardens are open to the public. A narrow-gauge steam railway runs from Torosay to the ferry terminal at Craignure about a mile and a quarter away. An enjoyable journey at little more than walking pace, it takes in views of sea and mountains, woodland and rhododendrons.

Joan accompanies the Robinsons to a party at Achnacroish, for which Powell used Duart Castle, just beyond Torosay, a much older castle dominating the Sound of Mull. Like Moy Castle, it is an ancient Clan MacLean stronghold. Although it was in ruins for a long time, it was restored in the early twentieth century and is open to the public in summer.

The interior of Duart was reconstructed at Denham Studios near London, but was reputedly so convincing that it fooled even the castle owner who thought he was being done out of a fee.

At Achnacroish Joan meets Torquil once more and, such are her feelings, she determines to attempt to cross to the island of Kiloran whatever the dangers. The island of Kiloran was really the island of Colonsay, 15 miles south of Carsaig. Powell had determined to use the Corrievrechan whirlpool, which lies between the islands of Scarba and Jura and would have involved Joan and Torquil, who is accompanying her, in a considerable diversion, but most viewers would not know that.

Their boat is sucked towards the whirlpool, but Torquil's calm nerve saves the day. In a wonderfully symbolic moment Joan's wedding dress is lost overboard and swept away. They manage to get back to Mull rather than Kiloran. The following day the weather is fine and Joan can cross safely. She kisses Torquil goodbye before finally admitting her love and deciding her future lies with him.

LOCAL HERO (1983)

Some people play Mark Knopfler's wistful soundtrack recording as they drive into the village, some make straight for the famous phone box, some arrive in tears – such is the power of Bill Forsyth's evocation of the simple life in *Local Hero*, though the idyllic setting was actually a combination of two places on opposite sides of Scotland.

Scenes of Ferness village were shot in the tiny Aberdeenshire village of Pennan – a few dozen whitewashed houses clinging to a narrow strip of land between cliffs and sea. The wide open beach scenes were shot on the other side of the country at Camusdarrach in Morar.

Thousands of visitors come from all over the world each summer to be captivated by the locations, just as oil executives MacIntyre (Peter Riegert) and Happer (Burt Lancaster) were captivated.

Happer is head of an oil company that wants to buy Ferness Bay for a refinery. He is also a keen amateur astronomer and MacIntyre uses the village phone not only to keep him informed of negotiations to buy the village but also to report on the night sky, including an eye-witness account of the aurora borealis. When Happer sees Ferness he is so charmed by it that he drops the refinery plans and decides to build an observatory instead.

Forsyth was inspired by *Whisky Galore!* to create a contemporary story of life in an isolated Scottish village, building stereotypes only to undermine them with his off-kilter sense of humour: the tranquil Highland setting shattered by a low-flying jet, the meal at the hotel turning out to be the rabbit that the visitors rescued during their drive. The film is quirky and unpredictable, but essentially eco-friendly and certainly very friendly to the tourist industries of those areas involved. 'We've a visitors' book in the bar here and I don't think there's a country that isn't represented,' says Norrie Grierson, owner of the Pennan Inn. 'It's a very, very busy place in the summer months.'

The most popular attraction of all is the village phone box which plays such a key role in the film. Ultimately, Happer stays on in Ferness and sends MacIntyre back to America with his revised plans. In the penultimate scene we see MacIntyre, who really has no Scottish blood and was reluctant to go to Scotland, back home in America but looking very disconsolate.

The final scene is simply a shot of Ferness with the phone box in the foreground and the phone ringing out unanswered. Grierson says: 'We've had a lot of phone calls from all over the world to the box at various times, just people who have watched the movie. They're just asking "Is that *Local Hero* village? How are things in Ferness?"'

Roger Livesey, Finlay Currie and Murdo Morrison silhouetted against Carsaig Bay, Mull, in I Know Where I'm Going *(The Archers)*

While other red metal phone boxes have been replaced by newer models, there is a preservation order on the Pennan one. It takes a fair battering from the elements because it is down at the seafront and BT paint it every year using paints developed for the North Sea oil industry.

Location manager David Brown says: 'I think there's a bit of mythology there now . . . There was a public phone box in Pennan, which was on the shoreline, but it was round by one of the sheds. It was in a really bad, unphotographic place, so a prop one was constructed and put on the pier. Otherwise it wouldn't have looked so pretty.' Grierson explains: 'It's virtually on the same situation. If they ask us we'll tell them, but if they don't ask, we just let them go away blissfully ignorant.'

The location of the phone box was the least of the film-makers' worries. They spent months looking for a single seaside village location, with a harbour and beach, and their first choice was on the Outer Hebridean island of Lewis – but it was 32 miles from Stornoway and was considered just too difficult for financial and logistical reasons. Eventually, they settled on the combination of Pennan and Morar, even though the choice presented problems of its own in terms of moving equipment and people, and in terms of continuity – making sure that there was nothing in shot that would betray the fact that Ferness was really two different places.

Pennan, Aberdeenshire,
which appeared as the
village of Ferness in
Local Hero

So it was on the west coast that Ben Knox (Fulton Mackay), the one man who refuses to sell out his interests to the oil company, had his tumble-down beach house. David

Brown says: 'It's south of Morar . . . The beaches there roll together. There's about six or seven in a row.' Ben Knox's beach is the one with the cottage at the north end, which doubled, in the film, as the church with the black minister. The film-makers simply adapted it to look like a church. Associate producer Iain Smith says: 'The real church is on the road to Arisaig, the road to the isles. We replicated the exterior of that church on the Camusdarrach Beach. Many people were amazed when they walked by, saying "I can never remember seeing that church before."' For interiors, the film-makers used the real thing, Our Lady of the Braes R. C. Church at Polnish. The church was in regular use at the time of the film, but is now empty.

Brown recalls that it was between the two main locations that MacIntyre and his assistant, Danny (Peter Capaldi), rescue the rabbit they have stunned with their car and which will ultimately end up on their dinner plate. 'Some of the road work was shot around Fort Augustus,' he says. 'It's the B862, which goes on the south side of Loch Ness.'

The actors stayed at the Pennan Inn, but the hotel in the film consisted of a couple of houses in the village, with a sign added. Interiors of the hotel were shot at the Lochailort Inn at Lochailort, near Morar. The village shop was the shop at Pole of Itlaw, Banffshire, where filming is commemorated by a small plaque, and the village hall, where the ceilidh takes place, was at Hilton a few miles away.

Although the film turned out to be a great critical, commercial and tourist success, the film-making proved difficult with arguments over access in both main locations. Brown says: 'There were days when I would get down on my knees and beg for the keys to a location which we'd already paid a lot of money for . . . Pennan was a very difficult village in terms of a very small community, tightly-knit, with a lot of disparate ideas about the way things should be, and everyone knowing everybody else's business.' Just like in the film? 'Exactly.'

LOCH NESS (1995)
THE PRIVATE LIFE OF SHERLOCK HOLMES (1970)

Actor Ted Danson and director John Henderson shot their story about an American scientist in search of the monster on location on Loch Ness itself. But they did decide to throw in a few extra ingredients to improve Scotland's most famous loch, quite apart from Nessie.

They wanted a picturesque lochside village with a pier and so they intercut footage from Loch Torridon with that of Loch Ness. And the ruins of Urquhart Castle were not thought dramatic enough, so they inserted shots of Eilean Donan, the dramatic west-coast castle that featured in *Highlander*. 'The majority of filming was actually on Loch Ness itself,' says location manager Mark Mostyn. 'But we needed a very attractive pier and a little bay, which you don't get on Loch Ness, and we found it at Lower Diabaig at Loch Torridon – so obviously there's a bit of artistic licence there.'

The exteriors of Joely Richardson's little hotel were shot at Lower Diabaig, a little village about fifty miles north-west of Loch Ness in what is undoubtedly one of the most scenically spectacular areas of Scotland, where wild mountains tower over deep sea lochs.

Loch Ness is an inland loch in the Great Glen, just south of the Highland capital of

Inverness. One mile wide, 23 miles long and over 350 fathoms deep, there is sufficient water there to accommodate several giant prehistoric beasties. The first recorded sighting of the monster is in a seventh-century biography of St Columba, and it is now the area's biggest tourist attraction. There is a permanent Nessie exhibition at Drumnadrochit on the west bank.

The film-makers also shot in the villages of Dores, Foyers and Fort Augustus on Loch Ness; at the Natural History Museum in London and elsewhere in the English capital; at Pinewood Studios and in the United States.

Writer John Fusco had to wait more than ten years to see his script go into production, but latterly it was only one of several Loch Ness scripts doing the rounds, including one by John Sayles, with interest intensifying after *Jurassic Park*.

The legendary American director Billy Wilder had filmed at Loch Ness a quarter of a century earlier on *The Private Life of Sherlock Holmes*, an atypical and unfairly neglected tale of the detective's rather poignant love life and of international espionage involving the Loch Ness Monster. Robert Stephens plays Sherlock and Christopher Lee is his smarter brother, Mycroft. Much of the action takes place around the ruins of the sixteenth-century Urquhart Castle. Once the largest castle in Scotland, it was blown up in 1691 to prevent its use by the Jacobites. The promontory, on which it is located, has been the location of many Nessie sightings.

MARY REILLY (1995)

Every summer thousands of tourists from all over the world pack the pavements of Edinburgh's Royal Mile and spend leisurely hours admiring and photographing churches, public buildings and the towering, tightly-packed tenements of Edinburgh's Royal Mile. Yet, even at the height of the tourist season it is possible to venture off the main thoroughfare opposite the Scandic Crown Hotel, into Carrubber's Close – the alley that runs from the Royal Mile down to Jeffrey Street – and never meet a soul.

They call alleys 'closes' in Edinburgh and there are dozens of these stone canyons branching off from the Royal Mile like thin fish bones from the central spine.

By the middle of the nineteenth century, when Hans Christian Andersen visited the city, the gentry of the capital had moved from the Royal Mile to Edinburgh's elegant New Town about half a mile away, leaving the poor in the overcrowded slums of the Old. Andersen observed: 'Many side streets are narrow, filthy and with six-storey houses . . . Poverty and misery seems to peep out of the open hatches which normally serve as windows.'

Some closes have been closed off or fallen victim to redevelopment. Other tenements have been modernised and provide central accommodation for young professionals. Flats that once had families of 12 and no running water now have all mod cons and a single occupant.

Tourists may be wary of leaving the safety of numbers in the Royal Mile to enter these side-routes. They were certainly a hotbed of prostitution and crime in the nineteenth century, but are quite safe now, at least during the day, even if some do retain a certain claustrophobic sinister quality.

Carrubber's Close remains a rather grim example, with stone tenements on one side and the unprepossessing blackened back of the Carlton Highland Hotel on the other. But it was just the sort of shady setting that the makers of *Mary Reilly* wanted for one of the few location scenes in their big-budget reinterpretation of the famous story of *Dr Jekyll and Mr Hyde*, retold from the point of view of Jekyll's maid, who was to be played by Julia Roberts in exchange for a reported world-record fee of $10 million.

Most of the filming was done at Pinewood Studios where joiners elaborately recreated the tenements, closes and cobbled streets of Victorian Edinburgh on four stages. The director, Stephen Frears, who made *My Beautiful Laundrette* and *Dangerous Liaisons*, felt Edinburgh was a much more dramatic setting than London would have been. Iain Smith, the film's Glaswegian co-producer, said: 'The look of the picture is very much derived from the "verticality" of Edinburgh.' But the film-makers were still determined to do some location shooting in Edinburgh and the arrival of the world's highest-paid actress provoked considerable excitement in the city.

While you may find Carrubber's Close completely empty today, it was buzzing with actors, extras, technicians and security men on 22 June 1994 and awash with 1,000 gallons of blood – made from dyed water thickened with golden syrup. Several hundred onlookers turned up during the day to try and catch a glimpse of the stars, but a black sheet was hung from the archway over the entrance at the foot of the close, preventing the crowd from seeing anything of the filming. Police and private security men stood sentry on the entrances, though the public got some idea of the excitement beyond the screen from the steady trickle of blood running beneath it and into the gutter.

Carrubber's Close had become Slaughterhouse Street, site of the city abattoir, to which Jekyll had gone to get transplant material for his sinister experiments. John Malkovich, the star of *Empire of the Sun, The Sheltering Sky* and *In the Line of Fire*, played Jekyll. And he may have been walking in the very footsteps of Deacon Brodie, who led a double life and inspired Robert Louis Stevenson to write his Gothic tale of dual personality. Brodie was a respected town councillor by day and a daring burglar by night. After a failed attempt to rob the General Excise Office in Chessel's Court, a few minutes' walk from Carrubber's Close, Brodie was hanged on a gallows of his own design in 1788.

Almost one hundred years after Brodie's execution, Stevenson wrote a play about him and subsequently used him as the inspiration for *The Strange Case of Dr Jekyll and Mr Hyde*, in which Jekyll carries out experiments on himself to separate the good and evil aspects of his personality. The latter, personified as Mr Hyde, increasingly takes control and embarks on a series of crimes, including murder.

It has often been filmed before, though frequently set elsewhere. Film-makers were often attracted by the theme, but played fast and loose with the story. There was even a film called *Dr Jekyll and Sister Hyde* in the seventies. *Mary Reilly* was not based directly on Stevenson's story, but on a novel by Valerie Martin which shifted the focus to Jekyll's maid, who comes to realise the awful truth about her handsome master.

Roberts and Malkovich showed the two faces of film stardom during their visit to Edinburgh. Malkovich seemed happy to hang around in flowing black wig and period costume and even cracked jokes about the Scottish weather. He thought Edinburgh very pretty. 'It's like a cross between Copenhagen and Barcelona,' he said, 'except in Copenhagen they speak more understandable English.' Roberts spent most of her time hidden away in her luxury trailer parked in Jeffrey Street. She had food sent in, while Malkovich ate with the crew in a church hall at the bottom of the close. The hall was that of Old St Paul's Episcopal Church which had a strongly Jacobite congregation and some of whose members were associates of Bonnie Prince Charlie some 40 years before Deacon Brodie was stalking the closes.

Roberts had had a reputation for being difficult since crew on Steven Spielberg's *Peter Pan* film *Hook* nicknamed her Tinkerhell three years earlier. She was no more than a flurry of long skirt, as her minders whisked her between the trailer and Carrubber's Close. She had a jacket over her head and was further obscured by a shield of umbrellas – like some shameful criminal coming out of court.

The public was able to catch a glimpse of her at a subsequent location, in Calton Road under the towering arch of Regent Bridge. Just beside the back entrance to Waverley railway station, the road had been covered with dirt and Roberts was filmed in a horse-drawn carriage. Iain Smith said she had very high standards and liked to keep her mind very much on the job. 'It's not that she's being difficult,' he said. 'She just creates a state of mind for her part and we don't want to disturb that.'

At one point, however, she did send out autographs for distribution among extras, and invited one local teenager into her trailer when told it was her sixteenth birthday. 'It was such a privilege,' said Claire Wilkie later. 'I watch her films and I wanted to see her on the set, but I got a lot closer. I can't think of words to express it. I will never forget it.'

The night before the Carrubber's Close scene, Roberts even stopped off in a local pub, the St Vincent Bar in St Vincent Street in the New Town. She had been checking another location, the nearby St Stephen's Centre, which was to play a hospital in the film. Her minders reccied the joint before she decided to take the plunge and have a quick Highland Park malt whisky, though she had earlier balked at the thought of haggis, and passed on to Iain Smith the haggis that one Scottish journalist had given her. 'I'd sooner starve,' she said at the press conference at the start of filming at Pinewood.

Smith insisted that away from the pressures of public and press, she was 'one of the family'.

MONTY PYTHON AND THE HOLY GRAIL (1975)

Quite apart from the quality of jokes on offer, Monty Python's comic take on King Arthur and the Knights of the Round Table was widely praised for its realistic recreation of the look of medieval England – even though it was shot in Scotland.

Arthur is one of the most English of legends. It seems ironic that he should be relocated in Scotland on film. But there again, considering it is a Monty Python film, it becomes curiously apt. In any case, there have been suggestions in the past that Arthur was, in fact, Scottish – Edinburgh's best-known hill is called Arthur's Seat.

The Pythons have Arthur and his knights tour various Scottish historical sights in their holy quest to find Christ's drinking-vessel, beginning near Stirling at Doune Castle. Built for the powerful Duke of Albany 600 years ago, it is now owned by Historic

Scotland and is one of the best preserved medieval castles in the country.

King Arthur (Graham Chapman) presents himself at Doune, along with a servant whose job it is to bang two half coconut shells together to simulate the sound of horses' hooves. The guards question how he got coconut shells in Mercia and Arthur suggests they were carried by migrating swallows.

The Pythons also filmed at nearby Sheriffmuir, a hill where Jacobites fought government troops under the command of the Duke of Argyll in 1715; at Arnhall Castle, Killin and Bracklinn Falls in Perthshire; and in Glen Coe, scene in 1692 of the famous massacre, where MacDonalds were slaughtered by government soldiers from the Earl of Argyll's regiment. (The earl was subsequently promoted to duke.)

Glen Coe is specified in the script, which was written by the whole Python team. 'The knights emerge from the mouth of the cave to find themselves in a breathtaking, barren landscape. Glencoe. They are half the way up the side of a mountain.'

It is at the Meeting of the Three Waters in Glen Coe that they come to the Bridge of Death across a deep gorge. The knights must answer three questions correctly before crossing, otherwise they are plunged to their death. Lancelot (John Cleese) gets asked his name, quest and favourite colour, but Robin (Eric Idle) is asked his name, quest and the capital of Assyria, and Arthur gets involved in a discussion on the air speed velocity of an unladen swallow.

Eventually, the knights believe they have reached the castle that holds the grail – in reality Castle Stalker, a bleak fortress on a small island about 25 miles north of Oban. It changed hands between the Stewarts and the Campbells (Argyll's lot) and was garrisoned by Government troops after the final defeat of the Jacobites at Culloden. It is now privately owned, but visitors can see it by appointment, with a boat laid on.

Sadly, King Arthur never gets to see the inside, for the police arrive just at the climactic moment and arrest him and all the remaining knights, and force the curtailment of the film.

THE PRIME OF MISS JEAN BRODIE (1969)

Maggie Smith won an Oscar for her performance as the monstrous Miss Jean Brodie, the Edinburgh schoolmistress who imposes not only her passion for art, but also her misguided political views on her pupils, particularly her special girls: the 'crème de la crème'. There were other excellent performances from Celia Johnson as the headmistress, Gordon Jackson and Robert Stephens as the fellow teachers Miss Brodie takes to bed, and Pamela Franklin and Jane Carr as two of her protégées.

But the city of Edinburgh is an important character itself, both in the film and in the short novel by Muriel Spark on which it was based. *The Prime of Miss Jean Brodie* is one of those films which perfectly capture the spirit of their setting, which in this case was douce, middle-class Edinburgh in the thirties – though some of the attitudes survived for many years after that and still linger amid the fur coats of Marchmont and Morningside.

Jean Brodie lives in a Calvinist society and teaches in a traditional school, but sees herself as a beacon of culture and sophistication in a fog of narrow-minded mediocrity. She champions Italy, Giotto and Mussolini, but dismisses Catholicism. All the while, Miss

Brodie remains as much of an Edinburgh snob in her own way as anyone else on the staff of the Marcia Blaine School for Girls.

Spark herself was born in Edinburgh in 1918 and was educated at James Gillespie's School for Girls. But the school in the film was housed in the nineteenth-century Donaldson's School for the Deaf building in Henderson Row. A few years after the film was made, it became part of the neighbouring Edinburgh Academy, a school just as exclusive as Marcia Blaine's. The building currently houses the rector's office.

Pupils and staff of Marcia Blaine's are seen arriving, full of hope, for the new term at the beginning of the film, and pouring out of the gates into Henderson Row two hours later, lives ended, shattered and changed forever by Miss Brodie's prime.

Miss Brodie and her girls are also seen in the grounds. Various other Edinburgh streets were used and there is a lengthy scene in Greyfriars Churchyard, not far from Edinburgh Castle and probably best known as the haunt of Greyfriars Bobby, the little dog who reputedly kept watch at his master's grave and who became the hero of his own Disney live-action feature film in the sixties. But such couthy tales were not the sort of thing to appeal to Miss Brodie who tells her girls how leading presbyterians signed the National Covenant against episcopalianism at Greyfriars, using their own blood.

Mr Lloyd, the art master (Robert Stephens), had his studio just across the street and comes to meet them in the churchyard. His rival, Mr Lowther (Gordon Jackson), invites Miss Brodie and her girls to his home in Cramond, a picturesque Edinburgh suburb down on the Firth of Forth dating back to Roman times. However, in the film Mr Lowther's home turns out to be a small castle, owned by Lord Rosebery – not bad on a teacher's salary. Barnbougle Castle is just along the coast from Cramond on the Dalmeny estate.

Lord and Lady Rosebery live in Dalmeny House, while the much older Barnbougle Castle, about half a mile away on the shore, provides accommodation for a caretaker. It was rebuilt in the nineteenth century and it is uncertain when the original was constructed. The castle is closed to the public, but the estate is open.

RESTLESS NATIVES (1985)

American director Michael Hoffman and Scottish scriptwriter Ninian Dunnett tried to tap into the quirky sense of humour demonstrated in Bill Forsyth's comedies, with this lightweight tale of highway robbers and locations spread right across Scotland.

A couple of bored young teenagers, Will (Vincent Friell) and Ronnie (Joe Mullaney) don clown and wolfman masks and hold up tourist coaches in the Highlands.

Their home base would seem to be Edinburgh, given that they get a good view of the capital's famous castle from the balcony of Will's parents' flat, but the city is not named and various locations in Edinburgh's great west-coast rival, Glasgow, are thrown into the mix.

Will, minus his wolfman disguise, is seen at Glasgow's Anderston Cross Bus Station, making clumsy overtures to the young tourist guide, Margot (Teri Lally), he has taken a shine to. Although Will's flat is in Edinburgh, it is on the very western edge at Wester Hailes – hardly the best place for a good view of the castle and well away from the tourist sights.

There was, however, considerable filming in Edinburgh city centre. Alan Wands, who

Jane Carr, Pamela Franklin, Maggie Smith, Diane Grayson and Shirley Steedman in The Vennel, off the Grassmarket, Edinburgh, for The Prime of Miss Jean Brodie *(20th Century-Fox)*

was unit manager, recalls: 'We had a police car chasing a motorbike which went right up the top of the High Street, down the Mound and on to Princes Street and we had to shut the whole place down on Sunday.'

Princes Street is the capital's main shopping street and an important east-west route, the High Street is the main road through the older part of the city and the Mound is the road that links the high-rise tenements of the Old Town with the elegant Georgian New Town.

'It was a nightmare,' says Wands. 'Edinburgh police and authorities were very helpful, but they had never had anything like that to deal with before.'

Several romantic scenes involving Will and Margot were shot at Newhaven, an old fishing village just a couple of miles from the city centre. Although right next to Leith Docks, it is a relatively tranquil spot, with a picturesque little lighthouse at the harbour mouth.

The robberies were shot up around Fort William, including Glen Coe, and on both sides of Loch Ness. The film-makers converted an empty warehouse in Fort William into a make-shift studio, where they could shoot interior scenes when bad weather prevented filming outside.

The chase sequence in which the highwaymen evade a road block by driving their motorbike off the road and along a beach was shot at the little town of Lochgilphead in Argyllshire.

The highwaymen end up in Latin America. Well, not quite; they end up on the American side of the Mexican-American border. Well, not quite again. The budget obviously did not run to a trip to New Mexico so the scene was shot in Glasgow's Barras market, named after the old habit of selling goods straight from the barrow.

The film-makers turned the area called the Square Yard into a New Mexican street scene, with the three main characters outside a cantina. 'The people who own it have given it a slight American look, which helped us,' says Wands. 'We only had to take away their junk and put in various other bits and pieces. We had a donkey, which just capped the fact it was Mexico, apart from the decor and the funny hats. The director said "I want a donkey," so here we had this bloody donkey in the Barras, which was quite amazing.'

ROB ROY (1995)

The makers of *Rob Roy* were determined to shoot in the Scottish Highlands close to the glens the legendary outlaw frequented in the late seventeenth and early eighteenth centuries. Director Michael Caton-Jones believed his native land had never been fully exploited on film before. The Highland village the film-makers constructed beneath Ben Nevis had to be rebuilt inside in Perth because of heavy rain, but they insist they have no regrets.

Rob Roy represented the first chance for Caton-Jones, director of *Scandal* and *Memphis Belle*, to make a feature film in Scotland. And it was a home-coming too for scriptwriter Alan Sharp, who had left Scotland for Hollywood after establishing himself as a novelist in the sixties. He wrote the classic 1972 western *Ulzana's Raid*, which starred Burt Lancaster. They brought with them a star-studded cast with Liam Neeson in the title role,

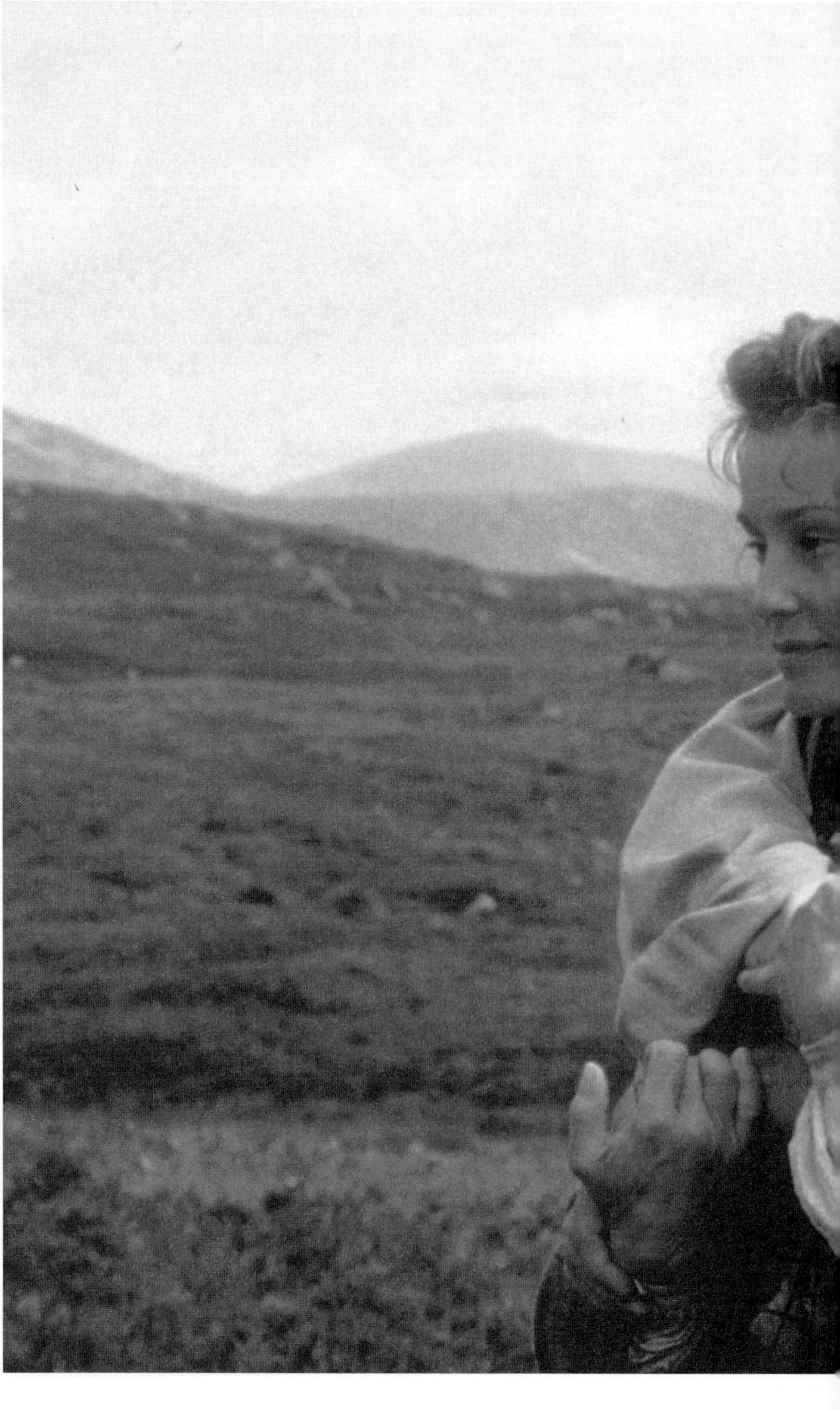

Liam Neeson and Jessica Lange in Rob Roy *(Talisman/UA)*

Jessica Lange as his wife, Mary; Eric Stoltz as his friend, Alan McDonald; John Hurt as the villainous Marquis of Montrose and Tim Roth as Montrose's henchman, Archibald Cunningham.

The Balquhidder area, where Rob Roy lived and where he is buried, was considered as a location and ruled out because of the extent of modern development and the spread of anachronistic pine plantations. It is one of the most easily accessible and popular parts of the Highlands. Location manager Keith Hatcher started scouting locations farther north and, eventually, filming was split between the Fort William and Perth areas.

The film-makers built a stone cottage for Rob Roy at Bracorina on the north side of Loch Morar, the deepest lake in Britain and home of a rival monster to Nessie called Morag. Bracorina is not far from the location used for beach scenes in *Local Hero* and *Highlander*. Rob Roy's cottage was entirely dismantled at the end of filming, though the location remains a quiet and scenic spot. A plaster house was built for Rob Roy on desolate Rannoch Moor and a third, prefabricated, dwelling was flown by helicopter to a remote location at Inversanda in Glen Tarbert.

The MacGregor village – an entire community of rudimentary stone cottages that seems to have risen from the very earth was originally built in Glen Nevis, near Fort William. 'There's a very large ceilidh [party] scene in the film and that's where the village comes into it,' says Hatcher. Co-producer Larry DeWaay adds: 'In hindsight, we should have planned to build it inside . . . The two nights we attempted to shoot – with 200 extras, 36 dancers and our cast – it poured with rain. It became basically just a mud-hole, so we thought "this is ridiculous". We got the essential shots we needed for the wide expanse of dusk and dawn and we decided to build it inside . . . We went to the Perth Equestrian Centre.' Jessica Lange had to be recalled from America to reshoot the ceilidh scenes.

The film-makers also built the stone hall at Perth for the duel between Rob Roy and Archibald Cunningham. The choice of the Perth area was largely dictated by the selection of nearby Drummond Castle as the seat of the Marquis of Montrose. Hatcher says: 'We needed a castle with an amazing garden because that's what Montrose had in the script. He was the sort of character who would have a splendid garden because he wanted to keep up with the French aristocracy.'

The castle is not open to the public but the ornamental terraced gardens are open in the summer months. They were laid out by the Earl of Perth in 1630 and were later embellished with statues from Italy. The castle tower-house dates from the fifteenth century, though the mansion house is Victorian. The Earls of Perth lost possession for supporting Bonnie Prince Charlie in the 1745 Jacobite Rising.

'I couldn't find the right type of castle gardens on the West Coast,' recalls Hatcher, 'so we upped sticks from Fort William and moved to the east.'

Perthshire also held out the prospect of fairer weather and the film-makers took over the grounds around Drummond Castle, shooting long into the cold nights.

Eric Stoltz's character is supposedly ambushed and killed in some lonely spot, but in reality Stoltz, looking every inch the Highland clansman with his kilt and his naturally red hair, meets his demise in woodland just a couple of minutes walk from the castle and from the reviving warmth of his trailer.

Glen Coe, a reliable and accessible source of spectacular Scottish scenery, was used while the film-makers were based at Fort William. One of the principal scenes shot in Glen Coe involved a clash between Rob Roy and cattle rustlers. The dramatic panorama right at the beginning of the film was shot above Kinlochleven.

The cobbled courtyard of Megginch Castle, near Perth, was used as a village square and Crichton Castle, south of Edinburgh, was used as the exterior of the gambling den where Rob Roy and Cunningham have their showdown. Mary Queen of Scots reputedly honeymooned at the castle, before the addition of its highly unusual piazza-style courtyard and Italianate portico – the work of the colourful fifth Earl of Bothwell, whose principal interests seemed to be Italy, treachery and witchcraft.

Crichton was a late substitute for another location on Rob Roy. 'Very early on I found a castle in the Borders called Hermitage, which is a beautiful castle,' says Hatcher. 'Unfortunately, on going back there, Historic Scotland had scaffolded the side that we needed to shoot and obviously it would have been too costly to take the scaffolding down, so we had to go out and find an alternative.'

Crichton Castle and the grounds of Megginch are both open to the public.

SHALLOW GRAVE (1994)

Although this stylish and violent black comedy is set in the elegant world of Edinburgh New Town, most of the filming was done in Edinburgh's great rival city, Glasgow.

The film-makers were lured west by £150,000 from the Glasgow Film Fund and they reconstructed the spacious flat – where most of the action takes place – in a warehouse in Anniesland. The film's opening narration says that the story could be taking place anywhere, but the introductory sequence is quite firmly rooted in Edinburgh's famous Georgian New Town. It is there that doctor Kerry Fox, accountant Chris Eccleston and journalist Ewan McGregor share a flat.

Director Danny Boyle says he wanted to avoid a sweeping panorama of the city, with viewers knowing that he was going to focus in on one particular point. Instead, he begins with the flatmates' car whizzing over the cobbles of Heriot Row – one of the most expensive residential streets in Edinburgh, just a few minutes walk from Princes Street. Robert Louis Stevenson lived at 17 Heriot Row. The car speeds along Great King Street and Drummond Place, down St Vincent Street towards St Stephen's Church, and into North East Circus Place, which is ostensibly the location of the flat. The fleeting glimpses of these streets establish that this is a long-established and up-market city neighbourhood.

Although *The Scotsman*'s Edinburgh head office is seen at one point in the film, McGregor's character has not quite made the grade there. He is working for the (Glasgow) *Evening Times* and the film-makers shot in its offices.

A fourth flatmate dies, leaving behind a suitcase full of money. Rather than reporting it to the police, the other three decide to dispose of the body. They are seen struggling with it down the stair.

The stair in question was some distance from North East Circus Place in Scotland Street, but the wood where they bury it was right on the other side of the country in

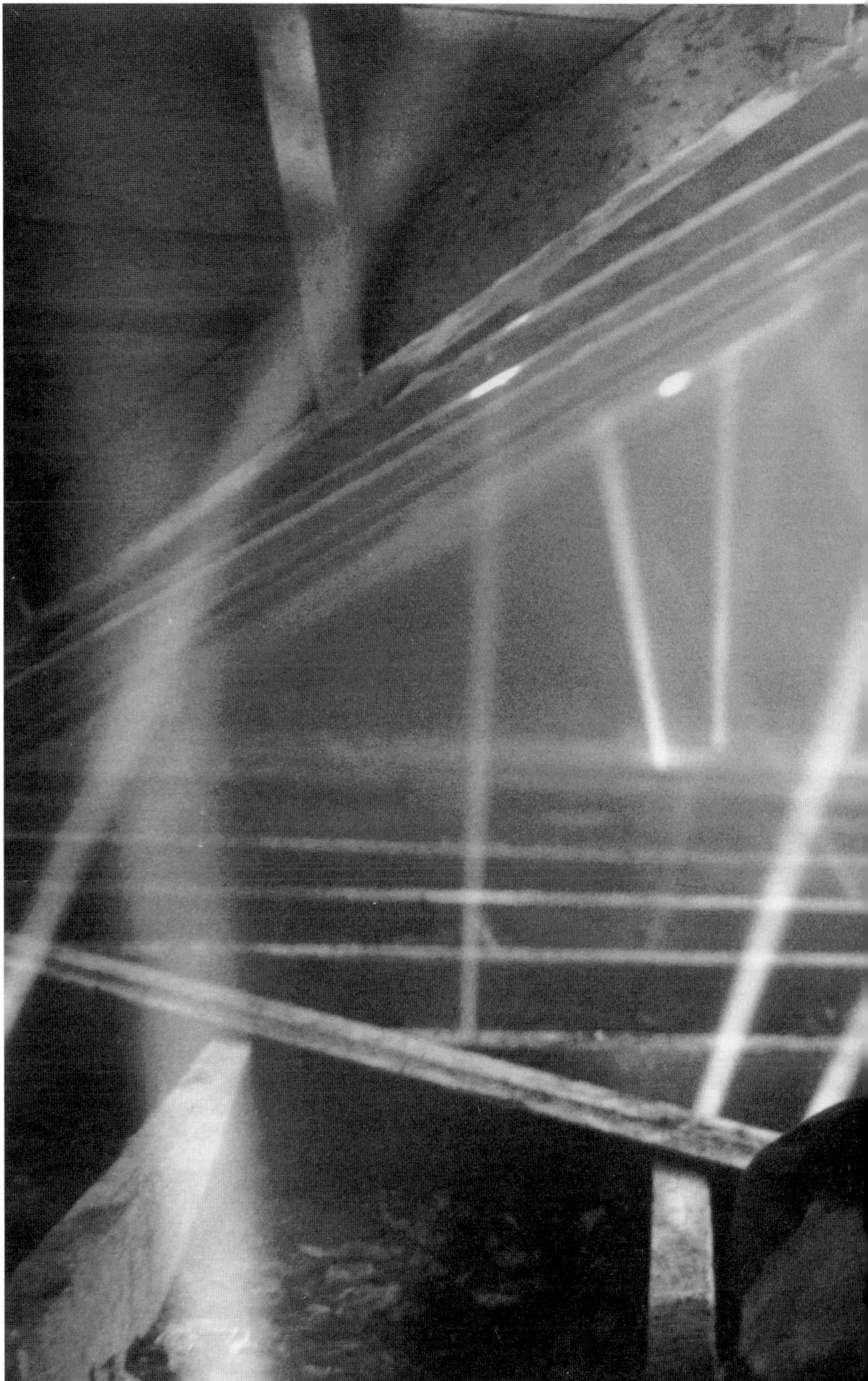

Chris Eccleston in Shallow Grave *(Channel Four)*

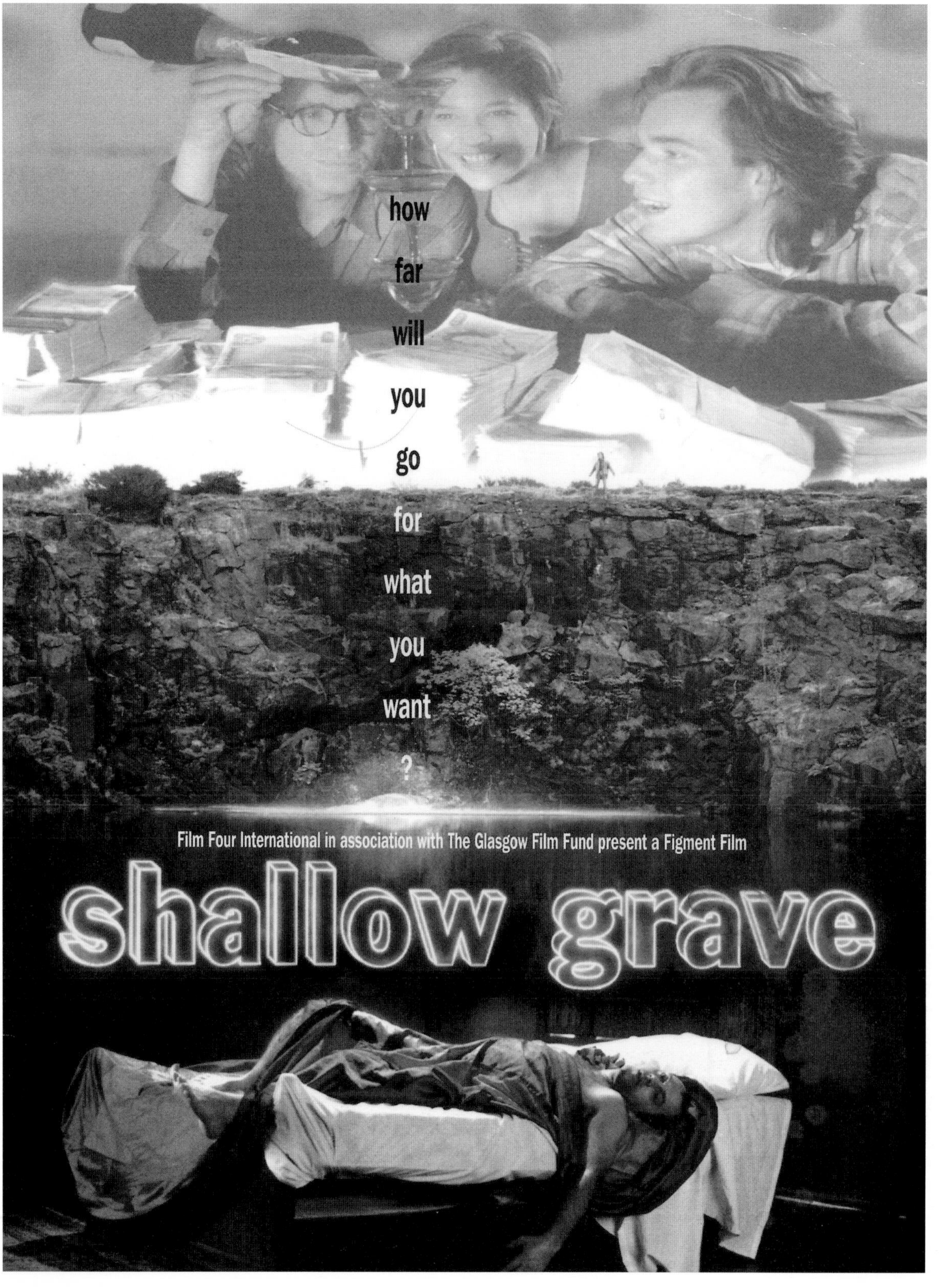

how

far

will

you

go

for

what

you

want

?

Film Four International in association with The Glasgow Film Fund present a Figment Film

shallow grave

Rouken Glen, a large park on the outskirts of Glasgow, with a boating pond and waterfalls as well as a wooded glen.

They also have to dump a car, which ended up in the flooded quarry at Mugdock Country Park, near Milngavie (pronounced Millguy), north of Glasgow. It may still be there. Producer Andrew Macdonald says they were meant to remove it after filming, but the flotation barrels did not work as planned. There was some talk of bringing in a helicopter, but, given that there were several other old cars in the quarry already and the budget was tight, it was decided to leave it where it was.

The Scottish country dancing was filmed at Glasgow's Townhouse Hotel in West George Street, which seems appropriate as it was once the home of the Royal Scottish Academy of Music and Drama.

Chris Eccleston, Kerry Fox and Ewan McGregor in Shallow Grave *(Channel Four)*

THE 39 STEPS (1935, 1959 and 1978)

Although much of the action in Alfred Hitchcock's classic spy film takes place in Scotland, it was virtually all shot at Lime Grove Studios in London. Even the scenes with sheep on the glens were done in the studio – though the animals disrupted production by eating the carefully arranged heather and bracken.

The most memorable location shot is that in which the hero, Richard Hannay (Robert Donat), escapes his pursuers by climbing out of a train on to the Forth Bridge, which spans the Firth of Forth near Edinburgh. One and half miles long, this spectacular metal cantilever bridge was one of the greatest engineering feats of its time. It is now over one

Godfrey Tearle and Robert Donat in The 39 Steps *(1935) (Gaumont-British)*

hundred years old and much the same as it was at the time of the film.

Hannay has been making his way north on the *Flying Scotsman* train from London after a mysterious woman is murdered in his flat. In one of cinema's great scenes, his charlady's scream on discovering the body turns into the whistle of a train emerging from a tunnel. The train in question is clearly not the *Flying Scotsman*, which the audience has just seen. It was a Great Western train, filmed coming out of a tunnel near Bath.

When this discrepancy was pointed out to Hitchcock, he responded by saying: 'There is something more important than logic; it is imagination.' That, presumably, also explains the fact that when Hannay makes his way off the Forth Bridge, he appears to be in the middle of the Highlands, rather than in Fife.

The Forth Bridge was used again in the lacklustre 1959 remake with Kenneth More, but the 1978 version, with Robert Powell, used the Victoria Bridge on the Severn Valley Railway. It stuck more closely to the plot of John Buchan's novel, which was not set in the Highlands at all, but in the south-west of Scotland.

This third version shot at Castlemilk House, a privately-owned nineteenth-century baronial castle near Lockerbie; Morton Castle, a ruin near Thornhill; the village of Durisdeer; the Forest of Ae; and the Duke of Buccleuch's Drumlanrig estate. Bill Cunningham, who was Powell's stand-in, recalls: 'Extensive use was made of local extras for the police search sequences and local amateur actors for walk-on parts. My main memory is of a great deal of rain and long waiting periods in cars or buses.'

2001: A SPACE ODYSSEY (1968)

British locations have doubled for America, China and India in the past, but one of the strangest uses was the employment of the Hebrides to represent the planet Jupiter in Stanley Kubrick's big-budget science-fiction movie. It was billed as 'the ultimate trip', it took two and a half years to make and it cost more than $10 million. But it was filmed primarily in the studios at Shepperton and Borehamwood, near London.

Most of the money was spent on special effects, including model spacecraft and rotating perspex representations of planets, as Kubrick charted Man's journey from prehistory, and the first use of a bone as a weapon, to space travel.

2001 was made against the background of the seemingly radical social and cultural upheaval of the sixties, when interest in space exploration and alternative religion were at their height. It was as the space traveller David Bowman (Keir Dullea) speeds towards the surface of Jupiter, that Kubrick brought into play the landscape of one of the most socially and culturally conservative areas of Britain.

Bowman is projected helplessly across a fleeting, world of ever-changing colour, sometimes hard, cold and rocky, sometimes soft, even molten. Aerial views were shot of the peat-bogs, crags and mountains of the Hebridean islands off the west coast of Scotland and of the dry, rocky terrain of Monument Valley in the United States, so favoured by John Ford in his westerns. Colour filters were then used to turn them into a multi-coloured psychedelic landscape that contributed to the ultimate trip for many members of the audience who were supplementing Kubrick's special effects with some chemical stimulus of their own.

TUNES OF GLORY (1960)

Director Ronald Neame had planned to film James Kennaway's story about personal and class tensions between army officers Alec Guinness and John Mills largely on location at Stirling Castle, one of Scotland's most famous fortresses. But the authorities' initial enthusiasm cooled when they saw the script.

Like Edinburgh Castle, Stirling Castle dominates its landscape from its vantage point atop a great rock. The English and Scots frequently fought over it, with Robert the Bruce gaining possession and securing Scottish independence at nearby Bannockburn in 1314, though most of the building dates from the fifteenth and sixteenth centuries. King James II stabbed the Earl of Douglas here and threw his body out of a window, and the infant Mary Queen of Scots was crowned in the Chapel Royal. Stirling Castle was long used as the barracks of the Argyll and Sutherland Highlanders.

'It had been our intention to use the Argylls, the regiment on which the book was based,' says Neame. 'With high hopes we went to Stirling Castle where the regiment was located and had a discussion with the colonel in command at that time. He was most friendly and said he would be delighted for us to shoot the film in and around the castle, and, even better, would allow his regiment to participate. He asked us to leave a copy of the book and script and meet with him again the next day.'

James Kennaway had adapted his own novel about the conflict between Colonel Jock Sinclair (Guinness), a hard-drinking, boorish war hero who has worked his way up through the ranks, and Colonel Basil Barrow (Mills), the suave, Oxford-educated officer imposed over his head as battalion commander. It ends with one colonel committing suicide and the other going mad.

Neame says: 'On the following morning when we returned, the reception was very different. The colonel was shocked and horrified that we intended to disgrace him and his men . . . No amount of persuasion was of any help; he was adamant. We asked if we could at least use a long shot of the castle and the picturesque cobbled road that led up to it. He at last grudgingly agreed to this provided that we disguised the castle so that it could never be recognised. This we did with the use of a "matte" shot that completely changed the shape of the roof and turrets.'

Much of the filming was done on a large exterior set at Shepperton Studios, near London, though Neame also shot 'in and around Windsor, in the shadow of the castle'. Windsor Castle in Berkshire was an official residence of the kings of England while Scottish history was forged hundreds of miles away at Stirling in the Middle Ages. It seemed once again that strategies were being worked out at Windsor to determine the fate of Stirling. Neame says: 'Jock's home was a small house on the edge of Windsor Park. The local pub was in a street alongside the castle. For the regiment we used the services of the Territorial Army. They had an excellent pipe band . . . The maddening part of all this was that when the film was finished the Argylls asked if we would allow them to use it for recruiting purposes.'

Stirling Castle is open to the public and includes the Argylls' regimental museum. Windsor Castle is also open to the public.

Guinness had initially been offered the role of Colonel Barrow, but felt it was too close to his character in *The Bridge on the River Kwai*. Although there were some reservations about his accent, he delivers a truly compelling performance. Kennaway was nominated for an Oscar for his script and the film remains a very powerful character drama.

VENUS PETER (1989)

The film-makers decided to shoot entirely on location in Orkney, even though it was a major inconvenience for their biggest star – a 60-foot fibreglass and latex whale. It had to be transported 500 miles by road from a workshop in Bristol to the port of Aberdeen, was then loaded on to a ferry and, finally, was given a police escort to the beach at Dingy's Howe, Deerness, where the three sections were stuck together for filming.

Venus Peter was based on Christopher Rush's book *A Twelvemonth and a Day*: memoirs of childhood in the much more convenient village of St Monans in Fife. Director Ian Sellar and producer Christopher Young opted for Stromness on Orkney because they wanted a working fishing port and considered mainland towns either too quiet or too picturesque.

Most of the film was shot in and around the harbour and the narrow streets and closes of Stromness – the smaller of Orkney's two towns with a population of about 1,700. It was once an important base for ships of the Hudson's Bay Company and many of the houses were erected along the waterfront in the eighteenth century.

The scene in which the young boy, Peter, almost drowns was shot just outside Stromness at Warbeth Beach. The other big beach scene, involving the whale, was shot right on the other side of Orkney at Dingy's Howe. Sellar also used Holm Parish Church.

A local boy, Gordon Strachan, played Peter and Ray McAnally played his grandfather. McAnally died a week before the film's British première in Orkney, at which point the whale was being used to house a hall of mirrors in a local funfair.

Fifty years earlier, Michael Powell sent a two-man unit to Orkney for location footage for *The Spy in Black*, his first film with partner Emeric Pressburger. Location filming was not the norm at the time and Powell dared not tell the producer about the trip, even though it accounted for only £350 of the film's £17,000 budget.

WHISKY GALORE! (1949)

You do not need to be rich to spend a few nights in the house that served as Gordon Jackson's schoolhouse in this wonderful Ealing comedy; you just need to be homeless, for the building has been turned into emergency accommodation for those with nowhere else to go.

The inhabitants of the Outer Hebrides have always been down-to-earth folk. 'A happy people with few and simple pleasures,' says the voice-over at the beginning of the film, as nine children appear one after the other through a croft-house door.

It was one of those pleasures, whisky, that was to inspire Compton Mackenzie to write his famous comic novel and Sandy Mackendrick to make one of the most enduring classics of British cinema, *Whisky Galore!*, or *Tight Little Island*, as it is known in America. Even now, if you visit an islander's home on Barra, where the film was shot, you will probably be offered (and will be expected to drink) a glass of whisky, quite possibly the size of a cup of tea.

Barra today will be instantly recognisable to fans of *Whisky Galore!* with the village of Castlebay spread out on the lower slopes of the mountain of Heaval just before it slips into the sea. Main Street or 'The Street', down on the seafront where the ferry berths, has changed little in the half-century since 'The Fillums' came from London and took over the island. Kisimul Castle, the picturesque little fortress that sits on a tiny island of its own just a stone's throw from 'The Street', still commands the bay as it has done for 800 years and commands the attention of any tourist with a camera.

Whisky Galore! is the story of a ship that runs aground carrying 50,000 cases of whisky and of the islanders' attempts to salvage and hang on to the cargo. Mackenzie was inspired by a real wreck and by his experiences living among the islanders on Barra. A prominent early figure in the revival of Scottish Nationalist politics, Mackenzie was actually born Edward Montague Compton in West Hartlepool, but took the family name Mackenzie to emphasise his Scottish heritage.

It was off another Hebridean island, Eriskay, where Bonnie Prince Charlie arrived in Scotland to begin the Jacobite Rising of 1745, that the SS *Politician* hit a rock in 1941 and islanders helped themselves from its cargo of whisky. There were those who said that it was the first time that a politician had ever brought anyone any good.

In his book Mackenzie called the island Todday, after the term for a hot alcoholic drink, and the film-makers considered several Scottish islands before settling on Barra.

It was not through any great ambition or vision that *Whisky Galore!* broke new ground as the first Ealing comedy made entirely on location. It was simply that there was no room in the studio. Sandy Mackendrick, an American-born Scot, had never directed a feature film before and the producer Monja Danischewsky was more accustomed to managing Ealing's press releases than managing films. Sir Michael Balcon, head of the studio, had doubts about the project right from the start. But in the summer of 1948 a cast and crew of about 80 descended on the island of Barra, a six-hour ferry journey from Oban on the Scottish mainland.

The cast included Gordon Jackson as the young schoolteacher; Jean Cadell as his fierce mother; James Robertson Justice as the doctor; Joan Greenwood, Wylie Watson, John Gregson and Duncan Macrae as various other islanders; and Basil Radford as Captain Waggett, the English incomer and commander of the Home Guard, who takes it upon himself to stop the pilfering of the whisky. Compton Mackenzie, who had, in fact, commanded the Home Guard, played the captain of the ill-fated ship, renamed the *Cabinet Minister*.

Barra is one of the most attractive of the Outer Hebrides; about ten miles long, with a few scattered communities, rough hill terrain and beautiful beaches. When the tide is out, planes land on the hard and expansive cockle beach at Traigh Mhor on the north of the island, sweeping down over the heads of tiny figures gathering cockles at the water's edge, to touch down with a splash and a surge of delight for those making the journey for the first time.

'The Fillums' were accommodated in the homes of the islanders, which helped them

Gordon Strachan in
Venus Peter
(BFI/Channel
Four/British Screen)

get the feel of the place, and no doubt a taste for the product which the film was all about. They used the old Castlebay village hall as a makeshift studio and shot exteriors and interiors all over the island, hampered by dreadful weather. The village hall was situated beneath the Church of Our Lady, Star of the Sea, but is no longer there. The church itself survives.

Barra is one of the few Roman Catholic islands in the Hebrides and is a relaxed place compared with the much larger island of Lewis to the north. But Our Lady, Star of the Sea, was supposed to be a Presbyterian church in the film. Its clock signalled the sabbath, thereby forcing the islanders to postpone salvage operations. Captain Roddy MacKinnon, the local councillor, says: 'That wouldn't have stopped anybody on this island going out to a whisky boat, I can tell you.'

Main Street has changed little since the film. The current post office served as The Island Store in the film and the bank is still a bank, albeit that it is now the Royal Bank of Scotland rather than the Commercial Bank of Scotland. Mackendrick shot beach scenes at Allasdale, Eoligarry and on the neighbouring island of Vatersay, which has subsequently been linked to Barra by causeway. As Captain Waggett's house, Mackendrick used the old police house, which is where the council offices in Castlebay stand today. But Jackson's house is still there. Captain MacKinnon says: 'They used the actual schoolhouse, not the school itself, but the actual headmaster's residence in Borve. It's detached from the school but sits right beside it. It's used now as an emergency unit for the homeless. If somebody, all of a sudden, finds themselves without a home they're put in there on a temporary basis until such time as a home can be found for them. It's just known as The Schoolhouse.'

It would be nice to say that when Mackendrick and Danischewsky showed Balcon their footage from Barra he suddenly realised he had a masterpiece on his hands. In fact, he still did not like it and another Ealing director, Charles Crichton, who made *The Lavender Hill Mob* and, many years later, *A Fish Called Wanda*, was called in at the editing stage to try to save the film. Looking at it now, it seems both beautifully shot and brilliantly edited. Who can forget the pace or the invention in the scene where the islanders have to quickly hide their whisky, pouring it into every conceivable household container, hiding it everywhere from down drains to underneath the baby.

Critics have called *Whisky Galore!* stereotypical, patronising and cosy comedy, but what has ensured its continued popularity is the dryness of its humour. The introductory voice-over sets the tone when talking about the isolation of Todday. 'To the west there is nothing,' says the narrator, before adding as a throwaway line ' . . . except America.'

Whisky Galore! has a hard subversive edge. Although they may be funny, other Ealing comedies ultimately take the side of the Establishment. Here a criminal Celtic brotherhood outwits authority in the shape of the straightlaced Waggett. In reality, several men who took whisky from the SS *Politician* were convicted and sent to jail. In the film, the islanders come out on top. Mackendrick told the story not as it happened, but as it should have happened. There was a sequel, *Rockets Galore!*, retitled *Mad Little Island* in America. It also shot on Barra and was a pleasant, but undistinguished, comedy.

THE WICKER MAN (1974)

Christopher Lee rates it the best film he ever made, *Cinefantastique* magazine called it the *Citizen Kane* of horror films: *The Wicker Man* is no less than a minor masterpiece of British cinema.

It was filmed entirely on location in Scotland, combining a number of sites in its construction of a close-knit twentieth-century pagan community. In many respects it is closer in form to a musical than a horror film. It is not just the way the cast frequently burst into song, but also their sustained jollity that give this impression and ultimately make the film all the more chilling. The only glum character is Sergeant Neil Howie (Edward Woodward), the policeman who goes to Summerisle to investigate an anonymous report of the disappearance of a child called Rowan.

Although the community is an island in the film, director Robin Hardy used various locations on the west coast of Scotland, beginning with Howie's seaplane flight over Skye and its arrival in the sheltered bay at Plockton, at the mouth of Loch Carron, in Wester Ross on the mainland. Plockton, which also featured in BBC TV's *Hamish Macbeth*, was built in the eighteenth century as a fishing village, though its neat painted waterfront cottages are now used largely by holidaymakers.

The strangeness of the film is established at once by the sight of palm trees, made viable by the warmth from the Gulf Stream and the absence of hard frosts in winter. Howie comes ashore and proceeds in a southerly direction, travelling almost 200 miles to the little market town of Kirkcudbright (pronounced Kircoobrie). Hardy used the colourfully painted houses and the little closes, or alleys, of Kirkcudbright High Street as part of the backdrop for his story, and the old police station, now a charity shop, served as Rowan's mother's store.

The Ellan Gowan Hotel, about fifteen miles away in Creetown, was used as the Green Man Inn – a den of iniquity run by Lindsay Kemp and his daughter, Britt Ekland. Legend has it that Ekland wanted to buy one of the hotel's old toilets and the owners have considered erecting a plaque saying: 'Britt Ekland sat here.'

The Cally Estate offices in nearby Gatehouse of Fleet served as the outside of the Green Man. Gatehouse's chemist's shop also appears in the film and still operates as the town's chemist today.

Howie visits the Summerisle school where one teacher (Walter Carr) leads the boys in a dance around the maypole while another (Diane Cilento) explains to the girls that the pole represents the penis and the regenerative power of nature. Hardy used both the old schoolhouse and the roofless old kirk at Anwoth – a hamlet up a quiet country lane, off the A75 between Gatehouse and Creetown.

By now Howie suspects that Rowan was the victim of human sacrifice and is buried in the kirkyard, where one headstone reads 'Here lieth Beech Buchanan, protected by the ejaculation of serpents.' The church, seen in ruins beside the graveyard, was the church of Samuel Rutherford, a famous seventeenth-century Scottish minister who was suspended for nonconformity, though his nonconformity did not extend as far as that of his latter-day parishioners.

Among the buttercups and daisies of the well-maintained kirkyard are graves dating

*Anwoth Old Kirkyard,
as featured in* The
Wicker Man *(British
Lion)*

back four centuries, some featuring skulls and crossbones, including one that appears prominently in the film. The old schoolhouse, which is right beside the kirkyard, has been turned into a delightful little cottage, available for holiday lets.

Christopher Lee played the local laird, Lord Summerisle, whose seat was Culzean Castle, a very grand National Trust property in Ayrshire. Its extensive grounds became Scotland's first country park in 1969. Culzean was originally one of a chain of Clan Kennedy castles though it was rebuilt and enlarged over the years. In the late eighteenth century, Robert Adam remodelled existing turrets and added new ones, giving the place a fancy, romantic look.

It is never entirely clear how big Summerisle is. Lord Summerisle occupies one of the finest houses in Scotland and the community merits its own registrar of births, deaths and marriages (Ingrid Pitt), but, conveniently, it does not have its own policeman.

Apart from the bouncy production numbers, *The Wicker Man* – for much of its length – seems a very predictable hammy film. But everything falls into place and Anthony Shaffer's cleverly contrived story makes perfect sense when we reach the final powerful sequence in which a human sacrifice must be burned inside the giant wicker man. The climax was filmed on the promontory at Burrow Head, the south-eastern tip of Wigtownshire.

The Wicker Man was originally released as the lower half of a double bill with *Don't Look Now*. It has now been re-evaluated, was included in Alex Cox's *Moviedrome* series on BBC TV and has acquired cult status.

In his time Christopher Lee played Frankenstein's monster and Dracula, and appeared in James Bond and Steven Spielberg movies, but when we discussed his career at the 1994 Cannes Film Festival, he unhesitatingly singled out *The Wicker Man* as his best film.

CHAPTER EIGHT
Educating Rita in Geography
DUBLIN

AN AWFULLY BIG ADVENTURE (1995)

Hugh Grant and director Mike Newell got together again after the enormous success of *Four Weddings and a Funeral* for this drama, set in Liverpool, but shot in Dublin. Grant is cast in an unsympathetic role as a dictatorial manager of a theatre company, Alan Rickman is one of the actors and Georgina Cates is a teenage actress torn between them.

Assistant director Martin O'Malley recalls: 'It was a very difficult one to do, because it's about a theatrical troupe that put on three plays in Liverpool in 1947 – *Peter Pan, Dangerous Corner* by Priestley, and *Caesar and Cleopatra* by George Bernard Shaw. They were all fairly big costume dramas and we shot in the Olympia Theatre in Dame Street for exteriors and interiors. We were in there for about eight days and we had to change all the sets each time, so there was quite a bit to do . . . We shot the dressing-room interiors in the old Richmond Hospital [near the Four Courts on the north bank of the Liffey]. You'd start off in the morning with *Cleopatra* because that was the heaviest make-up job, and then you'd go over to *Dangerous Corner*, which was a tuxedo, evening-wear thing, then that would give you a chance to get on to *Peter Pan*, a serious costume play.'

As a rehearsal hall, O'Malley used the old music hall he had discovered above Ricardo's Snooker Hall in Lower Camden Street when looking for locations for *The Commitments*. Other locations included Green Street – 'we did a lot of night stuff there. Georgina Cates was always going over to get the rasher sandwiches – the bacon sandwiches – from the little mobile tea wagon' – and Henrietta Street – 'They're very, very big old eighteenth-century houses and Alan Rickman's flat was up there.'

In *The Companion Guide to Ireland*, Brendan Lehane rates this the saddest street in Dublin. He maintains that one of the finest Georgian streets in the city was transformed into a forlorn slum earlier this century when the buildings were turned into tenements.

The film-makers shot in Ireland because of the tax incentives there. A few brief 'establishing shots' were done in Liverpool.

THE BLUE MAX (1966)

Dublin became Berlin in this action film, which sparked a minor boom in First World War dramas using Ireland and its air space as their locations.

In *The Blue Max* George Peppard is the ambitious German air ace and Ursula Andress is his mistress. The historic Dublin Castle and its state apartments were used for several sequences, ranging from a formal dinner party to steamy bedroom scenes. The castle dates from the thirteenth century and remained the centre of British power in Ireland and a hated symbol of British oppression until the establishment of the Free State in 1922. It is

Hugh Grant, Peter Firth and Georgina Cates in An Awfully Big Adventure *(Portman/British Screen/BBC/ Wolfhound)*

Dublin Castle doubled as imperial Berlin in The Blue Max *(20th Century-Fox)*

still used for official functions and conferences, though part of it is open to the public.

The Black Pool, or Dubh Linn, from which the city takes its name, was reputedly sited in the Great Courtyard. Other Dublin locations included Trinity College, Heuston Station and Winetavern Street.

At much the same time as *The Blue Max* was shooting, Dublin was doubling for Berlin in a second major feature film, *The Spy Who Came in From the Cold*, with Richard Burton in the title role. Checkpoint Charlie was reconstructed at Smithfield Market.

Battle sequences for *The Blue Max* were shot in the countryside around Kilpedder in County Wicklow and Leixlip in County Kildare. 'They were used for the battlefields; all the wide shots of the troops moving backwards and forwards,' says Seamus Byrne, who worked on the film. 'The planes fly over and troops move.'

The film-makers used Casement Aerodrome, at Baldonnel, near Dublin, which is the headquarters of the Army Air Corps; and Weston Airfield, near Leixlip.

Byrne says the deciding factors in shooting in Ireland were clear air space and the readiness of military personnel to service the planes and appear as extras in the big scenes. 'And I think the similarity to France would be a big factor from the air,' adds Byrne, 'because it's reasonably unspoiled. There wasn't too much industry and the aerial stuff was obviously terribly important . . . It started a kind of run of other aerial films like *Darling Lili* (Julie Andrews and Rock Hudson) and *Von Richthofen and Brown* (known in Britain as *The Red Baron*).'

THE COMMITMENTS (1991)

Forty-four different Dublin locations were used to transfer the world of Roddy Doyle's novel to the screen in Alan Parker's film. And the aim at the outset was to create an idea of a tough working-class community that might inspire the sort of heart-felt white soul music that was to become the hallmark of the band the Commitments. 'It was our intention at all times to avoid the picture-postcard locales traditionally associated with Ireland and show a contemporary world a little different from the romantic notions,' said Parker.

'Gradually, we put together a patchwork of places, streets and buildings of a world we could see, but could not find in one place. Not for the first time, I found myself climbing walls, avoiding guard dogs and knocking on doors that the occupants seemed wary to open. In Dublin it's not unusual to climb a ladder to get from one part of a garden to another, and I put this in the script at Joey's mother's house.'

The interior and garden scenes for Joey the Lips' mother's house were shot in Gardiner Street, near the Sinn Fein headquarters and opposite the St Francis Xavier Church, 'the SFX', which is used in the film for an impromptu rendition of 'A Whiter Shade of Pale'. The front exterior of Joey's house, however, was in another part of the city, in Pembroke Road, Ballsbridge.

Location manager Martin O'Malley recalls the film as presenting serious location headaches. 'Alan Parker likes to shoot on location and he likes to shoot all the roughest areas he can find, and make them, like, worse.'

O'Malley says the film-makers not only had to deal with the occasional local 'villain', but also community groups that were trying to improve their neighbourhoods and wanted them portrayed positively on screen. 'I thought at the time I had a very close working relationship with the art department, but all of a sudden they were dragging burning cars out and we had never agreed it with some of the communities,' says O'Malley.

'We shot in a very famous place in Dublin called Sheriff Street,' he continues. 'Sheriff Street was the opening scene at the market with Jimmy Rabbitte selling his T-shirts and cassettes, with all the horses and stuff.' It is a working-class area not far from the docks. 'It was where they did the rioting scene for *In the Name of the Father*. We were there before them, though. It was *The Commitments* that broke into that whole area and got the people on our side and gave them employment – we used them as extras, used them for security. And you know when you have them on your side there's not going to be any trouble.'

The cast were all recruited locally as well. The film has no big-star names. Parker needed 12 people to make up the band and decided that they should be singers and musicians who would play their own instruments, not actors whose music would be provided by others at a later stage. The film-makers auditioned more than 3,000 before drawing up a short leet for each role.

It was at this late stage that Parker discovered Andrew Strong, the son of a singer from the session band which had been helping to work out various possible songs for the film. He was only 16 but he had the voice of someone who had spent years in smoky bar-rooms and noisy gambling joints. Parker said: 'Young Andrew stood at the mike and belted into "Mustang Sally". I couldn't believe his mature voice and such extraordinary confidence from someone so young. His voice was exactly as Roddy had described it in the book – a real deep growl that scraped against the tongue and throat on the way out. It seemed I had at least found the Deco of our story.

'I sorted through the various permutations of our casting, juggling all the possibilities in a giant photographic grid on my hotel room floor. Finally, I decided on the chosen twelve Commitments.'

Doyle's original story was set in a fictional place called Barrytown, based on the Northside housing estate of Kilbarrack, where he taught. But Parker was keen to use inner-city locations as well. It was while checking out pool rooms that O'Malley stumbled upon the hall that they would use to film the Commitments in rehearsal. It was a room above Ricardo's Snooker Hall in Lower Camden Street. It had been a cinema but was simply being used as a storage room at the time.

'I sussed that there was a false ceiling in the cinema upstairs, so we pulled out a few tiles and saw that the original plasterwork was still there from an old music hall. So we did a deal and got the place . . . There's the pool hall downstairs, which was used for one or two scenes, but it was mostly upstairs for the rehearsals.' The hall was also used in *An Awfully Big Adventure*.

Several locations were used for the Commitments' concerts, beginning with the scene where Jimmy Rabbitte (Robert Arkins) tells Derek and Outspan they must get rid of their keyboard-player. It was filmed at the Bray Head Hotel, just outside Dublin in the seaside resort of Bray.

The Commitments
*(Beacon/First Film/
Dirty Hands)*

The Commitments graduate from playing local halls, including the Guide hall in Synge Street, to starring at one of Dublin's premier music venues – the Waterfront Rock Café on Sir John Rogerson's Quay – but the tensions and disagreements within the band finally come to a head in the dressing-room – a scene shot at the Olympic Ballroom, off Camden Street. Finally, a limousine carrying the legendary Wilson Pickett is seen stopping to ask Jimmy where the Commitments are playing, at which point we are back on Sir John Rogerson's Quay.

Parker also made extensive use of Darndale, which O'Malley rates as the roughest estate in Dublin. 'Darndale was used for where Jimmy Rabbitte lived. In Darndale itself there were three separate areas, Buttercup, Tulip and Primrose, lovely names . . . And you couldn't bring the security guards from Primrose into Buttercup because there were three different gangs . . . It was a terribly difficult film.'

At the end of the day, however, Parker not only succeeded in presenting a new and grittier image of Ireland on screen, but he wound up with a major international hit. In Britain, *The Commitments* was the only non-American film in the 1991 Top Ten.

THE DEAD (1987)

The film of James Joyce's short story, surely one of the very best examples of that form, was the great director John Huston's final film, shot partly on location in Ireland at the very house that featured in the original story. The Irish scenes, however, were not directed by Huston but by Seamus Byrne. For this was a film in two parts, shot on different sides of the world.

'All the actors' stuff was shot in California,' says Byrne, 'because John Huston couldn't travel, but all the other exteriors were shot in Ireland, all around the place, in Kildare and Wicklow mainly . . . The house was the house that's mentioned in the book.'

The film uses the same 'dark, gaunt house' at No. 15 Usher's Island, Dublin, on the south bank of the Liffey, that Joyce had used when constructing his fictional tale. It was once occupied by two elderly female relatives of Joyce and in his short story it was where the Misses Morkans held their annual dance – 'a great affair' – and where the sound of Bartell D'Arcy's singing of 'The Lass of Aughrim' reminds Gretta Conroy (Anjelica Huston) of Michael Furey, the boy who loved her, long ago in Galway. Despite poor health, he came out in the snow to say goodbye on the night of her departure from the village, and subsequently died. Her husband, Gabriel (Donal McCann), realises that he has never loved like that.

There has been extensive redevelopment at Usher's Island, but the townhouse at No. 15 remains. It was used by a seed merchant and a fabric import business, before being left empty – its windows broken, its brown paint peeling, occupied only by the ghosts of Joyce's drama.

Byrne shot various street scenes with synthetic snow in Anglesea Street, Henrietta Street, the quayside and Temple Bar. Kildare and Wicklow were used for country scenes because there was natural snow lying there. 'They were exteriors, you know, for when she talks about Michael Furey, her lost dead lover; the man she might have married,' says Byrne. 'The graveyard was in Kildare and the shots of the ice and snow were in Wicklow

and the various bits of Irish Irishness – like there's a round tower in one of the shots – that was in Glendalough.'

Glendalough is an area with a sixth-century monastic settlement, located in County Wicklow. The Round Tower is one hundred feet high, with a doorway ten feet off the ground. It looks like a Stone Age spaceship.

Joyce concludes his story with the image of snow falling over Ireland, including 'the lonely churchyard on the hill where Michael Furey lay buried'. Byrne says: 'It was a graveyard in the Curragh [the farming land east of Kildare]. It doesn't have a name, I don't think.'

He also shot at the Rock of Cashel in Tipperary, which rises high above the town of Cashel; the capital of the kings of Munster. It is said the devil bit the rock out of the mountains to the north and deposited it on the plain. It is crowned by the ruins of an ancient cathedral, with another round tower dating from the eleventh century.

Byrne's location footage was neatly sewn into the fabric of Huston's final film – a film that Huston, who had taken out Irish citizenship, had long wanted to make. It is an unusually calm, measured and introspective work from one of the great practitioners of cinema; a sensitive adaptation of a quietly devastating piece of literature.

EDUCATING RITA (1983)

Although playwright Willy Russell's work is set firmly in his native Merseyside, the film of *Educating Rita* was made entirely on location in and around Dublin. Judging by her accent, there was no doubt Rita (Julie Walters), hairdresser and Open University student, remains Liverpudlian in the film version, too. But her community appears to have been relocated in the Republic of Ireland.

Trinity College, Dublin, is where she attends English tutorials with boozy lecturer Frank (Michael Caine); the English working-class pub, where she feels so out of place at the sing-a-long, was the Stag's Head in Dame Court, Dublin; and her summer school was none other than the new Belfield campus of University College Dublin on the outskirts of the city. Even when Frank goes off on holiday to France he gets no farther than St Patrick's College in the village of Maynooth, which is about ten miles outside Dublin, but whose architecture was considered suitably Gallic in style.

Director Lewis Gilbert, who had previously worked with Caine on *Alfie*, shot extensively at Trinity College. It was founded in the late sixteenth century with a grant from Queen Elizabeth I of England in order to reduce the numbers seeking higher education in France, Italy and Spain, where students would be 'infected by popery'.

Trinity occupies a large area within the centre of the city. For a long time it had the reputation of being an enclosed fortress of Protestant English tradition and learning. It admitted women in the early years of the twentieth century, but until the sixties most of the students were Protestant. The grounds are now open to the public and there are guided tours. The buildings date largely from the eighteenth and nineteenth centuries.

Gilbert filmed in the squares, with their cobbles, lawns, trees and distinctive, central bell tower; in the Exam Hall, which is also used for concerts; and in the Graduates Memorial Building, which is where Frank's room is in the film. It is here Rita's unpretentious

Trinity College, one of the main locations for Educating Rita *(Acorn)*

enjoyment of literature reawakens Frank's interest in the possibilities of life beyond the bottle.

Although Trinity is the principal location, numerous other places in Dublin were used. Frank's house was in Burlington Road, which was formerly part of the red-light district. It is near the canal that divided two police precincts and meant that prostitutes simply had to cross the bridge when a police car came along. Exterior shots of the house and yard belonging to Rita and her husband, Denny, were filmed in Erne Street, and interiors in Ballsbridge.

Rita is berated by her father for not having children, at her sister's wedding, which takes place at the Church of the Holy Family, Aughrim Street. Rita subsequently leaves her husband and shares a flat with Trish (Maureen Lipman) in Crosthwaite Park and they work as waitresses in Dobbin's Wine Bistro in Stephens Lane, which has changed little since the film was made.

The Stag's Head in Dame Court, where Rita's mother cries and reflects that there must be better songs to sing, is one of Dublin's oldest pubs and celebrated its centenary in 1995. Mahogany, mirrors and stained glass contribute to an atmosphere as thick as the ale. The Stag's Head was also used in *December Bride* and has even appeared on an Irish postage stamp. The outside of Rita's bar was, however, the Dame Tavern, directly opposite. Frank is also seen at the disco at the Stillorgan Park Hotel. It is virtually the only location specifically mentioned by name in the film.

Tiger suggests to Frank that Rita might be at the Flamingo, a nice plug for the venue, though ironically, it has reinvented and renamed itself since the film.

Frank discusses Blake with Rita in the People's Gardens in Phoenix Park on the north-western edge of the city. Reputedly the largest enclosed park in Europe, it has a circumference of seven miles and includes playing fields, a zoo, a racecourse and the residences of the President of Ireland and the American ambassador. The Fifteen Acres playing fields were the traditional site for duels in the eighteenth century, but provided the venue for a mass Mass when the Pope visited in 1979.

Frank sees Rita off to summer school from Pearse Station and, ultimately, she sees him off to Australia from Dublin Airport – both of them having benefited from their association.

Russell, whose other plays include *Shirley Valentine; John, Paul, George, Ringo and Bert* and *Blood Brothers*, adapted *Educating Rita* for the screen himself. It won British Academy Awards for best film, best actor and best actress. Russell, Caine and Walters were all nominated for Oscars and *Educating Rita* remains a funny, and at times poignant, observation on the human condition.

HEAR MY SONG (1991)

John McDonnell is one of Ireland's leading location managers, having worked on *In the Name of the Father, Hidden Agenda* and *Into the West*. Of all the locations he has organised, he rates the main location for *Hear My Song* as his favourite. It was the hall used as Heartly's, the Liverpool club where the legendary singer Josef Locke was to make a comeback.

Duplicity and disappearance feature prominently in the film. It is a similar story with the location, which was in Dublin rather than Liverpool and has now disappeared . . . almost.

Adrian Dunbar plays Heartly's manager Micky O'Neill, who is facing dismissal because of declining audiences. He organises a concert by a mysterious Mr X and encourages speculation that this is Locke, who disappeared years before, owing the taxman a fortune. It turns out that Mr X is not Locke and the only way O'Neill can redeem himself is to track down the real Locke (Ned Beatty) and persuade him to appear at the club.

It was originally intended that the film would shoot mainly in Liverpool, but it ended up shooting almost entirely in Ireland.

As the Liverpool club, the film-makers used Merrion Hall, at Dublin's famous Georgian square, Merrion Square. 'It was just an amazing building,' says McDonnell. 'It was a Brethren meeting-house and the stage was their version of an altar . . . It burned down six months later. The façade was preserved and they built a hotel around it.' It is now the luxurious Davenport Hotel.

The original hall was built in 1863, with a neoclassical frontage incorporating three similar entrance doors and pillars on the upper level between elegant, slim windows.

O'Neill tracks Locke down to a farm in Ireland, surrounded by a loyal group of friends. He then finds himself being held upside down over a cliff – a scene which was

Davenport Hotel,
Hear My Song
(Limelight/Channel
Four/Windmill Lane)

shot at Howth (pronounced to rhyme with both), on the coast above Dublin. The film-makers also filmed in western Ireland, including the spectacular Cliffs of Moher in County Clare. For the tower where Locke and O'Neill go drinking, the film-makers used exterior shots of O'Brien's Tower, which is open to the public and gives spectacular views of the Cliffs of Moher and coastline.

IN THE NAME OF THE FATHER (1993)

Daniel Day-Lewis is famous for the lengths to which he will go to get himself into character for the role he is playing. It obviously must have helped him – in a film in which one of the themes is British oppression of the Irish – that he was acting within the walls of the Dublin jail which had held so many famous Irish patriots over the years and where James Connolly and Patrick Pearse were shot after the collapse of the Easter Rising in 1916.

In the Name of the Father was one of the most controversial films of its year, with its critics attacking the numerous deviations from recorded fact by Jim Sheridan, the writer-director who had earlier worked with Day-Lewis on *My Left Foot*. Day-Lewis plays Gerry Conlon, who was convicted of the 1974 Guildford pub bombing in London, in which five people died. The convictions against the 'Guildford Four' were finally overturned 15 years later, but the case remained highly contentious as Sheridan prepared his film version.

Although the action is set in Belfast and London, Sheridan opted to shoot in Dublin

Kilmainham Gaol, one of the main locations for In the Name of the Father *(Universal)*

and Liverpool, with the riot scene spilling over the Irish Sea – beginning in Ireland and ending up in England – just as Irish republican violence had done.

Early in the film, Conlon is seen stealing lead from a roof in Belfast. British soldiers mistake him for a gunman, give chase and, in one of the film's strongest and most exciting scenes, the chase escalates into a frightening confrontation and full-blown riot in which anything could happen – though the viewer's interest remains pinned to the fate of the young wide-boy, Conlon. Location manager John McDonnell says: 'Where he's up on the roof at the very start of the film, he is on the roof of the Guinness brewery in Dublin city centre. It switches from there to Ringsend, where they run through lanes.' Ringsend is the area where Oliver Cromwell landed with his army in 1646 to subjugate the Irish. It is now a traditional working-class area.

'They run through a house and out of another house and that was in Sheriff Street on the other side of the Liffey – that's where the bottle-throwing and Saracens were.'

Keith Hatcher, who was responsible for British locations, takes up the story. 'The driving of the armoured vehicles across burned-out cars and a lot of the street marches were done in Liverpool, in the Dingle mostly.

'I had a few problems with religion on that film. Liverpool is just as divided as Belfast in many ways . . . We put a mural on a wall in a Protestant area and the mural was sort of "IRA rule. Brits out", which was like a red rag to a bull. It was only supposed to be there for an hour but, unfortunately, our art department decided to do it the night before and upset a lot of people and caused me a lot of trouble.'

Conlon escapes from the British soldiers, but the IRA is preparing to knee-cap him for all the trouble he has caused, when his father, Guiseppe (Peter Postlethwaite), persuades them to let him off with a warning. Conlon goes to London, meets up with an old friend, Paul Hill, and moves into a squat, which was a derelict house in Liverpool's Huskisson Street. Conlon and Hill spend the night of the bombing sleeping rough in a park, which was another Liverpool location, Falkner Square.

The film's opening sequence of the pub being blown up was shot at the Brunswick Vaults, Tithebarn Street, Liverpool. 'We built an addition on to it to match with the pub and that's what went,' says Hatcher. 'We totally redecorated it afterwards, so it looked better than it was before.'

Conlon and Hill are picked up and interrogated in Sir Patrick Dun's Hospital, at Dublin's famous Georgian square – Merrion Square. Sir Patrick Dun's Hospital was empty at the time, though it has now been redeveloped as flats. McDonnell says: 'We used the basement, which had a lot of tunnels and rough-looking rooms.' Conlon, Hill and two others from the squat are sent to the Old Bailey for trial, the front of which was Liverpool Museum, the back was Manchester Town Hall and the interior was one of the former courtrooms in St George's Hall in Liverpool, rated by the *Blue Guide* as 'one of the best Greek revival buildings in England'. It is open to the public.

Hatcher: 'They're absolutely fantastic for matching with the Old Bailey. In fact, more films that portray the Old Bailey have been shot in No. 1 Court in St George's Hall than anywhere else.'

The film-makers also used Kilmainham Gaol. Erected at the end of the eighteenth century, behind high stone walls, it held the Fenian rebels of 1866, the Land Leaguers of 1881 (including Charles Stewart Parnell), the Invincibles in 1883 and many of those involved in the 1916 Rising. A hated symbol of British colonialism, it was abandoned in the twenties and was left empty for decades. It has now been turned into a museum including an exhibition on the struggle for independence.

Curator Niamh O'Sullivan recalls: 'In the summer of 1994 a group of young Spanish students visited the jail. One girl asked if she could go upstairs to see the cell Daniel Day-Lewis was in while here. I told them it was not permitted, but a group of them protested. I allowed the first girl to go up to take a photo; no one else was to join her. So she ended up bringing about sixteen cameras with her and proceeded to photograph the doorway 16 times for all her friends.'

The interior is actually quite light because of the glass roof. Cells are arranged around the sides of the main building, though the metal staircase rises in the centre, with caged walkways branching off at each level. As well as filming in cells and corridors, the production team built sets in the courtyard, for the traditional cell is hardly designed to accommodate a film crew.

Kilmainham has appeared in several other films, including Marty Feldman's *The Last Remake of Beau Geste*, and U2 and Sinead O'Connor have used it for videos. Two other Dublin penal establishments also appear in *In the Name of the Father*. St Patrick's Institution courtyard was used for some exterior shots and Mountjoy Prison was used for the scene

in which Conlon is transferred to Scotland.

The breakthrough in the campaign to free the Guildford Four comes when Gareth Peirce (Emma Thompson) manages to get a file to which she is not supposed to have access, a scene shot at Findlater wine merchant's premises in Harcourt Street, Dublin.

When the film came out, Sheridan was accused of playing fast and loose with the facts – a potentially serious charge against a film about the distortion of the truth. In the film, the Guildford Four are released because of fresh alibi evidence. In reality, although there was fresh alibi evidence, they were released because it was shown the original police notes had been amended. In the film, the Four are tried alongside the Maguire Seven, whereas there were separate trials. Conlon is shown sharing a cell with his father, one of the Seven, though that never happened; and Peirce is shown championing his case in the Appeal Court, whereas she was a solicitor and therefore unable to present the case there. There were even complaints from serious commentators that Emma Thompson did not look like Gareth Peirce.

Sheridan maintains that it is necessary to compress events and amalgamate characters at times for the sake of the film. 'The truth is that the courts let them out because of contemporaneous note changes. It was a damp squid. They slipped them out where we dramatised them out.' The details may be inaccurate but the basic storyline remains correct.

In the Name of the Father quickly became one of the highest-grossing films ever in Ireland. It was hailed as a masterpiece in America and won seven Oscar nominations, including best picture, director, script and actor, though it lost out to *Schindler's List*.

Stories had emerged from the set of Day-Lewis living on a prison diet of soup and slops, insisting on being called Gerry all the time and hiring people to wake him up every time he went to sleep. Sheridan later told me that it was true Day-Lewis went without sleep for several nights before the scene in which Conlon confesses to a bombing he had not carried out.

Sheridan maintained he had made a drama rather than a drama-documentary, but he hoped it would increase pressure for peace. Only months after the film's release, the IRA announced a cease-fire, and peace talks began.

Daniel Day-Lewis outside Liverpool Museum during the making of In the Name of the Father *(Universal). Photograph by Neville Elder*

CHAPTER NINE

Ryan's Daughter, Daniel's Foot and Tom's Dingle
IRELAND, EXCEPT DUBLIN

CAL (1984)

Like many films set in Northern Ireland during the Troubles, *Cal* was shot in the Republic, largely in the town of Drogheda, the area in and around Newbridge, County Kildare, and in the countryside of County Wicklow, which has proved a consistently popular location over the years.

John Lynch plays Cal, a young man who acts as driver for the IRA's killing of a policeman and subsequently becomes obsessed with the dead man's widow, Marcella Morton (Helen Mirren). He accepts an offer of work on her farm and they become lovers, but Cal is haunted by guilt and by IRA activists Crilly and Skeffington.

The Morton farm and Cal's cottage were about twenty-five miles south-west of Dublin, at Newbridge (Droichead Nua), but their potato field was at Delgany, County Wicklow, 30 miles away – a long way to go for potatoes. Marcella also finds time to work in the library at Charleville Mall, North Strand, Dublin; while Cal and Crilly rob the Lyric Cinema, in the town of Navan, almost thirty miles north of Dublin.

Crilly was living just along the road, however, in Ship Street in the industrial town of Drogheda. It provided several run-down urban sites, while County Wicklow provided many of the more rural ones, including the Sally Gap area of the Wicklow Mountains and Crone Wood, near the Powerscourt Waterfall.

Helen Mirren and John Lynch in Cal *(Goldcrest/Enigma)*

DECEMBER BRIDE (1991)

There was a time when Island Taggart, a tiny island in Strangford Lough, near Belfast, supported several families, but it was deserted when Saskia Reeves, Donal McCann and Ciaran Hinds set up home there for this film.

The story takes place at the turn of the century, with McCann and Hinds as two brothers living in the same house as Reeves – much to the disapproval of their Presbyterian neighbours. The film was shot largely on location in the area of Strangford Lough, a saltwater lough about 20 miles long and almost entirely surrounded by land. The principal location was Island Taggart, a strip of land less than a mile in length, opposite the village of Killyleagh.

Older villagers can remember farmers swimming their cattle over to the island, though it is more or less accessible by foot at low tide. It is still used for grazing, although it is now part of the National Trust's Strangford Lough Wildlife Scheme. The area is of interest to geologists, archaeologists and ornithologists, with large flocks of ducks, terns, waders, swans and geese.

The film-makers augmented the old farm buildings on the island with specially-built

December Bride (BFI/Channel Four/British Screen)

Nicole Kidman and Tom Cruise in Market Street, Dublin, doubling for Boston in Far and Away *(Imagine)*

sets. They also shot in Dublin's Stag's Head pub, in Dame Court, and in Anglesea Street, Dublin – which stood in for Belfast in the film.

EXCALIBUR (1981)

Strangely, films about the legendary English King Arthur, his Knights of the Round Table and his court at Camelot have been shot mainly on locations outside England. The makers of *First Knight* rebuilt Camelot in Wales; *Monty Python and the Holy Grail* filmed in Scotland; while the musical *Camelot*, with Richard Harris, was made in Spain and at Burbank in California.

John Boorman's *Excalibur* filmed in Ireland, with Camelot constructed on the backlot of Ardmore Studios, Bray, though Cahir Castle does feature in the film's early battle scenes in the dark ages before Arthur's reign. A twelfth-century fortress on a rock in the River Suir in Tipperary, Cahir was also used in *Barry Lyndon* and is open to the public.

Most of the location filming for *Excalibur* was done in County Wicklow, around Bray, often just a very short drive from the studios. Arthur (Nigel Terry) and Lancelot (Nicholas Clay) meet and duel at the famous Powerscourt Waterfall – the highest in the British Isles at 120 metres. Childers Wood, near Roundwood, was used for jousting scenes and for the wedding of Arthur and Guenevere (Cherie Lunghi). The knights go searching for the Holy Grail in the Sally Gap area of the Wicklow Mountains; and Wicklow Head appears in battle scenes.

The Rock of Cashel in Tipperary also makes an appearance, while the king's final departure was filmed on the shore at Derrynane, County Kerry.

FAR AND AWAY (1992)

Interiors are smoky, exteriors are misty, except when the film-makers want to show off the dramatic Dingle coastline, in this sprawling $68 million Mills and Boon of a movie. American Tom Cruise plays a poor but spunky country boy and his Australian wife, Nicole Kidman, is a rich but spunky young lady in this celebration of Irish clichés.

The film opens in western Ireland in 1892 with Joseph Donelly (Tom Cruise) scrapping with his brothers on the farm, just for fun, against the backdrop of the shimmering sea and the cliffs of the Dingle peninsula. The rural village in *Far and Away* was constructed near the village of Dunquin, much the same area as was used for *Ryan's Daughter*, looking out towards the Blasket Islands. Nothing remains to be seen at the location, except, of course, the spectacular landscape. 'Looking at this countryside it is astonishing that the immigrants of the last century actually wanted to leave,' said Ron Howard, who was a well-known juvenile television star as Richie Cunningham in the American sitcom *Happy Days* before directing such films as *Splash, Cocoon* and *Parenthood*. 'But beautiful as it was, it was land they didn't own. And if there's anything stronger in Irish blood than the love of the land, it's their spirit of independence. That's what brought them to America.'

Donelly blames the landlord for the death of his father and goes to shoot him at his country estate, represented in the film by Kilruddery, near Bray, seat of the Earls of Meath. It is celebrated principally for its formal gardens, which date from the seventeenth century.

After failing to kill the landlord, Donelly elopes with his daughter, Shannon Christie (Nicole Kidman), and sails across Dublin Bay, on one of the Guinness company's ships, to Boston.

Although the film shot both in Ireland and America, Dublin was used to represent the nineteenth-century melting pot of Boston. The scene in which the couple first arrive in Boston and witness a shooting was filmed at the back of the Guinness brewery in Market Street and other scenes were shot in and around Temple Lane in the Temple Bar area – Dublin's equivalent of the Left Bank, with its cafés and cobblestones, alleys and artists' studios, and a general air of old world bohemianism.

The film subsequently moves west, where Donelly and Christie take part in the Oklahoma land rush. This section of the film was shot in Montana, prior to the Irish filming.

Howard is of Irish descent himself, among other things, including Cherokee. 'One of my earliest memories is of my great-grandmother, who married this Irishman, calling me over and showing me this family album and a photograph from the newspaper of the land race . . . just blurs, but she pointed to this one blur that was out in front on horseback and said "That was your grandpa."'

Howard, who worked on the storyline for *Far and Away* as well as directing it, had long wanted to make a film about the old country and the emigrants of the last century. The reaction of critics and public alike suggest he need not have bothered.

THE FIELD (1991)

An Irish-American arrives back in the old country to buy a plot of land from a widow, but in so doing provokes the wrath of a local man who believes he has a right to the land; and they end up battering away at each other to settle their differences. That synopsis serves not only for John Ford's Irish classic *The Quiet Man* but also for Jim Sheridan's *The Field*.

While Ford made a romantic comedy, Sheridan managed to turn the same basic ingredients into a dark tragedy about land and about obsession, described as an Irish *King Lear* by one reviewer. Ford shot his film in the lush, low-lying countryside around Ashford Castle Hotel at Cong, while Sheridan found a very different landscape less than an hour's drive away at Leenane, a village overshadowed by the wet, misty, limestone mountains of Connemara and Mayo. It clings to the shore at the eastern end of a long, deep sea lough called Killary Harbour, reminiscent of the Scandinavian fjords.

The film was set in the 1930s and writer-director Sheridan said he wanted somewhere with an untouched, edge-of-the-world feel; more remote than *The Quiet Man*, more savage. Tom Berenger plays the American in Sheridan's film and, in his first major film for over ten years, the Irish actor Richard Harris is his rival, Bull McCabe.

Leenane itself was the principal location, with pub scenes shot in Gaynor's, one of three bars that serve this tiny one-street village, though Gaynor's sign makes it clear it is a 'family grocer' as well as 'select bar'. Photographs from the film decorate the walls of the dark, atmospheric interior where customers can sup their porter while looking out across the lough to the mountains beyond.

Richard Harris beside
The Field *(Granada*
Film/Ferndale)

Bull's house was a spartan stone cottage, subsequently inhabited by sheep, just beyond the village on the road to Clifden. The field at the centre of the dispute is a little patch of bright green, enclosed by a dry-stane dyke, beneath the dark Partry Mountains. It is about six miles outside Leenane on the right-hand side of the road to Westport beside a little bridge. The scene of the fight was a couple of miles from Leenane at the Aasleagh Falls on the Erriff River.

Whereas John Wayne and Victor McLaglen could hammer away at each other all over the place without much damage, Bull ends up killing the American and is driven mad by guilt over the murder and by the suicide of his own son many years before.

The white-bearded Harris was nicknamed 'The Ayatollah' by the film crew, partly in affection, but perhaps also partly in fear, for he gave a towering performance, full of incipient violence, in sympathy with the dramatic landscape around him. It is the landscape and Harris's performance that sear themselves on viewers' memories.

Harris won an Oscar nomination as best actor, though originally he was offered only a cameo role in the film, with Ray McAnally playing Bull. It was McAnally who pressed Jim Sheridan to make a film based on John B. Keane's play, but McAnally died a few months prior to filming, giving Harris the chance to take over the main role.

HENRY V (1944)

Agincourt was occupied by the Germans when Laurence Olivier translated Shakespeare's play to the big screen; and wartime conditions in England ruled it out as a possible site for the recreation of the famous battle of 1415 in which Henry V led the English to victory, against the odds, over the French. So, Olivier took himself across the Irish Sea, hired extras from all over Ireland and spent eight weeks getting the battle scenes that were so vital for the film's success.

The film begins with a recreation of the Globe Theatre and then opens out against highly stylised sets, scenes shot at Denham Studios, near London, before reaching its climax with the realism of the battle. Many of the Irish extras were farmers and Olivier noted in his autobiography, *Confessions of an Actor*, that 'all the Irish could ride'. He had 200 on horseback and 500 on foot.

The location he chose was the Powerscourt estate, at Enniskerry, about ten miles south of Dublin. The estate was granted to Viscount Powerscourt by James I in 1609. The extensive grounds, which are open to the public, provided Olivier with his Agincourt. Powerscourt House itself, an eighteenth-century Palladian house, was gutted by fire in 1974, just before a gala reopening. But Powerscourt remains famous for its formal gardens and waterfall.

Ireland was neutral during the Second World War but it gave Olivier the location, the men and the conditions he needed to make what was intended as a great statement of British patriotism and a rallying call for the war effort. It was dedicated to British commandos and airborne troops.

Olivier himself was wounded during the Powerscourt campaign. The most serious of a number of injuries occurred when he directed a rider to gallop straight towards the camera through which he was looking, expecting the horse to veer away at the last minute

Peter O'Toole in High
Spirits *(Palace)*

of its own accord. But it galloped straight into the camera sending a piece of metal through Olivier's top lip and gum, leaving him scarred for life. He concealed the scar under a moustache.

Kenneth Branagh's *Henry V* (1989) shot in and around Shepperton Studios, near London, though one of Chorus's speeches was filmed on the National Trust clifftops at Crowlink in Sussex.

HIGH SPIRITS (1988)

The story behind the real spooky castle that appears in Neil Jordan's film is as bizarre as the storyline of the film itself, in which Peter O'Toole heads a stellar cast as a drunken Irishman who has turned his ancestral castle into a hotel but cannot attract any guests until he hits upon the notion of getting his staff to pretend they are ghosts. He advertises Castle Plunkett Hotel as the most haunted place in Ireland. Then, of course, the real ghosts turn up.

The film was shot only partly in Ireland, but Neil Jordan, who wrote and directed it, did go on location in County Limerick. As Castle Plunkett, he used Dromore, a Victorian Gothic Revival castle, with round tower, near Askeaton. Built for the Earl of Limerick in the 1860s, it was abandoned to the ghosts less than a hundred years later. It was put up for sale in 1950, but, like Castle Plunkett, found no takers. With a roof on it, Dromore was liable for rates, so the roof was deliberately removed and the building was left to rot, though it remains an extremely impressive sight.

Jordan also shot in the surrounding countryside. His cast included Daryl Hannah, Steve Guttenberg, Liam Neeson, Ray McAnally and Connie Booth.

Jordan quarrelled with his backers over the final shape of the film and was disheart-ened by the experience. He said: 'I wanted to make the film in Ireland. I wanted it to be magical and worldly in the sense that does still exist in Irish mythology and legend . . . Getting what I wanted was extremely difficult.' He later admitted the end-result was 'very ungainly'.

Smash Hits magazine called it 'a brilliantly executed, supernatural romantic comedy', but most of the reviews were closer to that in *Monthly Film Bulletin*, which said the film 'hasn't a flicker of comic sensibility or a funny line'.

INTO THE WEST (1992)

Director Mike Newell, who would later achieve enormous international success with *Four Weddings and a Funeral*, crossed Ireland from the Galway coast to the high-rise flats of Dublin and then back again in this charming and underrated tale about two boys, Tito and Ossie, who are led across the countryside by a mysterious white horse called Tir na nOg. They are the children of a traveller (Gabriel Byrne) who, following the death of his wife, whose spirit the horse seems to represent, spends his time drowning his sorrows and simply vegetating in a flat in Dublin's Ballymun scheme.

Exteriors were shot at Ballymun and the interiors, in which the boys take the horse up to their flat, were shot in the studio at Ardmore, outside Dublin. Tir na nOg is first seen on the white shelly beach at Dog's Bay, near Roundstone in Galway, before

accompanying the boys' grandfather (David Kelly) to Ballymun.

The horse is taken away from the boys, but they steal it back and head off with the police and their father in pursuit. Most of the cross-country scenes were shot in County Wicklow, though Tito and Ossie are seen making a meal of baked beans for themselves in the shadow of Lea Castle, near the little town of Portarlington, on the county boundary between Laois and Offaly. The castle is no stranger to mysterious comings and goings involving horses, for its last occupant was Cathal na gCapall, Charles the Horse, not, in fact, a horse but a noted horse thief who used the castle vaults as stables. The castle's gateway and round bastion survive.

The boys spend a night in Portarlington itself, site of a seventeenth-century Huguenot community and also of the first Irish power station driven by peat. The boys shelter in the Savoy cinema, an operational cinema in the film, though in reality it has been empty for years.

Tir na nOg leads them to their mother's grave, on Turlough Hill, near Wicklow Gap in the Wicklow Mountains, which would have meant they were doubling back on themselves. They pass Powerscourt Waterfall – undoubtedly one of the most frequently used locations in Irish films – before ending up back at Dog's Bay, where their mother's soul is finally set free.

THE MIRACLE (1991)

After working in America with Robert De Niro and an eight-figure budget, Neil Jordan decided to make his next film at home – not just in Ireland but in his own house in Bray, the Edwardian seaside resort where James Joyce lived for a few years in the late ninteenth century. *The Miracle* is literally Jordan's home movie.

Jordan told me at the time that he felt the need to make a small-budget Irish film after a couple of 'ungainly' Hollywood projects – *High Spirits* and *We're No Angels* – and his script for *The Miracle* drew on his own feelings about growing up in Ireland and about small-town Irish life. He had bought the house in Bray, just south of Dublin, about eight years earlier and always thought it had film potential, so he lent it to two of the characters in *The Miracle*.

Niall Byrne is Jimmy, a teenager living with his father, Sam (Donal McCann). Sam is an alcoholic who plays saxophone in a dance-band. Jimmy's mother supposedly died when he was small. Jimmy whiles away the time with his friend, Rose (Lorraine Pilkington), inventing stories about people they encounter, such as a group of bathing nuns. They are particularly intrigued by a glamorous American stranger (Beverly d'Angelo) who turns up at the railway station one day. Jimmy becomes obsessed with her and follows her to a Dublin theatre, where she is playing Frenchy in a production of *Destry Rides Again*.

The film-makers used the exterior of the Olympia in Dame Street, Dublin, and the interior of the older Gaiety Theatre in South King Street, but most of the locations were in Bray – the beach, the promenade, the railway station, the hill called Bray Head and Jordan's house – the exact position of which has, of course, not been publicised. In fact, the press notes on the film simply state that 'the house in which much of the action

Beverly D'Angelo and Niall Byrne in The Miracle *(Palace/Channel Four/British Screen)*

happens is like Jordan's own house' and that a series of other scenes 'takes place in the stretch of seaside promenade that Neil Jordan can see from his window as he writes'.

MOBY DICK (1956)

John Huston filmed in, or off, four different countries to translate Herman Melville's great novel of whales, obsession and vengeance to the screen, with a cast that included Orson Welles and Gregory Peck as Captain Ahab. Huston later described the film in his autobiography, *An Open Book*, as the most difficult he ever made and admitted he was lucky no one was killed as he strove to recreate the excitement and danger of a nineteenth-century whaling expedition.

Production began routinely enough at Shepperton and the ABC Studios, near London, where the film-makers worked with small-scale whale models in a tank, but very little of that footage was used. Most of the filming was done at sea, with a 104-foot, wooden-hulled sailing ship and 90-foot models of the title character – the great white whale that tore off Ahab's leg and which he is now bent on tracking down and killing.

The film itself begins with the arrival of Ishmael (Richard Basehart) in New Bedford, Massachusetts, where he signs up with Ahab. For New Bedford, Huston used the little market town, resort and fishing port of Youghal (pronounced Yawl), in County Cork, on the St George's Channel. The harbour scenes were shot there and the film-makers had all the houses painted to look like New England, except the public house, where the landlord wanted more money. Huston recalls in his autobiography that the pub was not vital to the film, but the locals boycotted it and when Huston expressed regret the publican said: 'I had it coming; I was trying to get something for nothing.' Huston notes: 'Where but in Ireland would you ever hear such an admission?'

For filming at sea, Huston used the Welsh port of Fishguard, on the other side of St George's Channel, as his initial base, but was hampered by bad weather and lost two whales when the two-inch thick nylon cable snapped in stormy seas. The whales consisted of steel and wood covered with latex and cost about $25,000 each. When the American producers visited Fishguard and saw the conditions under which Huston was filming they agreed to the extra expense involved in shooting the remaining sea scenes off the Canary Islands.

Moby Dick came out to mixed reviews, with many critics feeling that Peck lacked the depth necessary for Ahab, but *Leonard Maltin's Movie and Video Guide* reckons he brought a 'deranged dignity' to the part and the *Virgin Film Guide* now rates the film as 'one of the most historically authentic, visually stunning and powerful adventures ever made'.

MY LEFT FOOT (1989)

Daniel Day-Lewis upset the bookies' odds when he won the best actor's Oscar for his portrayal of the crippled writer and artist Christy Brown in this low-budget film – in preference to Tom Cruise's performance as the crippled Ron Kovic in Oliver Stone's *Born on the Fourth of July*. Day-Lewis also established his reputation as one of the most single-minded and committed actors in cinema. He spent every day of the six-week shoot in a wheelchair and would speak only in the same distorted manner as the late Christy Brown. Members of the cast took it in turns to feed him.

Gene Lambert, an artist and photographer crippled in a car crash, acted as consultant on the film. He said: 'He had to be washed, fed, dressed; he had to experience the thousand little humiliations that occur, irrespective of your abilities.'

Day-Lewis also learned to write and paint with his left foot, just like Brown, who suffered from cerebral palsy.

The film begins with Brown's meeting with nurse Mary Carr (Ruth McCabe) at a charity gala, where there is to be a reading from his autobiography. Kilruddery House, the mock-Tudor home of the Earl of Meath, just south of Bray, served as the location. It is noted for its formal garden, with lake, canals and amphitheatre, as well as its panelled great hall.

The film is told partly in flashback, with the exterior of Brown's house filmed at St Kevin's Square, Bray, and the interiors at Bray's Ardmore Studios. Christy Brown's art exhibition, which was a mixture of paintings by Brown, Lambert and Day-Lewis, was staged at the private residence of the film's producer, Noel Pearson, at Old Conna, just outside Bray.

Brown is desperately upset to learn that his doctor, Eileen Cole (Fiona Shaw), who has encouraged his art, is to marry the gallery owner and he creates an embarrassing scene in a restaurant, Locks Restaurant, in Windsor Terrace in the Portobello area of Dublin.

The film ends with Brown and Mary Carr drinking champagne and watching dawn break over the city, beside the nondescript stone monument on top of Victoria Hill at Killiney, a coastal suburb of Dublin. The hilltop is just a short walk from the roadside, up steps and a paved path, and it affords fine views over the surrounding land and sea.

Brenda Fricker won an Oscar as Brown's mother, while Ray McAnally won a posthumous British Academy Award as his father. Day-Lewis was acclaimed best actor in both the American and British Academy Awards.

THE PLAYBOYS (1992)

After the phenomenal success of *My Left Foot*, writer Shane Connaughton had the pleasure of seeing a major feature film being shot in the remote village of Redhills where he grew up and knowing he was responsible for bringing some unaccustomed glamour to the little community.

The playboys of the title were the travelling actors on whom the villagers relied for occasional entertainment before the days of television. They were the lowest rung on the acting scale. Connaughton recalls: 'They would go to the cinema and see a film and then come and act it out for the locals that night.' Now Redhills had somewhat more distinguished visitors in the shape of Albert Finney, Aidan Quinn and Robin Wright, subsequently Tom Hanks's girlfriend in *Forrest Gump*.

Redhills is a mile or so south of the Irish border in County Cavan, little more than a village green with a handful of houses round it, deep in a region of green countryside and hundreds of lakes. Connaughton's father had been police sergeant there and Connaughton made the village sergeant one of the principal characters in his story, which is set in the fifties.

Wright plays a young woman who has scandalised the village by having an illegitimate

baby and refusing to name the father. Finney is the policeman who wants to marry her and Quinn is the 'playboy' who is Finney's rival for her affections.

Connaughton remembered the playboys from his childhood and said they had had a tremendous effect on him. He began his career as an actor. 'The actors were very important because no one else would come to us,' he says. 'We never got the circus or the big companies. The only people who did come were people like The Playboys, who would set up on the village green and put on a show.'

There were serious doubts about the practicalities of shooting in Redhills. Producer Bill Cartlidge said at the time: 'We agonised over making the film here because of its remoteness. The attraction obviously was that it is the real place that Shane wrote about and therefore it fits into the action of the movie quite easily.' In the end, it was shot entirely on location there. Director Gillies MacKinnon says: 'That includes the interior sets, which were built in a local garage (McMahon's). The rest of it was mostly done around the village green. There was incredible co-operation from the people of Redhills.'

The village shop had remained empty and unchanged since Connaughton was a boy and it was used as Robin Wright's shop in the film. One of the few locations outside Redhills was the church a few miles away at Corig, where Wright's character is denounced for immorality.

At the end of eight weeks' filming, there were emotional farewells. On completing his last scene, Finney was presented with a large Cavan crystal goblet. Two policemen arrived, arrested him for impersonating a police officer and led him away in handcuffs. Finney said later: 'Thank goodness they came and removed me. I was about to make a fool of myself and burst into tears.' But Finney and Connaughton were to return to Redhills in summer 1994 for another film *The Run of the Country*, again inspired by Connaughton's youth there, with Finney once again playing a police sergeant.

THE QUIET MAN (1952)

John Ford, one of cinema's greatest directors, had been wanting to film *The Quiet Man* since the thirties, but had been continually thwarted by Hollywood's doubts about a romantic comedy set in far-off Ireland. Finally, Ford secured a deal with Republic Pictures, and he, John Wayne, Maureen O'Hara and Victor McLaglen took themselves off to County Mayo for extensive location shooting that would eventually have to be married with studio footage shot in Hollywood.

But Ford's belief in the project was well placed and in due course he won a record fourth Oscar as best director. The film won another for cinematography, thanks to the lush location shots, and picked up five more nominations, including best picture. Many people now cite it as their favourite film of all time and, 30 years after it was made, it would become one of the best-selling videos in Britain.

In June 1951, John Wayne, who had just established himself as Hollywood's biggest box-office draw, arrived with the production team in the village of Cong, following the footsteps of ancient kings who had sought solace in its historic abbey. Although John Ford was born in America, his parents were Irish and his real name was Sean Aloysius O'Feeney;

Maureen O'Hara was born in Dublin and John Wayne had Irish blood in him. Although he made a career of playing Irishmen, Victor McLaglen was born in England.

It is easy to see the appeal to Ford of Maurice Walsh's short story about a man who leaves his home in America to return to a simpler life in rural Ireland. John Wayne, who had already worked with Ford on several westerns, including *Stagecoach*, was to play Sean Thornton, the central character – the quiet man of the title. O'Hara was Mary Kate Danaher, the colleen who both enchants and enrages him, before he literally takes her in hand. It is difficult to make a case for *The Quiet Man* from a feminist perspective. McLaglen was her brute of a brother, Red Will, who is angry because Thornton has bought back the Thornton family's former land and prevented Red Will from getting it.

The film opens with a shot of Lough Corrib and the magnificent, greystone Ashford Castle, which looks like a boy's over-imaginative vision of a giant medieval fortress, though it was built in the nineteenth century. In reality, the castle seems out of all proportion to the neighbouring village of Cong, which is little more than a single street of whitewashed houses on a strip of land that separates Lough Mask and Lough Corrib; County Mayo and County Galway. The village is called Inisfree in the film, a name that immediately evokes the romance of Ireland through its associations with W. B. Yeats's poem *The Lake Isle of Innisfree*.

I will arise and go now, and go to Innisfree,
And a small cabin build there, of clay and wattles made;
Nine bean rows will I have there, a hive for the honey bee,
And live alone in the bee-loud glade.

Pat Cohan's bar in Cong in The Quiet Man *(Argosy)*

Maureen O'Hara
and John Wayne in
The Quiet Man
(Argosy)

There is a real island called Innisfree in Lough Gill, near Sligo, about sixty miles north-east of Cong.

Ashford Castle had belonged to the Guinness family, but was already a hotel at the time of filming, and provided accommodation for the stars – even if Cong could not provide them with all the modern conveniences to which they were accustomed, such things as electricity.

The area around the hotel was to provide the location for much of the filming. The Danaher house was in reality the Ashford farmhouse, which is still there, and Thornton first sees Mary Kate tending her sheep in the grounds of Ashford Castle, on land which became part of the Ashford Castle golf course. At that point, Thornton is just arriving in Inisfree, having been picked up by Barry Fitzgerald's horse and trap at Castletown railway station, described as being about five and a half miles from Inisfree. It is seen again later in the film when Thornton prevents Mary Kate from leaving and drags her from the station and across country back to Inisfree.

Ford used the little station at Ballyglunin, about 20 miles away, between Athenry and Tuam. A colourful picture-postcard of a station, in green and white, with neat beds of daffodils and wallflowers, it has changed little since filming. The station sign proclaims 'Castletown for Ballyglunin'. The main difference is that there are no longer any regular passenger services, only the occasional goods train and special excursions.

The Quiet Man is a film that manages to be both lyrical and brawling, and provides one of the best-known, most expansive fights in the history of cinema, with Thornton and Red Will – Wayne and McLaglen – hammering away at each other over the length and breadth of the village. Of course, Wayne wins in the film, but he would have had little chance in real life, for McLaglen had been a professional boxer, good enough to fight a tied bout with the world heavyweight champion Jack Johnson.

The fight for the Inisfree championship began at the farm but climaxed at the village pub. For the pub, the film-makers decided on Murphy's general store and the sign 'Pat Cohan – Bar' was hung above it and left in place after filming finished; it was still there more than forty years later. Cohan's was the only bar in the area allowed to open on a Sunday.

Ford used both Roman Catholic and Protestant Church of Ireland churches. He shot interiors at the Catholic church, which had a Harry Clarke stained-glass window, and exteriors at the Protestant church nearby. The Catholic church's holy water font was moved to the Protestant church and left there by mistake. The Protestant worshippers were outraged by its presence the following Sunday, and complained to the bishop about their minister, who had given permission for filming. The bishop came up with a simple solution – all would be well if Ford promised to scrap all the footage from the church. It is not known what Ford said at the time, but the footage remains in the film. The Catholic church has been rebuilt and is a spectacularly ugly building that looks like a concrete, or rather asbestos, blockhouse – though it is pleasant enough inside, where Clarke's windows have pride of place. The traditional Church of Ireland building, with its high steeple, is just along the road, inside the grounds of Ashford Castle.

Just at the gates at the exit from the castle's one-way road system is the picturesque cottage, covered in red creeper, where the Reverend Playfair lived in the film. The castle is a five-star hotel whose guests have included former film stars President Reagan and Princess Grace of Monaco. Boards declaring 'Residents Only' are posted at the entrance to the building, but it is possible to spend hours wandering around the grounds, visiting *Quiet Man* sites and enjoying the expansive views of the lough with its many little islands. Use of Ashford's 25,000 acres was one of the main reasons Ford chose the region.

Ford shot the film's horse-race at Tully Strand in Connemara and Thornton's home, White o' Morn', was at Teernakill in Maam Valley, about ten miles west of Cong. O'Hara said: 'It is a beautiful little cottage, with a stream in front and with stepping-stones across. One would think some set designer just dreamed it as it is.' The irony was that the owners made so much money from the film that they built a new house alongside and let the cottage fall into ruin.

O'Hara was already a major Hollywood star, through films such as *The Hunchback of Notre Dame* and Ford's Oscar-winning *How Green Was My Valley* (which was set in Wales, but filmed in Hollywood). She was determined to return to her homeland for *The Quiet Man*. 'As far as I'm concerned, Ireland is the star of the picture,' she told the local *Connacht Tribune*. 'No one has ever put Ireland on the screen in Technicolor before.'

John Wayne went back to America in buoyant mood, convinced *The Quiet Man* was one of his best films. Many would agree.

RYAN'S DAUGHTER (1970)

Cameras had to be chained to rocks, Leo McKern lost an eye in stormy seas (a glass one, though not everyone knew it at the time) and Trevor Howard and John Mills almost drowned, as David Lean strove to capture the power of the elements for his sprawling drama of rural passion.

After *The Bridge on the River Kwai, Lawrence of Arabia* and *Doctor Zhivago*, Lean turned to Ireland for his next film. An original love story for the screen, set against the backdrop of the Irish Rebellion of 1916, it is the only one of David Lean's epics which is set mainly in Britain or Ireland. It was written by the playwright Robert Bolt, who had provided the scripts for *Lawrence* and *Zhivago*.

Sarah Miles, who was married to Bolt at the time, is the publican's daughter, Rosy Ryan, whose romantic dreams fail to find fulfilment in her marriage to a much older man – Robert Mitchum, brilliantly cast against type as the gentle, patient schoolmaster Charles Shaughnessy. She turns instead to Major Doryan (Christopher Jones), the shellshocked officer in command of the local British garrison.

The film took a year to shoot and was done mainly on location in County Kerry, on the Dingle peninsula, a wild and remote strip of land jutting out into the Atlantic in south-west Ireland. Eventually, Lean and his unit went off to South Africa to shoot the final scenes there, but not before the film had made an enormous impact on the local community and had captured footage of the beaches, cliffs and countryside that was to enchant audiences around the world and give a long-term boost to the tourist industry.

Rosy Ryan's village of Kirrary was built by the film-makers in the winter of 1968-69

Ryan's Daughter
(MGM/Faraway)

A story of love.
Filmed by David Lean
Ryan's Daughter

starring
ROBERT MITCHUM · TREVOR HOWARD · CHRISTOPHER JONES
JOHN MILLS · LEO McKERN and SARAH MILES · BARRY FOSTER
Screenplay by ROBERT BOLT · Produced by ANTHONY HAVELOCK-ALLEN
METROCOLOR and 70mm SUPER-PANAVISION · Released by MGM-EMI DISTRIBUTORS

MGM

ⒶⒷⒸ 2 EDINBURGH COMMENCING 15th FEBRUARY

Evenings Commence 7.10 p.m. Sundays Commence 6.45 p.m. Matinees Held Monday to Saturday
Programmes Commence 1.45 p.m. ADVANCE BOOKING OFFICE NOW OPEN FROM 11 a.m. to 8 p.m. For The Booking
of all Seats Evenings Only One Week in Advance   Stalls 75p (15/-) 50p (10/-)

on a hill called Maoilinn na Ceathrun, behind the village of Carhoo in the parish of Dunquin – popularly known as the last parish before America. Lean said: 'It was cheaper that way. To find a village of the period in the first place is next-door to impossible, and then add to that a village in a desolate spot. Also, in a rural village the shopkeepers want payments.' A specially-built village meant he had greater control over the place and could keep sightseers away.

Nothing remains of Kirrary today except a cobblestone street and the stone foundations of some houses, though the local people were asked if they wanted it left intact. 'The trouble is that the village was built on a commonage,' says Micheal de Mordha, a local man who wrote *The Best Government We Ever Had*, an Irish-language account of the impact of the film on the local community – it takes its title from one old woman's view of the film-makers.

De Mordha adds: 'A commonage means that several people have title and it's for common use . . . Some of the houses, you know, only the fronts were built properly. The backs were built with timber and that sort of thing. So they weren't really sound structures and they were on top of a mountain as well, which was susceptible to gales and all that. They were afraid, maybe, of hooliganism, because just after the film was finished people were going up there and thinking of squatting. And they didn't like that sort of thing being brought on the parish, so eventually it was demolished completely.'

However, the single-storey stone schoolhouse is still standing about a mile away, on the cliffs looking out towards the Blasket Islands. Both the schoolhouse and Ryan's pub, where Major Doryan suffers a spasm of shellshock and is comforted by Rosy, were built with walls that opened to allow cameras and lights in. The schoolhouse looks solid enough from the front, but is now partly open at the back.

Much of the story takes place away from the village on the beach. Rosy and the major spend time together there; the village idiot Michael (John Mills) finds the major's brass button on the beach and subsequently parades through the village with it; IRA arms come ashore in a dreadful storm; and the major blows himself up on the beach. The film's poster shows Rosy standing on a clifftop as her parasol blows down towards the stretch of yellow sand, on which stands a single darkened figure.

Being the perfectionist he was, Lean was never going to settle for one beach. Most of the filming was done at Inch Strand, a long stretch of beach about twelve miles east of the town of Dingle, and at Coumeenoole Strand, a little beach surrounded by cliffs in the Dunquin area. The steep road that runs right down on to it was used in the scene where the villagers appear *en masse* to help rescue the arms shipment.

It was at Coumeenoole that a curragh (a small rowing boat) was overturned by a high wave and Mills and Trevor Howard, weighed down by heavy boots and a priest's cassock, were caught in the dangerous off-shore currents and had to be rescued by frogmen. Sarah Miles wrote in her highly readable autobiography, *Serves Me Right*: 'Both disappeared into the rough sea, but David refused to say "Cut!" The stuntmen finally pulled them to shore, where they were rushed off to hospital either stunned or unconscious.'

She recalls another occasion when Leo McKern (Ryan) had to be rescued from a watery grave. 'The shock of Leo's soaking appearance was most macabre if you weren't

Sarah Miles and Robert Mitchum in Ryan's Daughter *(MGM/Faraway)*

expecting to see a mass of sand oozing out from an empty eye-socket. No one had told me Leo wore a glass eye.'

Lean also filmed on Barrow Strand, north of Tralee.

Storm scenes were shot way to the north in County Clare, not, however, at the famous Cliffs of Moher, though they do appear at the start of the film when Rosy loses her parasol. A sheer precipice five miles long, rising to a height of almost seven hundred feet, they afford a view of virtually the whole ragged coast of County Clare and they certainly do not lack for drama.

That was the problem as far as the storm was concerned. Associate producer Roy Stevens explains: 'It doesn't matter how big the storm is, the cliffs are so big that it looks like nothing. So, while I looked at it, we didn't actually film anything there.'

They filmed about thirty miles to the south in the area of the Bridges of Ross, where there are a number of striking rock formations, including a natural rock bridge. Many of the rocks are very flat and look like roads that have been ripped up by an earthquake and left at an angle. Stevens says: 'The place that I found that was very good was a huge rock where at the right tide the waves would come over the rock and crunch down, and it was safe enough to get people in.'

Coumeenoole Strand, one of the locations for Ryan's Daughter

Cinematographer Freddie Young later told an interviewer: 'David spent months on the storm scene. It was a two-hour journey to that particular bit of the coast. We got the whole force of the storm coming across the Atlantic. We'd get a storm warning and off

we'd go and we'd arrive and there would be this storm happening. We'd start shooting, work perhaps for an hour or two and then the storm would die away.'

The cameramen worked in wet suits with their cameras and themselves chained to the rocks to get unforgettable footage of the Atlantic tossing and heaving as the villagers attempt to salvage the IRA arms.

At the end of 1969, cast and crew left Ireland for six weeks' filming in South Africa. In the depth of Irish winter it was impossible to get the sort of bright beach scenes Lean needed to match earlier footage. The light was right in South Africa, but the rocks were wrong. The problem was the rocks were too light and the art department was instructed to paint them a darker colour, like the rocks in Ireland.

But that still was not the end of the storm sequence. Lean remained dissatisfied with the footage he had got, so he left Roy Stevens and a second unit team in Ireland to get more. They stayed in the town of Ennis and every time the wind got up they drove off down the coast towards the Bridges of Ross. But that was not often. 'It was more like a Mediterranean flat sea and cloudless sky.' Stevens says they were there for almost two months before they had the shots they needed.

Originally, *Ryan's Daughter* was scheduled as a 16-week shoot, but it took a year to film and a further six months to edit.

There was considerable tension within the production team, as Lean demanded take after take after take. Robert Mitchum liked to give the impression he did not take films very seriously, while David Lean was the ultimate perfectionist; though he dismissed reports that he waited months before filming clouds because they were not the right shape.

The scenery was spectacular, but Mitchum found the social scene rather limiting. He drank to excess – claiming to have drunk more Scotch on *Ryan's Daughter* than at any other time in his life. He grew his own cannabis in the back garden of the Milltown House guest house – which he took over for the duration – and he got himself involved in a brawl with one of the locals, which resulted in a badly bruised eye for Mitchum and disruption of filming. Close-ups of Mitchum were impossible for six weeks.

The greatest problems were with Christopher Jones as the major. Marlon Brando had been mooted for the role at one point, but Jones was being touted as the new James Dean at the time and Lean cast Jones after seeing him in *The Looking Glass War*, which he was watching to consider Anthony Hopkins. What Lean apparently did not know at the time was that all Jones's dialogue had to be re-recorded by another actor. Eventually, Lean would also get someone else to dub Jones's lines and Jones did not fulfil his potential as the new James Dean.

All those involved in *Ryan's Daughter* have vivid memories of the problems he had going through with a love scene with Sarah Miles. In her book, Miles said that eventually they had to drug him to do it and he was asleep on top of her while she had to pretend to be in the throes of passion. She wrote that, years later, Jones said that he had been deeply in love with the actress Sharon Tate (though she was married to Roman Polanski at the time), and was devastated by news of her murder during filming.

The British critics came close to murdering the film and it was to be more than ten

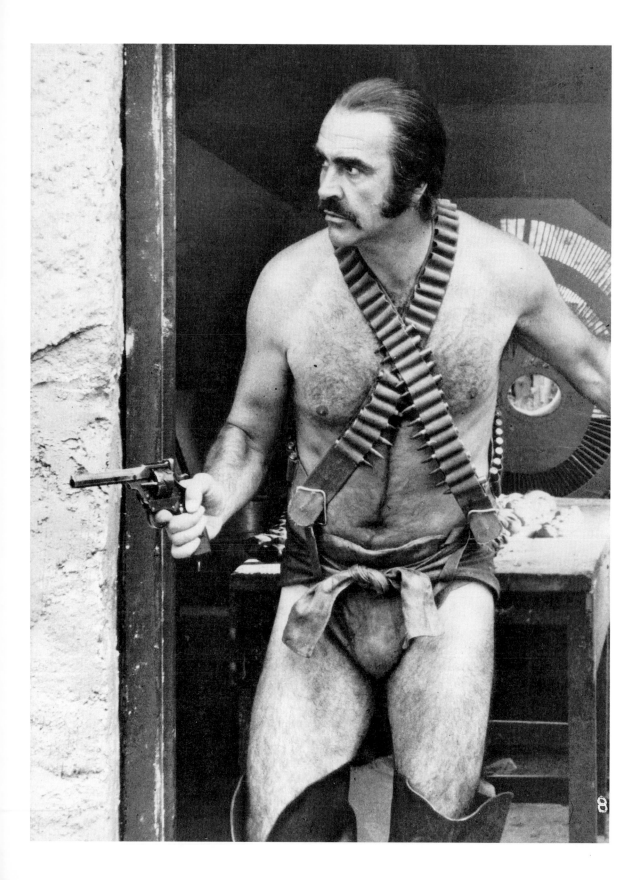

8

years before Lean made another, *A Passage to India*. *Ryan's Daughter* exploits its landscape as few other films have done, but that seemed to be the main problem as far as many critics were concerned. 'Lean's film succumbs ... to a debilitating travelogue prettiness,' said Nigel Andrews in *Monthly Film Bulletin*.

The American critics were kinder, as was the American Academy of Motion Picture Arts and Sciences. Mills won an Oscar as best supporting actor, Young won the Oscar for cinematography and Sarah Miles was nominated as best actress. In reality, it was a flawed masterpiece, with the story, music, location filming and several performances, including those of Mitchum and Howard, contributing to a hugely enjoyable film.

Sean Connery in Zardoz (John Boorman/ 20th Century-Fox)

WAR OF THE BUTTONS (1994)

The novel on which David Puttnam's film is based is set in France where it had been filmed in the early sixties, but Puttnam chose to relocate Louis Pergaud's story of two gangs of boys from neighbouring villages to the southern coast of Ireland. 'In rural Ireland there is still a real sense of community that is dead or dying in rural Britain,' said Puttnam.

With international financial backing, including funds from the United States, Japan and France, Puttnam hired an experienced English writer, Colin Welland, with whom he had worked on *Chariots of Fire*, a first-time director John Roberts, a recent graduate of England's National Film School, and an Irish cast – many of them children.

The action centres on the rivalry between gangs from the villages of Ballydowse and Carrickdowse, for which Puttnam chose Union Hall and Castletownshend; traditional fishing villages on neighbouring inlets on the coast of County Cork. Castletownshend was the home of Edith Somerville and Martin Ross (Violet Martin), authors of the Irish R. M. stories. They are buried in a local cemetery.

The film is set in the recent past and the film-makers used the villages very much as they found them. Production designer Jim Clay said: 'We've gone for a very natural look, but, in its own way, it's more colourful than almost anything I've ever done. You can understand why they call it the Emerald Isle. To tamper with it would have been mad.'

There was a naval engagement between the English and Spanish off Castletownshend in 1602. The war between the Ballys and Carricks is an altogether different affair, taking its name from the practice of cutting off the enemies' buttons as a symbol of victory.

The climactic Battle of Bunduff Castle takes place beside the Gothic ruins of Castle Freke, former home of the Barons Carbery.

ZARDOZ (1974)

Sean Connery ran riot in a Zapata moustache, Engelbert sideburns, thigh-length boots and bright orange swimming-trunks as an Exterminator in the wastelands of the twenty-third century – known as the Outlands and represented by Wicklow Mountains.

The film itself was a little ahead of the game in its mix of post-industrial collapse and old-fashioned action, but very much rooted to its time by its attitudes and the fashion sense of its characters. It might have succeeded as junk entertainment, but clearly writer-director John Boorman, fresh from the success of *Deliverance*, was aiming for something more cerebral.

His élite live in isolated luxury, sealed off from the masses, who are killed or enslaved by the Exterminators, including Zed (Connery). The Exterminators worship a flying godhead Zardoz who delivers their guns and in the course of the plot is revealed to be a creation of one of the élite; its name derived from the Wizard of Oz.

Much of the filming was done in the area off the L161 road, in spectacular, wild mountain scenery around the Sally Gap, the Luggala estate, Lough Dan and Lough Tay.

It seems appropriate that while the élite live in a stately home, Hollybrook, near Bray, the Brutals should be scratching a living about five miles away at a former reformatory, Glencree, north of the Sally Gap junction on a backroad from the Wicklow Mountains to Dublin. It was built as a barracks in the late eighteenth century, served as a reformatory in the nineteenth and as a centre for victims of the Troubles in Northern Ireland in the twentieth.

While Boorman's settings have a strange timeless quality, everything else about the film is firmly stamped with the mark of the early seventies and, ultimately, it gets bogged down in its intellectual aspirations.

CHAPTER TEN
Robin Hood Goes on Tour
EVERYWHERE EXCEPT SHERWOOD FOREST

BARRY LYNDON (1975)

Stanley Kubrick set out to make his period drama in Ireland, but after ten weeks he had spent the entire $2. 5 million budget, completed only about a tenth of the film and had become the subject of terrorist threats. So he packed up and moved over to England where he finished the film using some of the grandest houses in the country.

The film is based on a William Thackeray novel about a womanising Irish scoundrel and is set in the eighteenth century, with its pronounced class differences.

Among the Irish locations was Cahir Castle, on the River Suir, in Tipperary. An imposing structure dating back to the twelfth century, it has been the subject of several sieges over the years, led by Essex and Cromwell among others. Rebuilt several times, it is open to the public in summer.

Kubrick subsequently spent about three months at Longleat House, the Wiltshire home of the Marquess of Bath. It was built for his ancestors in the sixteenth century, an enormous Italian Renaissance building. In 1949 it became the first English stately home to open to the public and in 1966 Lord Bath and Jimmy Chipperfield established the first safari park outside Africa. Longleat also featured in *The Missionary* and *Splitting Heirs*.

Other locations for *Barry Lyndon* included Wilton House, the home of the Earl of Pembroke, near Salisbury, and Corsham Court, an Elizabethan and Georgian house, also in Wiltshire. It was one of the locations for *The Remains of the Day*. Wilton House is a magnificent sixteenth/seventeenth-century mansion famous for its state rooms. The elaborately decorated Double Cube room, hung with Van Dycks, was the scene of a banquet in the film. The Double Cube was also the location used in the 1984 film *The Bounty* for the court-martial of Lieutenant Bligh (Anthony Hopkins). Wilton House is open to the public except in winter and was used by various other films, including *Lady Caroline Lamb*, *The Return of a Man Called Horse* and *The Madness of King George*.

Barry Lyndon's wedding was shot at the chapel of Petworth House, a National Trust property in Sussex, which also appears in *Silver Bears*, starring Michael Caine. The chapel, with its arched windows and gallery, is the oldest part of the house, dating back to the thirteenth century. Most of the house was built in the seventeenth century by the Duke of Somerset, who had married into the Percy family, owners of Petworth since Norman times. The west front of the house is over one hundred yards long and the wall round the surrounding parkland is 13 miles in length.

But what makes Petworth most remarkable is its paintings. The collection, which includes Van Dyck, Holbein, Rembrandt and Reynolds, is considered one of the finest in England outwith the public art galleries. It includes paintings of Petworth's landscaped park by Turner. He spent long periods at Petworth and had his own studio above the chapel.

Kubrick appears to have been attempting much the same effect as a painter in his elegantly composed film, using slow backward zoom shots outside and specially designed lighting and camera techniques for interior shots. He even shot by candlelight, showing the dimly lit rooms as the people of the eighteenth century would have seen them. Kubrick spent a great deal of time on research and endeavoured to make sure every detail was correct. Many of the costumes were genuine costumes of the period. Kubrick also shot Prussian scenes on location in Germany, using Potsdam for Berlin.

The film is a long way from the usual Hollywood costume drama. Critics complained it was too dark, too slow, too long. Many attacked the blandness of Ryan O'Neal, best known as the star of *Love Story*, in the title role. Others felt his blandness was appropriate for the role. Leonard Rossiter, best known for his television role as Reggie Perrin, appears as Captain Quin, Barry Lyndon's rival in love. Rossiter was also in Kubrick's *2001*.

Barry Lyndon was nominated for the best-picture Oscar and won awards for cinematography, music, costumes and art direction. It has many supporters and it seems likely to undergo critical revaluation in the future.

CHARIOTS OF FIRE (1981)

It was always going to be the case that Scotland and England would share the gold medals on the track, but as with all Olympic Games there was another earlier contest to decide who would host them. It was a close-run thing between Scotland and England, before the film-makers decided against Murrayfield, home of Scottish rugby, and opted instead for the Bebington Oval, an athletics venue in Merseyside smaller than most Third Division football stadiums. It was its modest size which won it the right to appear in the film as the venue for the 1924 Olympic Games in Paris. 'The Olympics in 1924 were almost like a big school sports day,' says location manager Iain Smith.

Although Bebington may have been historically accurate, Smith himself felt there was a danger that it would simply look wrong to audiences with modern perceptions of the Olympics as the world's biggest sports jamboree. 'I argued that we should be looking for a bigger location of the period rather than one that was absolutely precise, so that we're dealing with a modern audience's expectations. Murrayfield would have been perfect.' Murrayfield was not, of course, the modern superstructure it is today. However, producer David Puttnam and director Hugh Hudson opted for Bebington and the town across the Mersey from Liverpool got its moment of Olympic glory.

Another consideration may have been the tightness of the budget, which restricted filming to Britain in the first place. It was, of course, much easier to fill Bebington than Murrayfield. It needed only about 7,000 people. Nevertheless, most of the shooting was done with a hundred extras strategically placed to give the impression of a full house.

Despite the arguments that Bebington would be more authentic than Murrayfield, the stadium itself was built as recently as 1972, though there had been a running track there for many years before that. Bebington Oval continues to serve as a local sports ground, with club athletics and county championships.

Chariots of Fire filmed entirely on location in England and Scotland, opening and closing with the famous sequences of the British athletes running barefoot across the West Sands at St Andrews to the sound of Vangelis's triumphal Oscar-winning music. The audience is told this is Broadstairs in Kent, though not only is the town of St Andrews clearly visible but the athletes are seen leaving the beach and running past the most famous golf clubhouse in the world, that of the Royal and Ancient. 'We shot it a couple of times actually,' says Smith. 'We had a technical problem the first go and had to do it again . . . The first time we shot it we had the full co-operation of the town of St Andrews in removing cars and television aerials and so on. The second time that we came to shoot it – because of a technical problem – for a variety of reasons they'd had enough of us and we had to borrow camouflage netting from the RAF at Leuchars and put it up all along the frontage of St Andrews to conceal the parked cars. In fact, in the shot that's in the film, as you turn towards the town, if you look closely, you'll see that there's a camouflage net up with a whole load of cars behind it.'

The first half of the film is really in two parts, one following Eric Liddell (Ian Charleson), a rugby-playing Christian in Scotland, and the other following Harold Abrahams (Ben Cross), the son of a Lithuanian Jew, and his friends, Lord Lindsay (Nigel Havers) and Aubrey Montague (Nicholas Farrell), at Cambridge University, though shooting in the city was limited to a few street scenes.

'Cambridge had decided they couldn't help the film; they refused to allow filming,' says Smith. 'My suspicion was that they didn't like the content of the film, the presumption that they were anti-semitic. I think they found that offensive.'

Certainly, derogatory comments about the fact that Abrahams is Jewish are heard coming from various university figures, ranging from the porter to the masters of Trinity and Caius – two delightful cameos from John Gielgud and the film director Lindsay Anderson – who come over like the two grumpy old men in *The Muppets*, observing cynically from the wings.

Director Hugh Hudson managed to get permission from his alma mater, Eton College in Berkshire, to film there, including the race around the Trinity courtyard between Abrahams and Lindsay while the college clock chimes twelve. Eton College was founded in 1440 and offered a similar atmosphere of tradition and history. Despite the term public school, Eton is, of course, one of the most exclusive schools in the country. However, the grounds are open to the public during afternoons in term and all day in the holidays.

Hall Barn, a private estate at Beaconsfield, in Buckinghamshire, was the location for the shots of Lord Lindsay jumping over hurdles on which he had balanced glasses of champagne.

Meanwhile, Liddell is seen handing out prizes and being persuaded to run in a Highland Games, in the Sma' Glen, north of Crieff in Perthshire. Inverleith, home of Stewarts-Melville, one of Edinburgh's top rugby clubs, was the location for a Scotland-Ireland athletics meeting, after which Liddell preaches to the crowd in the pouring rain, comparing faith to running a race. He gets knocked over in a Scotland-France international, but picks himself up and goes on to win, a sequence shot at Goldenacre, home of Heriot's F. P. rugby club, just a few minutes walk from Inverleith.

The next time we see Liddell racing, it is past John Knox's statue to a religious meeting in the Assembly Hall on the Mound, Edinburgh, where he is confronted by his sister, Jennie (Cheryl Campbell), who is unhappy about the amount of time he is devoting to running. They go for a walk in Holyrood Park to discuss his future against the backdrop of the city skyline and he reveals that he will shortly be going to China as a missionary. Edinburgh also provided the locations for Abrahams' romantic dinner with singer Sybil Gordon (Alice Krige), which was filmed in the oyster bar of the Café Royal, a nineteenth-century hostelry with tiled murals and stained-glass windows; and for the Church of Scotland church in Paris, where Liddell preaches after refusing to run in a heat on a Sunday – a decision that means he will have to run in the 400 metres rather than the hundred. The church was the Broughton McDonald Church in Broughton Place – a nineteenth-century building with a graceful Greek Doric pillared entrance. It is no longer in use as a church.

The athletes' port of departure for Paris was Birkenhead in Merseyside and the formal Olympic dance attended by the Prince of Wales was shot at Liverpool Town Hall. Abrahams duly wins the Bebington sprint and Liddell the 400 metres before they return to Britain, disembarking from the boat train at York. Smith says: 'York Station is the place for period railway scenes because it has the National Railway Museum there and, of course, it's a beautiful station with big curving platforms.' The station also has an extremely distinctive curving iron and glass roof, which is very picturesque on sunny days.

The 1924 Olympics and, as it turned out, the film *Chariots of Fire* were both triumphs for Britain. But, while the film celebrates the success of Liddell and Abrahams, it ignores the achievements of Douglas Lowe, another British athlete who won the 800 metres in 1924, went to the following games four years later and won the title again. It would clearly have been difficult to fit a third champion into the structure of the film, so while Liddell and Abrahams are now household names, Lowe lingers in obscurity.

Chariots of Fire was the second-highest grossing film of the year in Britain in 1982 and was in the US Top Ten the previous year. It won four Oscars, including best picture, and scriptwriter Colin Welland made an embarrassing speech about the British coming. Neither Cross nor Charleson made it to the top flight of film stardom and Charleson died of AIDS in 1990. However, one person who did go on to greater things was Ruby Wax, who makes a brief appearance in the film.

The title *Chariots of Fire* comes from William Blake's poem.

> *Bring me my bow of burning gold!*
> *Bring me my arrows of desire!*
> *Bring me my spear! O clouds, unfold!*
> *Bring me my chariot of fire!*
> *I will not cease from mental fight,*
> *Nor shall my sword sleep in my hand,*
> *Till we have built Jerusalem,*
> *In England's green and pleasant land.*

KING RALPH (1991)

A dozen of England's finest stately homes were called into service to double for Buckingham Palace and Windsor Castle in this comedy about a vulgar American singer Ralph Jones (John Goodman) who becomes king when the entire British royal family is wiped out in a freak electrical accident.

The film opens with a long shot of Buckingham Palace, but that was the closest the film-makers got. The Royal Naval College in Greenwich, London, was used for some exterior shots, including those of Ralph coming and going through the gates. The buildings started off as a palace for King Charles II in 1664 and later served as Greenwich Hospital for disabled seamen.

Ralph's predecessor and his family were killed while posing for a photograph on a rainy day in front of Wrotham Park, near Barnet, in Hertfordshire. The back of the palace and the lawn were shot at Harewood House, an eighteenth-century Robert Adam mansion, near Leeds, and other shots of the back were filmed at Somerset House – an eighteenth-century building on the site of the palace of the Duke of Somerset, who was executed in 1552, thereby forfeiting the building. The old palace was demolished in 1776 and the present building was designed to house the Royal Academy of Art and for other public uses. George III gave it to the nation in exchange for formal title to Buckingham Palace. More recently Somerset House has been used as the registry of births, marriages and deaths.

The film-makers shot in South Carriage Drive and The Mall – the main approach road to Buckingham Palace. Location manager Bill Lang says: 'We had to shoot it between five o'clock and eight o'clock on three separate Sunday mornings because traffic is forbidden on a Sunday in The Mall. We put the traffic in there. We had all the royal processions then.'

King Ralph welcomes the Finnish royal family at St Pancras Station, with Joely Richardson, as Princess Anna, looking like Princess Di and sounding like a posh version of Boris Karloff. The royal train looks like a standard train with a couple of flags stuck on the front.

Several rooms at Syon House, Brentford, were used to represent the reception room, hall, conservatory and picture gallery at Buckingham Palace. Syon House was also built by the ill-fated Duke of Somerset. Apsley House, in Piccadilly, was used for shots of the royal picture gallery as well. Another Robert Adam mansion, it was the London home of the first Duke of Wellington. It contains paintings by Goya, Velazquez and Rubens. Buckingham Palace's anteroom, stairs and the entrances to the ballroom and state dining-room were filmed at Lancaster House, in London; a nineteenth-century mansion commissioned for George III's second son, the Grand Old Duke of York of popular song. It is now used for conferences and government banquets. The film's big banquet and ball scenes, however, were done on sets at Pinewood Studios.

Buckingham Palace's white room is represented by a room at Belvoir Castle, near Grantham, in Lincolnshire, seat of the Dukes of Rutland since Henry VIII's time. The office of the king's private secretary, Willingham (Peter O'Toole), was in Hagley Hall, the last of England's great Palladian houses, near Birmingham.

*The Royal Naval
College, Greenwich,
which serves as
Buckingham Palace in*
King Ralph
(Universal)

Various places were used for Windsor Castle. 'The exterior at Windsor Castle . . . was the long walk at Windsor Castle,' says Bill Lang. 'I don't know how we worked that one, but we got away with it until they found out what we were doing.' The Georgian hall at Windsor was represented by Warwick Castle. Hever Castle, in Kent, formerly the home of Anne Boleyn and of the Astors, was also used for Windsor.

The home of Lord Graves (John Hurt), the Stuart pretender to the throne, was Highclere Castle, near Newbury, in Berkshire, home of the Earls of Carnarvon. The fifth earl discovered the tomb of Tutankhamun and some of his Egyptian finds are on display at Highclere.

Escaping from the pressures of the palace, King Ralph visits a strip show, shot in the Café de Paris, in London's Coventry Street. He takes the girl he meets there, Miranda (Camille Coduri), for a burger at the Burger King in Slough and later visits the poorer quarters of his realm with her, including allotments in Rotherham.

He takes a visiting African king for a game of darts in the Prince Alfred bar in London's Formosa Street. Despite the name, it turns out to be a traditional pub, about as cultured as King Ralph himself, and a welcome break from all the gilt and finery.

Most of the locations are open to the public.

ROBIN HOOD: PRINCE OF THIEVES (1991)

For the sake of authenticity, the Morgan Creek production company determined they would film their big-budget version of the Robin Hood story on location in England, unlike Warner Brothers who made *The Adventures of Robin Hood*, with Errol Flynn, in California in 1938, largely on studio sets. But the decision to film *Robin Hood: Prince of Thieves* in England, with Kevin Costner in the title role, was about as far as Morgan Creek's commitment to authenticity went.

Virtually nothing is known about Robin Hood, the outlaw who stole from the rich and gave to the poor. Tradition has it that he lived in Sherwood Forest in Nottinghamshire, though he is mentioned in Wyntoun's *Chronicle of Scotland* in the fifteenth century, and other accounts suggest he lived in Yorkshire or that he was a little forest elf – which gives considerable scope to film-makers.

The decision to shoot in England was just about the film-makers' only concession to tradition. They turned the Sheriff of Nottingham (Alan Rickman) into a Satanist, Will Scarlett (Christian Slater) into James Dean and Robin Hood's right-hand man into a politically correct, black-skinned Moor called Azeem (Morgan Freeman). They have Robin Hood's father, Lord Locksley (Brian Blessed), murdered by what looks like the Ku-Klux Klan and send Robin Hood on a grand tour of England, before finally he stumbles on the lost city of Nottingham in the south of France.

After escaping from imprisonment in Jerusalem, Robin Hood and Azeem arrive in England, beneath the white chalk cliffs of the Seven Sisters, near Eastbourne. Costner ended up directing this scene himself. The original attempt to film the homecoming was hampered by rough seas and heavy rain. With the film falling way behind schedule, Costner wound up going back to Seven Sisters with one crew, while director Kevin Reynolds continued work on the hanging scene at Shepperton Studios.

Just west of Eastbourne, the Sussex Downs are sliced away by the sea in a spectacular series of cliffs. There is a country park there which includes a cliff-top walk. And, if you are in this area, then the next port of call must obviously be . . . Hadrian's Wall, 350 miles or so to the north. By a strange coincidence Robin Hood, while supposedly making his way home to Nottingham, and the Sheriff of Nottingham's men both turn up sight-seeing at the old Roman wall at the same time, at Sycamore Gap, near Housesteads in Northumberland. It is, as they say, a small world.

In a previous age this was just about the limit of the Roman world. A significant part of the Roman Empire's defence budget around AD 122 was spent on the construction of this 75-mile stone wall that stretched across England from the River Tyne to the Solway Firth, punctuated by a series of turrets and forts. It took 20,000 men seven years to build. It was 20 feet high and seven to ten feet thick, with a wide ditch on the north side of it. It was probably always more impressive in its length than its height and was intended simply as a defensive line rather than an insurmountable barrier. Several stretches survive, though time has taken its toll. Nowhere does the wall reach its former height and in the film it looks just like any old dyke. It may have been a sense of disappointment at the much reduced scale of the wall that ended up in the violence between Robin Hood and the Sheriff's men.

Robin goes home to Locksley Castle, represented by Old Wardour Castle – a fourteenth-century castle with an unusual hexagonal tower, in the Wiltshire countryside, north of Shaftesbury. It was besieged and subsequently abandoned during the English Civil War in the seventeenth century and is now run by English Heritage. Among the relics at Old Wardour is Kevin Costner's sword, with which visitors can be photographed.

Next stop on Robin's tour is Hulne Priory at Alnwick in Northumberland, which served as the home of Maid Marian (Mary Elizabeth Mastrantonio). Dating from the thirteenth century, it is the earliest example of a Carmelite friary in England. It is located on a hill above the River Aln and is privately occupied.

After a further altercation with the Sheriff's men, Robin Hood escapes into the supposedly haunted Sherwood Forest, for which the film-makers used a combination of Hampshire's New Forest, the Yorkshire Dales National Park and Burnham Beeches, near London.

Despite its name, the New Forest dates from the eleventh century. It was named the New Forest by William the Conqueror. Forest was a legal term meaning, at that time, that the deer were reserved for the crown. The forest includes the best relics of oak, beech and holly woodland in England, and it is home to deer, badgers, foxes and the hardy New Forest ponies. Today, the New Forest extends to almost 100,000 acres of woodland, heath, bog and farmland. It was never, however, so large that it extended into Yorkshire, which provided the location for the fight, with wooden staffs, between Robin Hood and Little John (Nick Brimble), shot at Aysgarth Falls, where the River Ure drops over a series of limestone edges in the Yorkshire Dales National Park. Costner and Brimble spent several cold, uncomfortable days being walloped by staffs and knocked into the fast-flowing waters.

Robin never had a chance to repair the damage of a bitter argument with his father, and by this time he has also had a fight with Maid Marian. It certainly seems like he is destined not to get on with anyone in England when the Sherwood Forest outlaws accept him into their camp. It was built in Burnham Beeches, a 440-acre forest not far from Shepperton Studios in Buckinghamshire.

Hadrian's Wall was clearly not doing its job, for Robin Hood and the outlaws are disturbed by a mercenary army of Celts from the north. The scriptwriters assure us that the Celts worship the same god as the Sheriff of Nottingham, though they look like they have turned up in the wrong film.

A large exterior set was constructed at Shepperton to represent Nottingham's town square, where many of Robin's men are due to hang, though the impressive, high-ceilinged stone interior of the twelfth-century Priory Church of St Bartholomew the Great at Smithfield in London was employed as Nottingham Cathedral. It was subsequently used in *Four Weddings and a Funeral*. Finally, Carcassonne, a medieval walled city in the south of France, was used for exteriors of Nottingham.

During filming and post-production, Reynolds and Costner clashed repeatedly. The audience at a test screening said they preferred Rickman's pantomime sheriff to Costner's rather glum and anti-social hero. Reynolds's film editor was apparently locked out while the film was re-edited. Reynolds was unhappy with the finished product and Costner does not rank it as one of his better movies.

Rarely have the critics shown such unanimity in their dismissal of a film which at times seems almost Pythonesque in its absurdities, and yet audiences loved it. Perhaps the combination of those absurdities and the dashing enthusiasm of the participants worked for a public that was prepared to treat it as light-hearted swashbuckling nonsense, which is what the 1938 version was, after all.

No reputable critic would suggest the 1991 version comes anywhere near the accomplishments of the earlier film. But *The Adventures of Robin Hood* lost money at the box-office back in the thirties, while *Robin Hood: Prince of Thieves* was the second-highest-grossing film of 1991 in North America and topped the British chart, beating *Terminator 2* and *The Silence of the Lambs*, and taking twice as much money as Costner's Oscar-winning *Dances with Wolves*.

BIBLIOGRAPHY

Biographies and Autobiographies

Alec Guinness: Master of Disguise by Garry O'Connor, Hodder & Stoughton

Beginning by Kenneth Branagh, Chatto & Windus

Brando by Peter Manso, Weidenfeld & Nicolson

Brando: Songs My Mother Taught Me by Marlon Brando with Robert Lindsay, Century

Coming Attractions by Terence Stamp, Bloomsbury

Confessions of an Actor by Laurence Olivier, Weidenfeld & Nicolson

David Lean by Stephen M. Silverman, Andre Deutsch

Double Feature by Terence Stamp, Bloomsbury

Fred Zinnemann: An Autobiography, Bloomsbury

Joseph Losey by Edith de Rham, Andre Deutsch

A Life in Movies by Michael Powell, Heinemann

Long Distance Runner by Tony Richardson, Faber & Faber

Million-Dollar Movie by Michael Powell, Heinemann

An Open Book by John Huston, Macmillan

Polanski by John Parker, Gollancz

Polanski – His Life and Films by Barbara Leaming, Hamish Hamilton

Rex by Rex Harrison, Macmillan

Rex Harrison by Allen Eyles, W. H. Allen

Richard Harris: A Sporting Life by Michael Feeney Callan, Sidgwick & Jackson

The Robert Mitchum Story by Mike Tomkies, W. H. Allen

Roman Polanski by Virginia Wright Wexman, Columbus

Trevor Howard: The Man and His Films by Michael Munn, Robson

Serves Me Right by Sarah Miles, Macmillan

Film Books

BFI Film and Television Handbook, ed. Nick Thomas, BFI

Ealing Studios by Charles Barr, Cameron & Tayleur

Edge of the World by Michael Powell, Faber & Faber

The Films of Merchant Ivory by Robert Emmet Long, Viking

Final Cut by Stephen Bach, Jonathan Cape

Forever Ealing by George Perry, Pavilion

The Guinness Book of Movie Facts and Feats by Patrick Robertson, Guinness

Halliwell's Film Guide by Leslie Halliwell (subsequently ed. by John Walker), HarperCollins

Halliwell's Hundred by Leslie Halliwell, Granada

Halliwell's Television Companion by Leslie Halliwell with Philip Purser, Granada

VENUS *Peter*

Producer **Christopher Young**
Director **Ian Sellar**
Written by **Christopher Rush & Ian Sellar**
Starring **Ray McAnally**
David Hayman
Sinead Cusack

British Screen in association with Film Four International, The Scottish Film Production Fund and the

Hollywood, England by Alexander Walker, Michael Joseph

In the Footsteps of 'The Quiet Man' by Gerry McNee, Mainstream

Leonard Maltin's Movie and Video Guide, ed. Leonard Maltin, Signet

Local Hero: The Making of the Film by Allan Hunter and Mark Astaire, Polygon

The Making of David Lean's 'Lawrence of Arabia' by Adrian Turner, Dragon's World

The Making of Stanley Kubrick's '2001' by Jerome Agel, New American Library (New York)

National Heroes by Alexander Walker, Harrap

The New Official James Bond 007 Movie Book by Sally Hibbin, Hamlyn

Offscreen, Onscreen by Peter van Gelder, Aurum

Radio Times Film and Video Guide by Derek Winnert, Hodder & Stoughton

The Story of Tommy by Richard Barnes & Pete Townshend, Eel Pie

The Virgin Film Guide by James Pallot, Virgin

What A Carry On by Sally Hibbin and Nina Hibbin, Hamlyn

Venus Peter
(BFI/Channel Four/British Screen)

Other Books

Blue Guide: Country Houses of England by Geoffrey Tyack and Steven Brindle, A. & C. Black

Blue Guide: England by Ian Ousby, A. & C. Black

Blue Guide: Ireland by Ernes Benn, A. & C. Black

Blue Guide: Literary Britain and Ireland by Ian Ousby, A. & C. Black

Blue Guide: Wales by John Tomes, A. & C. Black

Cadogan Guides: Scotland, Cadogan

Collins Encyclopaedia of Scotland, ed. John Keay and Julia Keay, HarperCollins

The Companion Guide to Ireland by Brendan Lehane, Collins

The Complete Beatles Chronicle by Mark Lewisohn, Pyramid

The Concise Dictionary of National Biography, Oxford University Press

Fodor's Ireland, Fodor

Guide to National Trust Properties in Britain, ed. Richard Powell, A. A.

A Guide to the Steam Railways of Great Britain by Revd W. Awdry and Chris Cook, Pelham

Historic Houses, Castles and Gardens Open to the Public, ed. Sheila Alcock, British Leisure Publications

The New Shell Guide to England, ed. John Hadfield, Michael Joseph

The Oxford Illustrated Literary Guide to Great Britain and Ireland, ed. Dorothy Eagle and Hilary Carnell, Oxford University Press

The Reader's Encyclopaedia by William Rose Benet, Guild

The Shell Guide to Ireland by Lord Killanin, Michael V. Duignan, and Peter Harbison, Macmillan

The Shell Guide to Wales by Wynford Vaughan-Thomas and Alun Llewellyn, Michael Joseph

INDEX

Locations in Edinburgh, Dublin, Glasgow, Liverpool, London and Oxford are indexed under the name of each city.